IMAGES
of America

CAPITOLA

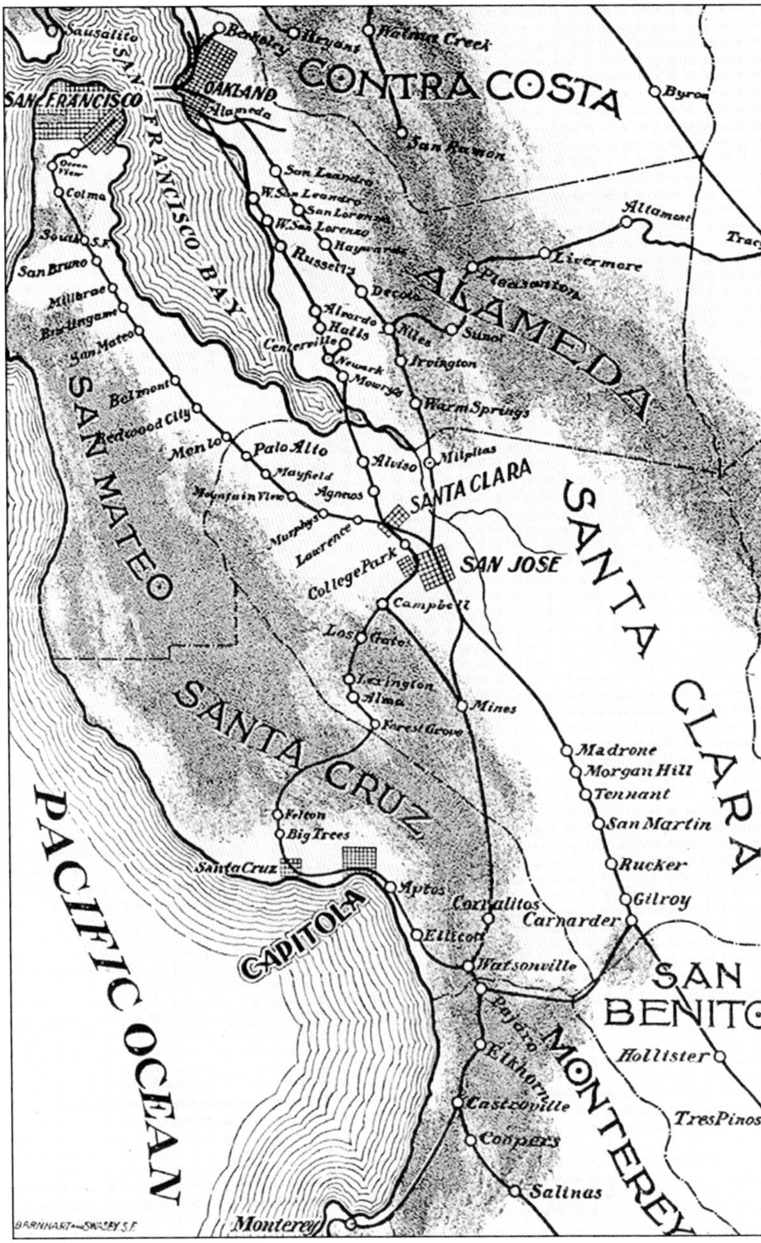

This early 1900s map shows the location of Capitola on Monterey Bay. Although the resort was open only in the summertime and had fewer than 100 year-round residents, the artist sketched its name so large that Capitola appears more prominent than the cities of Santa Cruz or Monterey. (Courtesy of the Capitola Historical Museum.)

On the Cover: Taken about 1908 by photographer Ole Ravnos (1864–1945), this image captures Capitola's enduringly youthful spirit. Ravnos and his wife, artist Amelia Norder, moved to Santa Cruz and set up a commercial studio in 1906. The clarity and composition of the Ravnos photographs have provided Capitola with some of its finest historical views. (Courtesy of the Capitola Historical Museum.)

IMAGES
of America

CAPITOLA

Carolyn Swift

ARCADIA
PUBLISHING

ISBN 978-0-7385-9690-7

Published by Arcadia Publishing
Charleston, South Carolina

Printed in the United States of America

Library of Congress Control Number: 2012942166

For all general information, please contact Arcadia Publishing:
Telephone 843-853-2070
Fax 843-853-0044
E-mail sales@arcadiapublishing.com
For customer service and orders:
Toll-Free 1-888-313-2665

Visit us on the Internet at www.arcadiapublishing.com

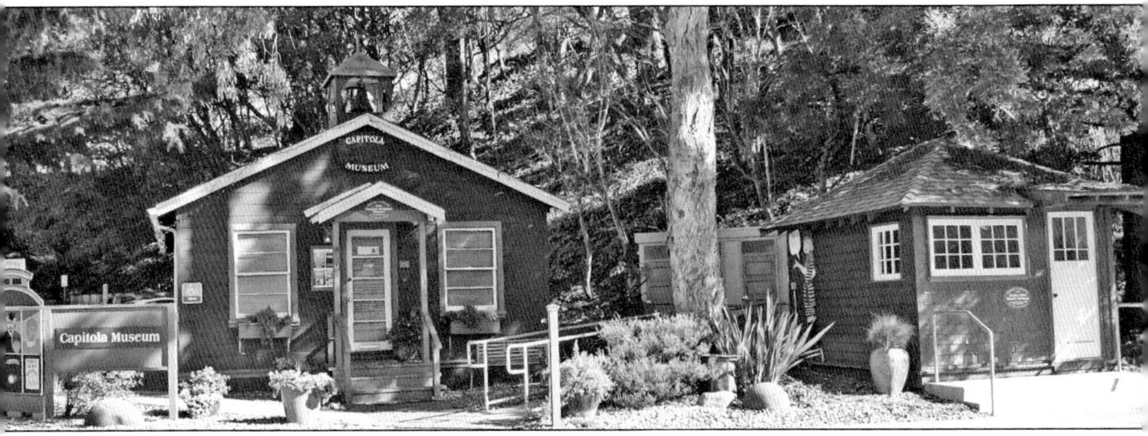

This book is dedicated to the city of Capitola and all its citizens and visitors who love and preserve its past. (Courtesy of the Capitola Historical Museum, 2013 photograph by Linda K.T. Banks.)

Contents

ACKNOWLEDGMENTS

After 48 years of work to collect, preserve, and interpret the past, Capitola Historical Museum brings to light its collection of images, matching them with text to illustrate and clarify the history of the oldest camping ground on the Pacific Coast. I am grateful to those who made it possible to get the job done, especially Linda Smith, museum board president; Gordon van Zuiden and Niels Kisling, board trustees; and Judith Steen, researcher and editor. I also thank those who have shared photographs, knowledge, and supportive help, especially Steve Swift, Joe Michalak, John Nicol, Eric Fingal of Covello and Covello Photography, Stanley D. Stevens, Sandy Lydon, and the staff and council of the city of Capitola. Unless otherwise noted, all images appearing in this book were provided by the Capitola Historical Museum.

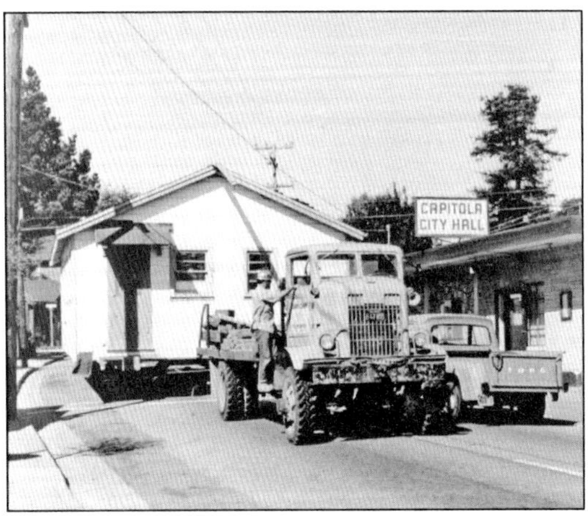

Capitola City Council member Phil Walker had pledged in his election campaign to establish a city museum. Borrowing artifacts and photographs, he created an exhibit in a tiny space behind the chamber of commerce on Capitola Avenue in 1966. The next year, Walker found a 700-square-foot farm cottage on Thompson Avenue in Live Oak that was slated for demolition. He bought it for $25 and convinced city leaders to provide a site for the museum next to Capitola City Hall. The building was moved to its present site on October 24, 1967. (Courtesy of Covello and Covello Photography.)

INTRODUCTION

As a slice of paradise, Capitola needs no introduction. The sun-kissed coastline and the lagoon on a summer afternoon say it all. Asked if they know what fun youngsters may have had a century ago, children are quick to say that kids did then as they do now. It's true—the splashing, swimming, sand-digging joy of a day at the beach is timeless.

Narrating the historical background is more challenging. Connections between people and the landscape go back thousands of years. The story of early inhabitants has been buried, literally, under the footprint of today's Capitola village. Those who lived the longest at the site where Soquel Creek meets the sea are the ones about whom only a little has been recorded, understood, or interpreted with fairness.

Prior to the arrival and impact of Spanish and Portuguese explorers, close to 40 culturally diverse native tribes, now collectively known as Ohlone (a Miwok Indian word that translates to "western people"), were living in the coastal region between the San Francisco Bay and Monterey Bay. They lived at sites that grew bigger or smaller as village locations shifted to fish, hunt, and harvest food. Coastal lands were cleared each year by fires that were deliberately set to assist the growth of seed-bearing plants and to attract deer and other game.

A tribal body of about 200 people lived along Soquel Creek. The Uypi spoke a dialect of the Ohlone language but were an independent unit that communicated, traded, and, at times, intermarried with their neighbors.

When Gaspar de Portolà's Spanish expedition reached Soquel Creek on its way up the coast in October 1769, the stream was recorded as El Rosario del Beato Serafin de Asculi. Twenty-two years later, after the founding of Mission Santa Cruz four miles up the coast, the Uypi were removed from their familiar territory and taken to the mission compound. It is believed they were grouped under the name Suquer, a Uypi leader who had been the second person baptized. Later attempts at translation led to Osocales, Osocali, and Osoquales, then to Usuacalis, Sakel, and Shoquel. Eventually, the word Soquel was applied to the people, the creek, and land that had been their home.

Santa Cruz Mission reached its peak when the population rose to 523 in 1796. Native inhabitants died from disease and poor nutrition. When the California missions were secularized in 1833, few from the present boundaries of Capitola were known to be among the survivors.

On the east side of the San Lorenzo River, and within sight of the mission, the pueblo of Villa de Branciforte was founded in 1797 as one of three Spanish towns—Los Angeles and San Jose were the other two—that were built to help defend and colonize Alta California. After Mexican independence in 1822, when the government began to give land grants, among those best positioned to receive title were the Villa de Branciforte's retired military. As second-generation native Californios, their children were also favored with property in the region.

The city of Capitola exists today within the margins of two Mexican grants, Rancho Arroyo del Rodeo and Rancho Soquel. By modern boundaries, Rancho Rodeo took in territory on the west side of Soquel Creek, including Forty-First Avenue. Francisco de Sales Rodriguez had been given title to this 1,473-acre property in 1834. His ownership was transferred in 1847 to John Hames and John Daubenbiss, the pioneers and founders of the town of Soquel. Rancho Soquel covered the expanse of the town of Soquel east of Soquel Creek, including a major portion of the present city of Capitola, including New Brighton Beach State Park. This was a strip of land one-and-a-half miles wide and two miles long, spreading across 1,668 acres. The land was given by the Mexican government in November 1833 to Maria Martina Castro Lodge.

Martina was a granddaughter of Joaquin Isidro (Ysidro) Castro, a member of the Anza Party, which had marched from Sonora, Mexico, to Alta California in 1776. Born at Branciforte about 1807, Martina first married Cpl. Simon Cota, a soldier stationed at Monterey. The Cotas had four children in the six years before he died in 1830. Within a year, Martina remarried, choosing Michael Lodge of Ireland. He was a sailor who had been on a whaling ship and came ashore years before. He had married and was a widower when he met Martina.

Soon after they married, the couple applied for a grant from the Mexican government. Granted the Rancho Soquel, they settled into a small hilltop adobe home within sight of the ocean and near a series of freshwater springs. Over the next decade, living space in the house was expanded for additional children and servants. For their growing cattle herd, Michael and Martina Lodge applied in 1843 for more land, seeking extension to a point called Palo de Yesca (Tinder Tree). A generous addition of 32,702 acres was granted as the Soquel Augmentation Rancho.

The augmentation was heavily forested with redwoods. Michael Lodge, aware that the trees had potential value, contracted with Hames and Daubenbiss to build a sawmill in 1846. Although it was washed away within the year, the venture gave a start to the logging industry that led to the founding of Soquel in 1852.

The finding of gold in 1848 set in motion a sequence of events that were for the Lodge family at first promising and then abruptly catastrophic. Martina, caught in the turmoil, suffered the most.

The gold discovery at Sutter's Mill lured thousands of prospectors. Joining them, Michael Lodge temporarily moved his family to Mokelumne Hill in Calaveras County. Tragically, the three youngest Lodge children died in a typhoid outbreak. Martina returned to the Rancho Soquel and waited for her husband to close his store and freighting business, but he never came back. The family was told that he was murdered.

With the coming of California statehood and formation of Santa Cruz County in 1850, American settlers came through in increasing numbers, seeking to buy or otherwise acquire title to Mexican land grants and to start industrial enterprises. Martina's English-speaking sons-in-law closed ranks and forced her to partition her lands, dividing them between herself and eight surviving children. Unable to read, write, or speak English, Martina also faced the bewildering challenge of proving title to her ranchos in the American courts. Seeking support, the widow made an unfortunate choice and married Louis Depeaux.

Martina was betrayed by Depeaux, several of her in-laws, her church, and the attorneys and officials who sought to make a profit from the sale of her property. Within a half-dozen years, she had lost her home and property, many personal belongings, her way of life, and for a time, her freedom. After her death in 1890, several family members hoped to retrieve some of the property by arguing in court that she was insane at the time she put her mark on the sale agreements.

Ironically, one of those who testified in 1896 that he knew Martina Castro Lodge to be sane was Frederick Augustus Hihn. He had good reason, since he owned a significant part of the land in question.

Sailing from his native Germany to the California Gold Rush, F.A. Hihn (1829–1913) came to Santa Cruz in 1851. As an entrepreneur with superior skills and a fierce drive to succeed, Hihn soon acquired sizeable territories in the Soquel and Soquel Augmentation Ranchos. Among his 1856 acquisitions were a two-mile stretch between Borregas Gulch and Soquel Creek and another parcel nearby that was part of the Rancho Arroyo del Rodeo. This land was to become Capitola.

One

Oldest Campground on the Pacific Coast

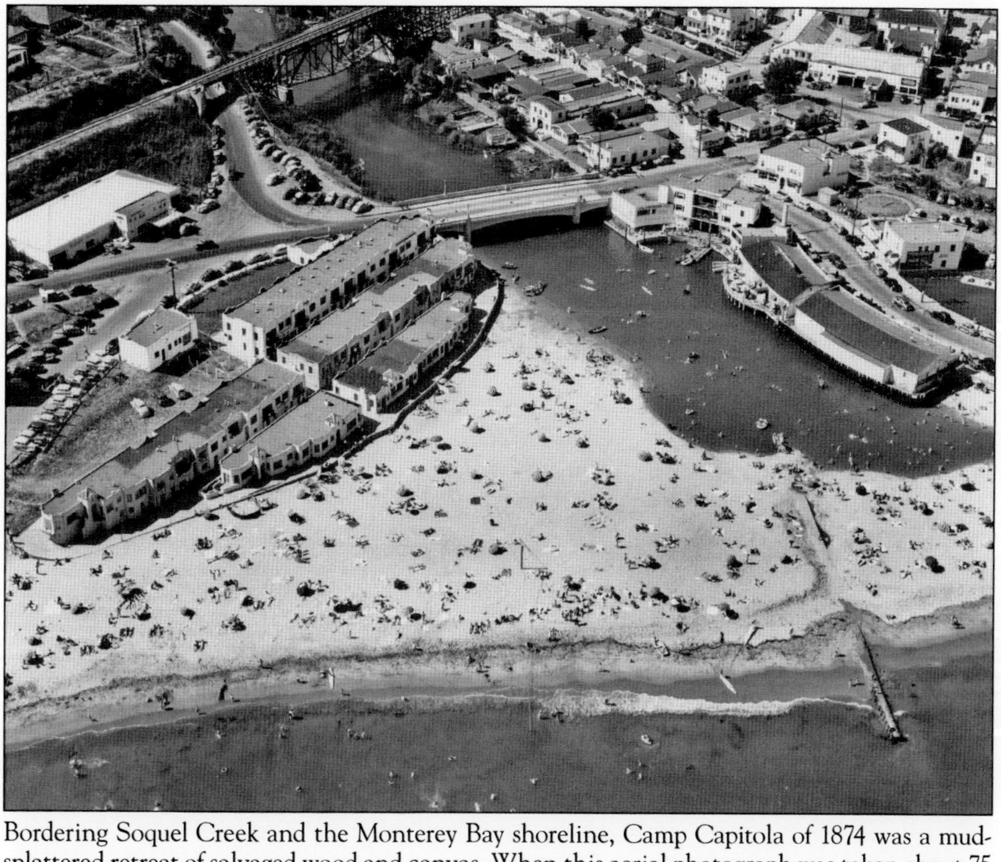

Bordering Soquel Creek and the Monterey Bay shoreline, Camp Capitola of 1874 was a mud-splattered retreat of salvaged wood and canvas. When this aerial photograph was taken about 75 years later, Capitola's modern character was framed within the historic outline. On this Fourth of July holiday—Capitola's birthday—inner tubes and paddleboats crisscrossed the lagoon. Blankets and umbrellas sprinkled the beach. Cars squeezed in every open space. Six months later, on January 4, 1949, the historic resort became an incorporated city. (Courtesy of Covello and Covello Photography.)

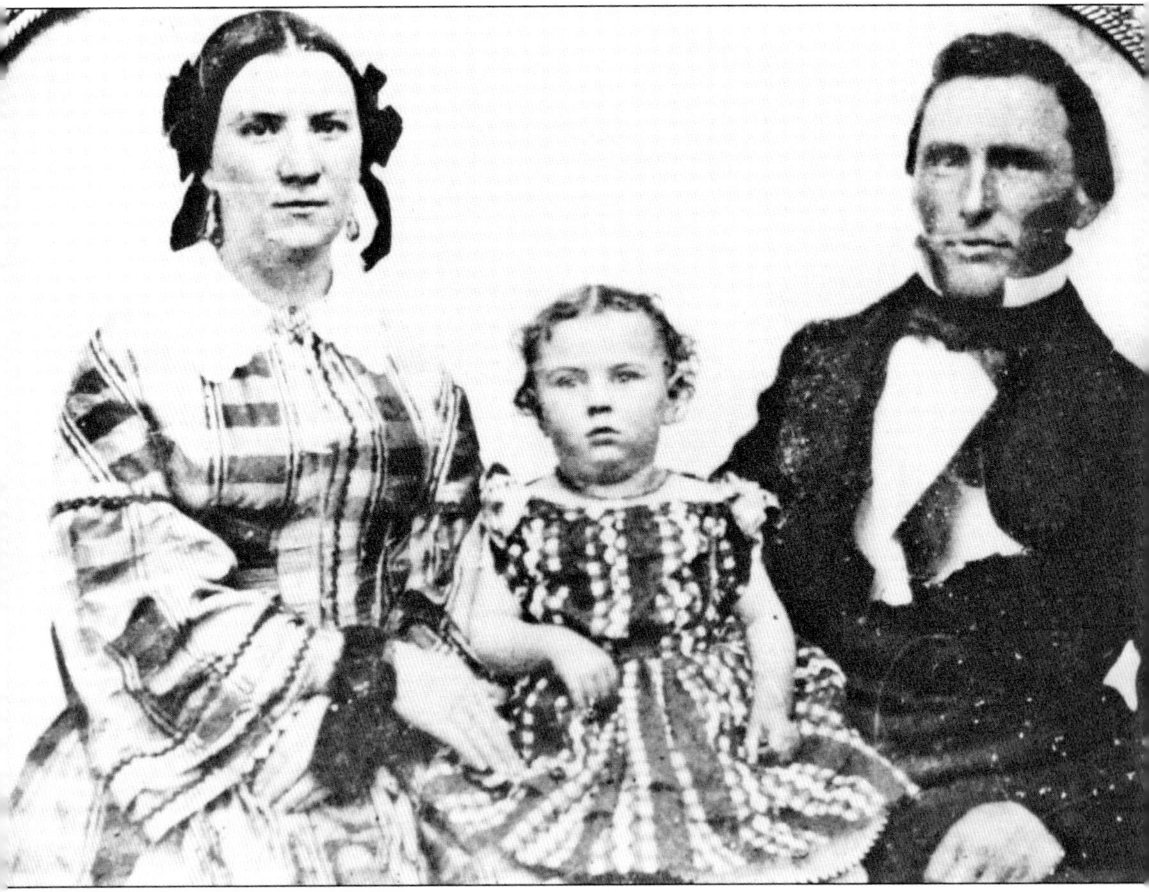

Frederick Augustus Hihn, Capitola's owner, was about 30 years old and a prospering merchant at the time this portrait was taken with his wife, Therese Paggen Hihn, and eldest child, Katherine, in 1857. The previous year, Hihn purchased La Playa de Soquel, a wetland at the mouth of Soquel Creek. Here he would build the resort that Katherine would inherit in 1913. (Courtesy of Stanley D. Stevens and the Hihn-Younger Archive, Special Collections, University Library, University of California, Santa Cruz.)

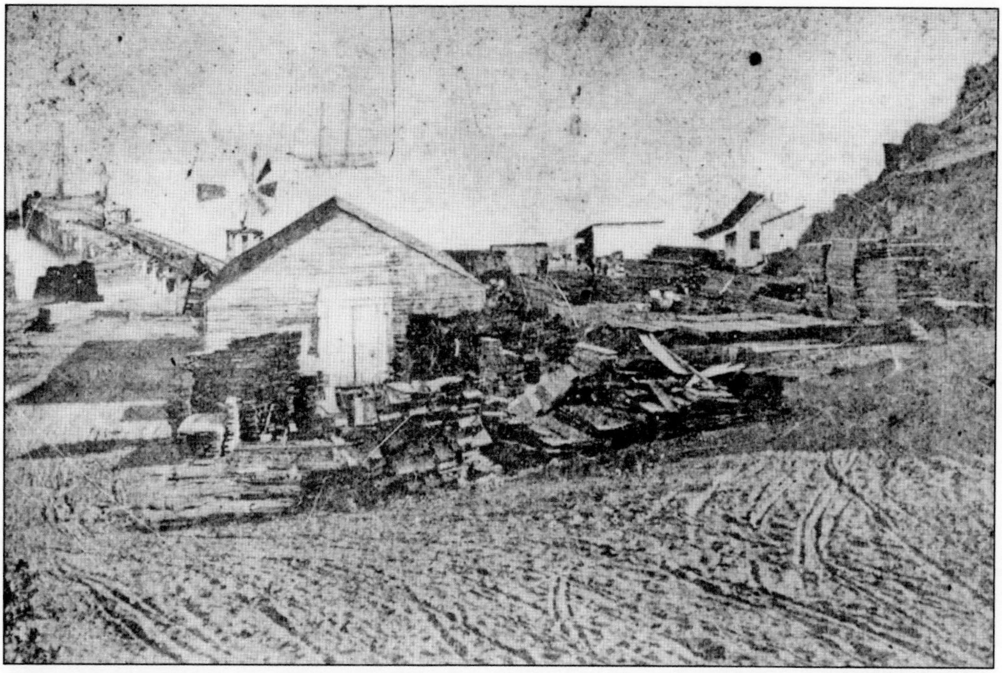

Once Hihn bought the beach and warehouse on the west side of the creek in 1856, he partnered with Sedgwick Lynch to build a 450-foot wharf. The shipping point became known as Soquel Landing, and by 1858, it was connected by way of Wharf Road to the Soquel Turnpike (Soquel–San Jose Road). (Courtesy of Dan Matthews.)

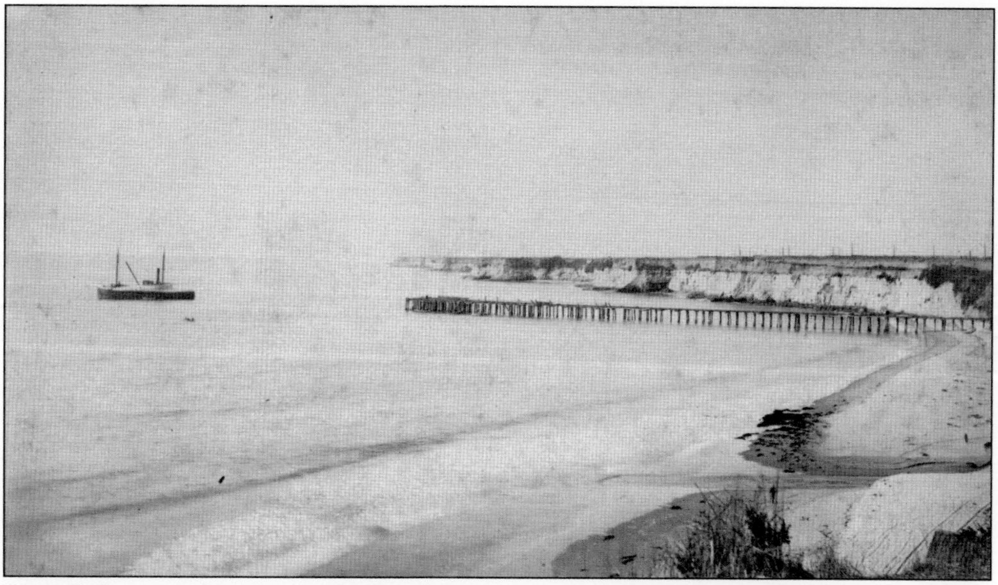

Expanded to 1,200 feet in 1863, the wharf was shortened to 700 feet by a high tide two years later. Steamship company freighters made scheduled stops at Capitola for more than 25 years. Here, a schooner approaches in the late 1880s.

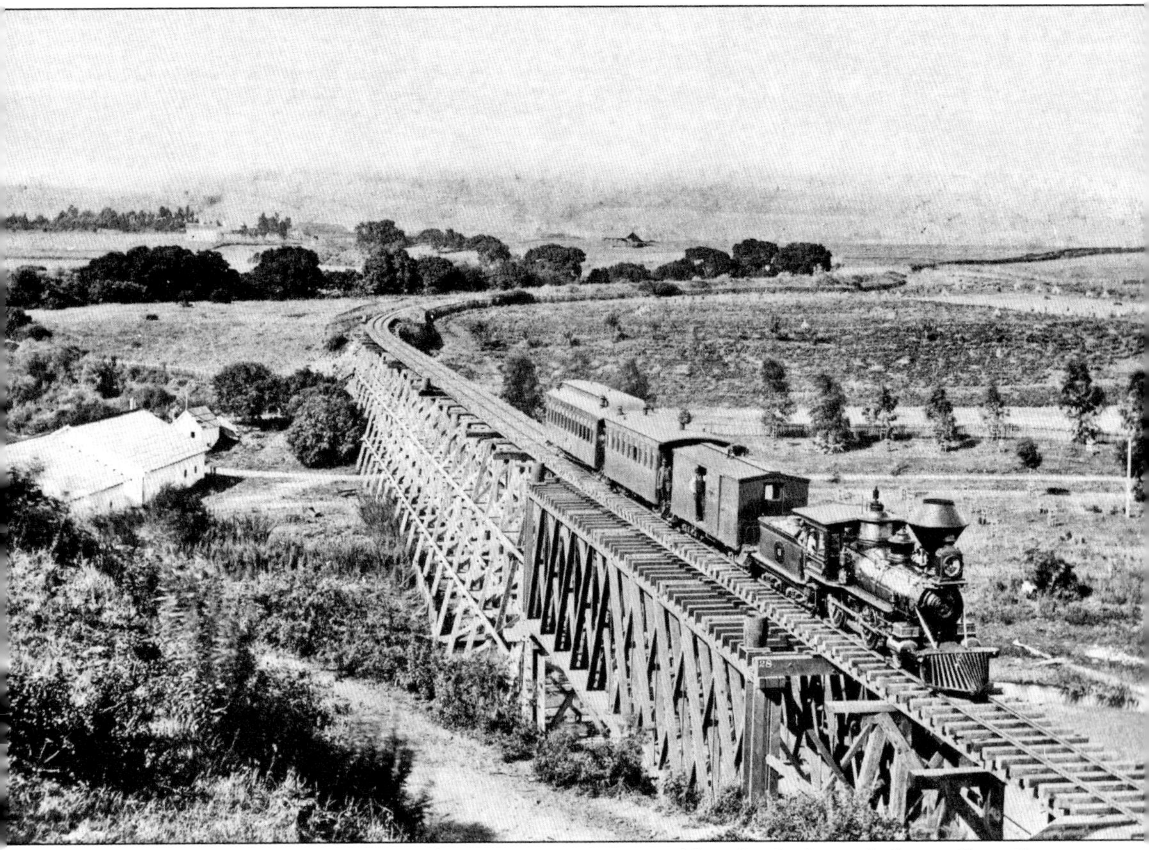

F.A. Hihn's steadfast ambition for years was to see a rail line built through Santa Cruz County. In 1872, he led a determined push for a narrow-gauge line that crossed, wherever possible, through his own properties along the coast. Preparations began in May 1874 to build the railroad bridge over Soquel Creek. The 105-foot-long Howe truss span was one of the first built for the route that was completed two years later. The wharf and trestle are today Capitola's most distinctive landmarks.

In 1869, Samuel Alonzo Hall (1816–1902) and his wife, Rachel, leased the beach flat at Soquel Landing. Although he was a farmer, Hall allowed people to come and cool off at the beach during July and August. Eventually, with Hihn's blessing, he made visitors more comfortable with a row of privies. Once the trestle for the Santa Cruz Railroad was in sight, Hall decided to invest in a livery stable and two excursion boats. He set up a campground in 1874.

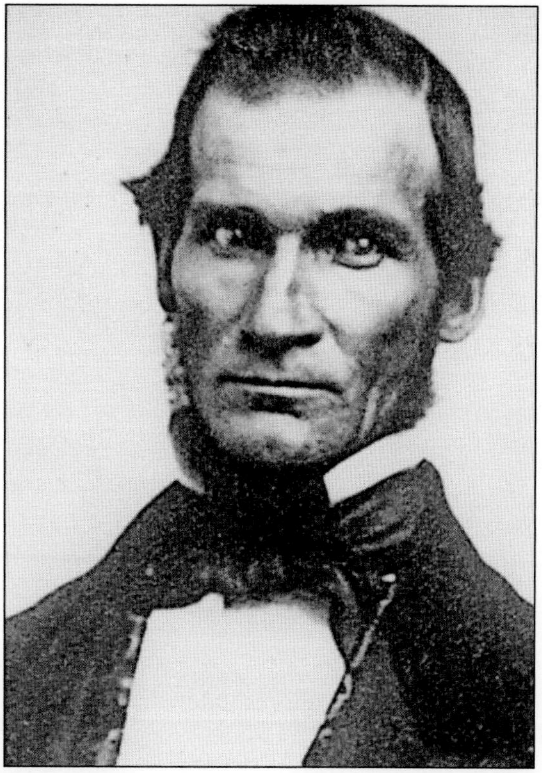

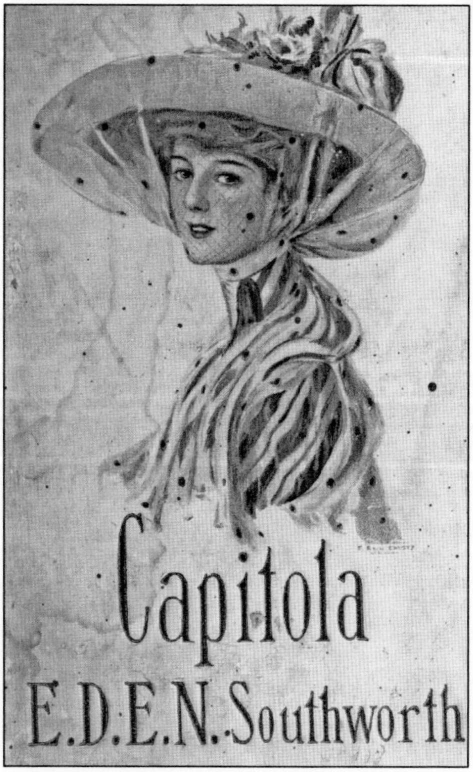

S.A. Hall's daughter, Lulu Hall Green Wolbach, a former Soquel School teacher, named Capitola for the lively fictional character created by author E.D.E.N. Southworth. A news article from an 1889 edition of the *Santa Cruz Surf* noted that Capitola, "like the little heroine for whom it was named, has long made for itself a place in the hearts of many admirers."

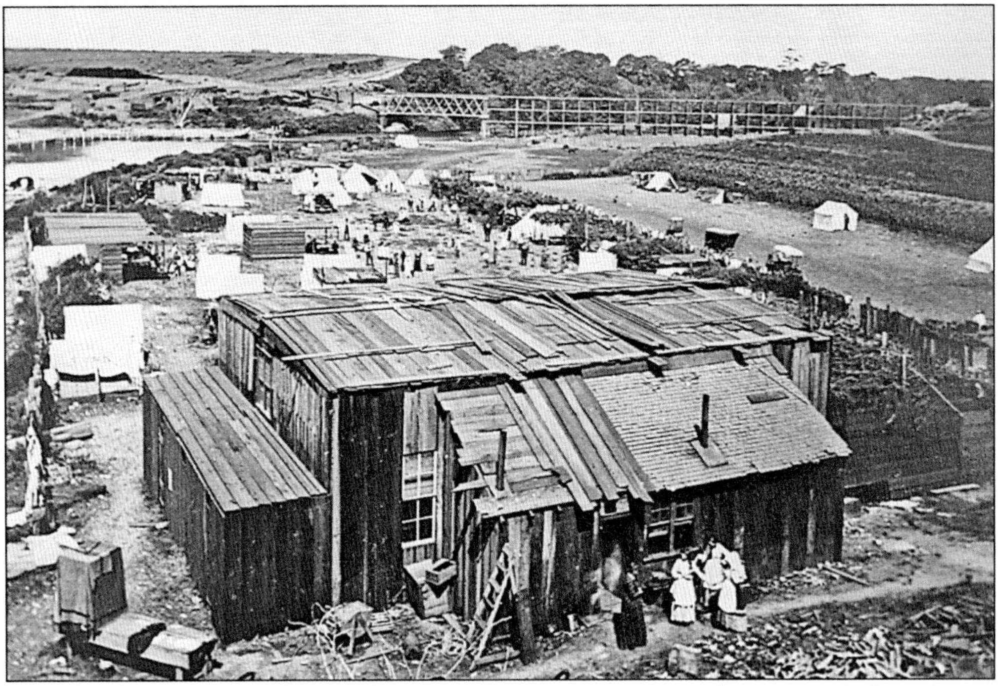

Camp Capitola officially opened on July 4, 1874. The season was only a few weeks long, but its success encouraged Hall to put a roof on the dance floor and build cabins for the next year. Campers did return the following June, paying $1 a night to sleep on beds of fresh hay. Children and horses cost 50¢. Adjacent to the campground were Hall's grain crops and the sugar beet fields of his Soquel neighbors. The California Beet Sugar Company had just begun operations at a factory along the creek, upstream from the trestle. Beyond it to the north was Soquel village, shown below. The white church with the steeple had been built by Hall in 1869.

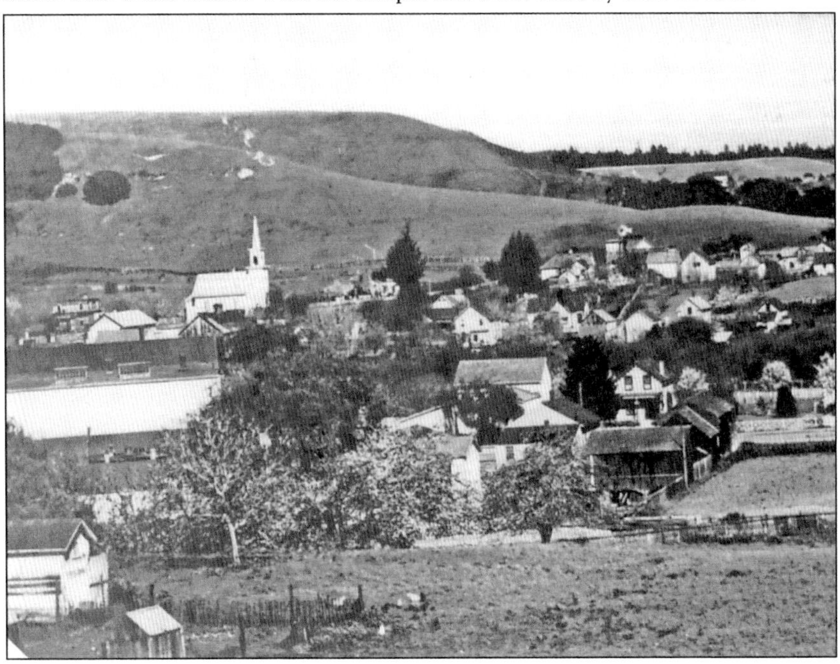

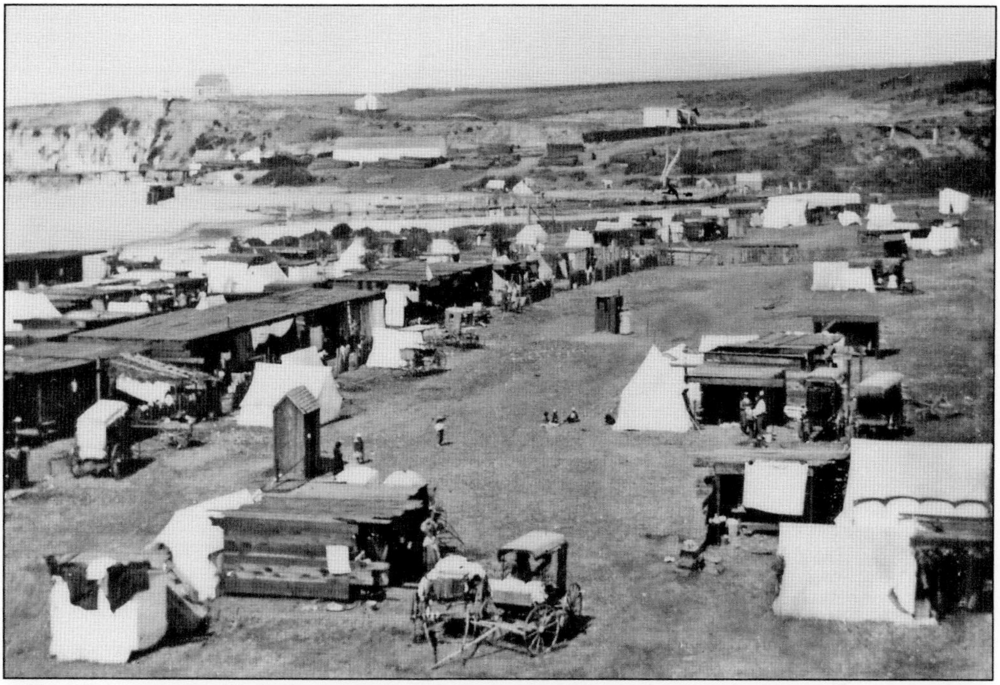

Officially known as the Soquel Depot, the Capitola railroad station rested on an incline along the western bluff, above and to the right of the wharf warehouse. Finished in time for the 1876 inauguration of the rail line, it soon became the brisk industrious shipping point that Hihn had intended. Vacationers arriving by train entered the resort by traveling along the beach to the narrow crossing where Soquel Creek met the sea. Once passenger trains began to deliver vacationers who stayed the whole summer, S.A. Hall laid separate grounds for cottages and tents.

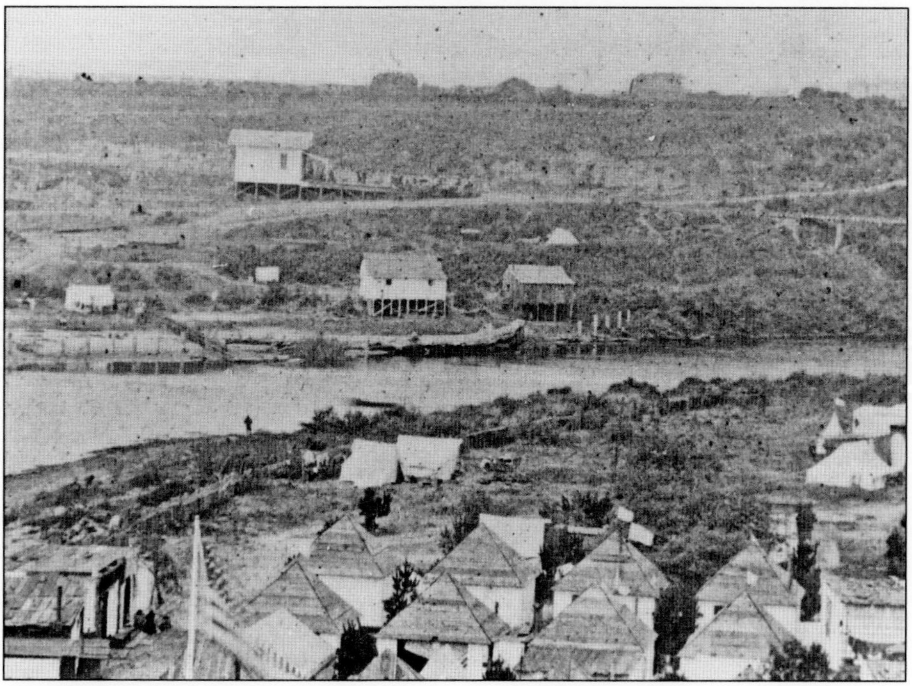

CAMP CAPITOLA,

"THE GREAT CAMPING GROUND OF THE PACIFIC COAST."

Situated on the Beautiful Bay of Monterey,

NEAR SOQUEL, SANTA CRUZ CO., CAL.

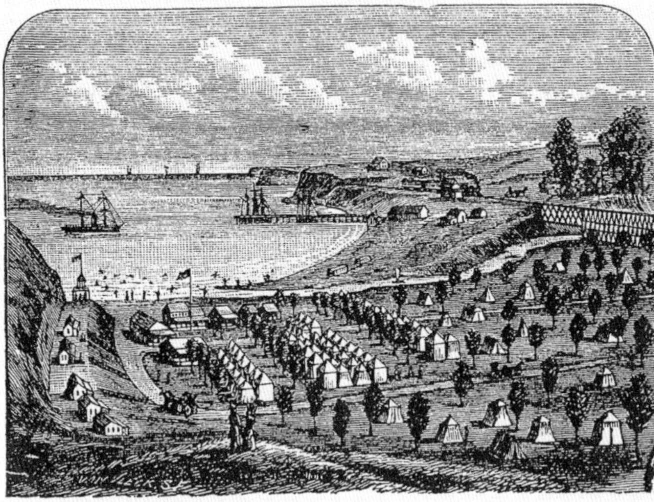

CAMP CAPITOLA.

FIRST-CLASS HOTEL—Situated on the Beach.
COTTAGES TO RENT—Furnished or Unfurnished, at Reasonable Rates.
LIVERY AND FEED STABLES—On the Ground, where good Carriage and Saddle Horses can be furnished.
TELEGRAPH, EXPRESS AND MAIL FACILITIES—To all parts of the State.
THE FINEST BEACH FOR SURF BATHING ON THE COAST.
GOOD TROUT FISHING AND ABUNDANCE OF GAME—In the Vicinity.
BEAUTIFUL DRIVES TO POINTS OF GREAT INTEREST.
THE RAILROAD DEPOT—Where all trains stop, is situated close to the Camp Grounds.
HAVE YOUR BAGGAGE CHECKED TO SOQUEL—The name of the Railroad Station.
FOR DESCRIPTION OF "CAMP CAPITOLA"—See opposite page.
FOR ROUTE OF TRAVEL—See page No. 187 of this book.

—CAMP CAPITOLA—

IS OPEN ALL THE YEAR ROUND.

RATES MODERATE.

For further particulars, address—

BERRY & BRANDON,

See opposite page. SOQUEL, CAL.

Capitola's first cottages lined the oceanfront and the ridge to the east. A small hotel was built in 1877–1878 near the entrance to the resort. When S.A. Hall's lease expired the next season, F.A. Hihn reasoned that since the camp appeared successful, the rent should be higher. Hall disagreed and left with his family, moving on to manage another retreat near Santa Cruz. R.D. Berry and Frank Brandon took charge in 1879, promoting Capitola as the oldest camping ground on the Pacific Coast. They further advertised it as open "all the year round," even though it was closed tight by late August.

The South Pacific Coast Railroad from Alameda was connected to the Santa Cruz Railroad in 1880, dramatically boosting the number of vacationers who headed to Capitola. A year later, however, the narrow-gauge route through Santa Cruz County fiscally collapsed. Southern Pacific Railroad bought it and had the line broad-gauged in 1883, about the time these photographs were taken. The trestle was rebuilt in 1886 with a span that was longer and higher than the original, allowing Wharf Road to pass beneath it.

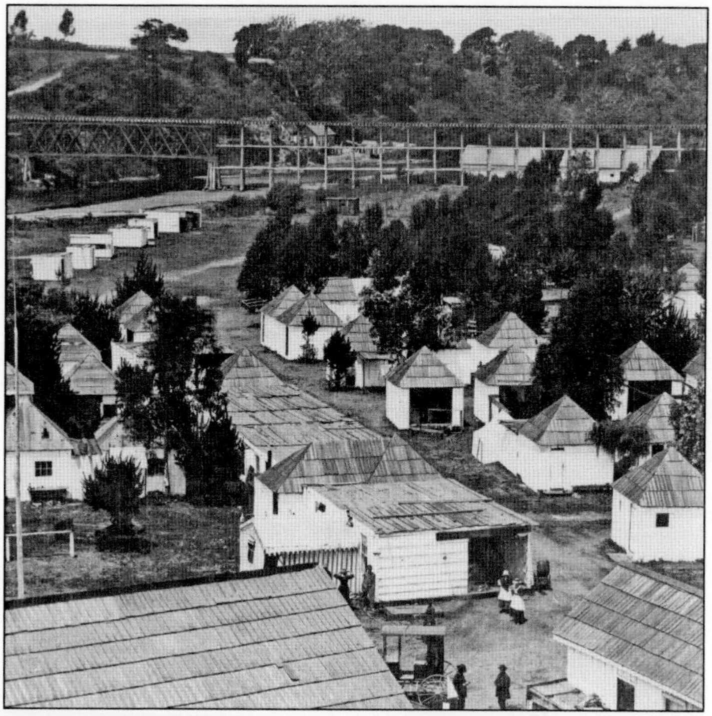

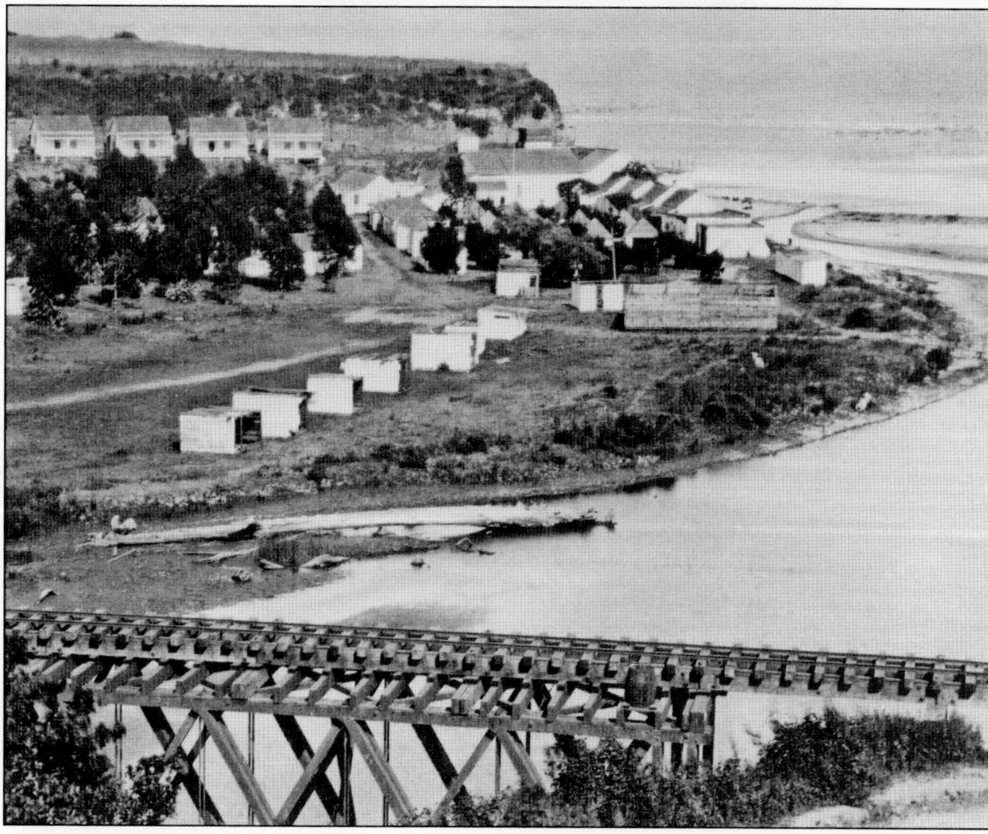

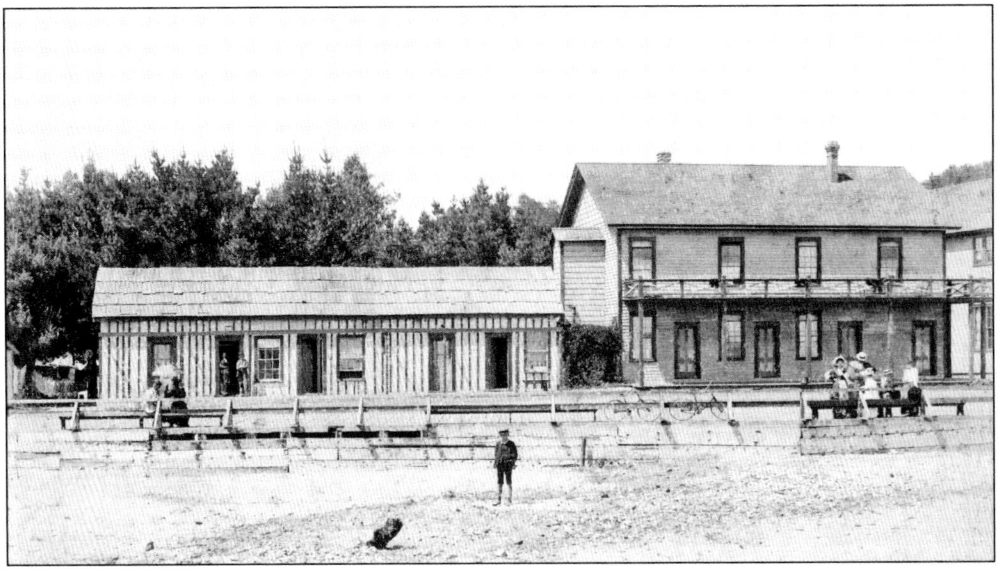

A *Santa Cruz Daily Surf* journalist noted in the 1880s that Capitola buildings were brightly painted "in stripes of red, green, blue, yellow, brown, violet, crimson, mauve, poppy, gold, daisy and abalone tints." News reports of camp life were typically filled with society news but could imply juicy gossip. In September 1885, for instance, the *Santa Cruz Daily Sentinel* noted "Camp Capitola has been prolific of sensations during the present season in the way of elopements, escapades, marriages at sea, out of reach of indignant papas or mammas." (Below, courtesy of Frank Perry.)

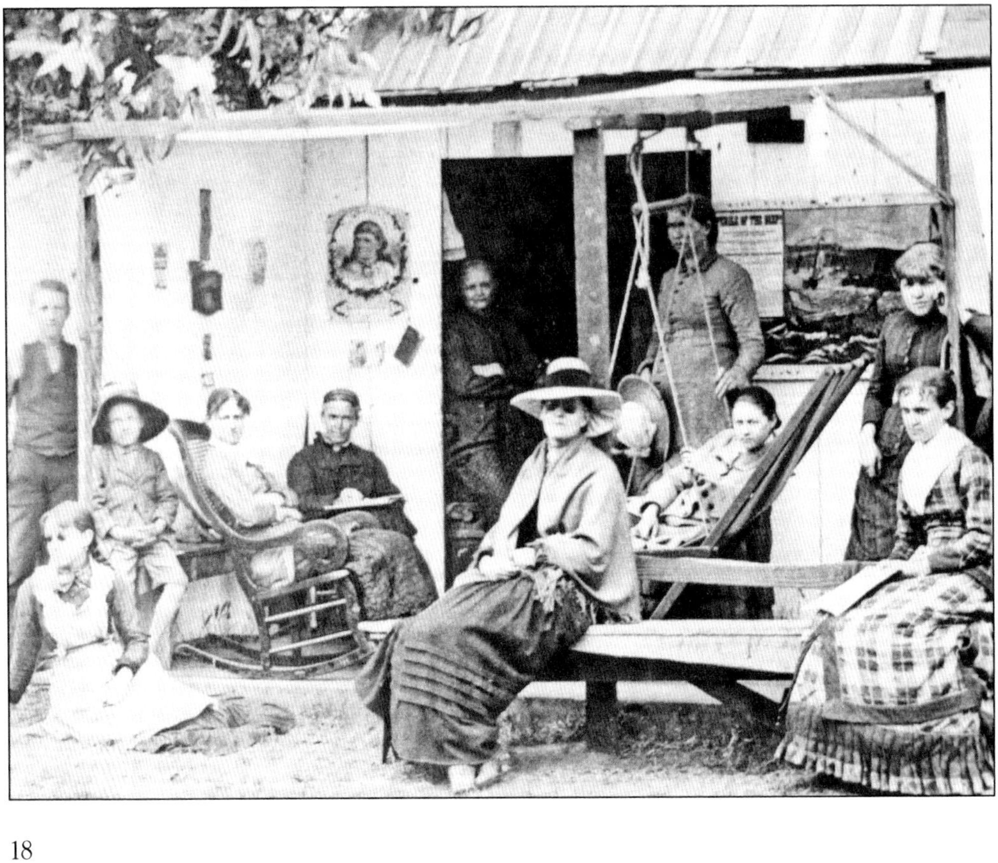

Two

In the Company of Frederick Hihn

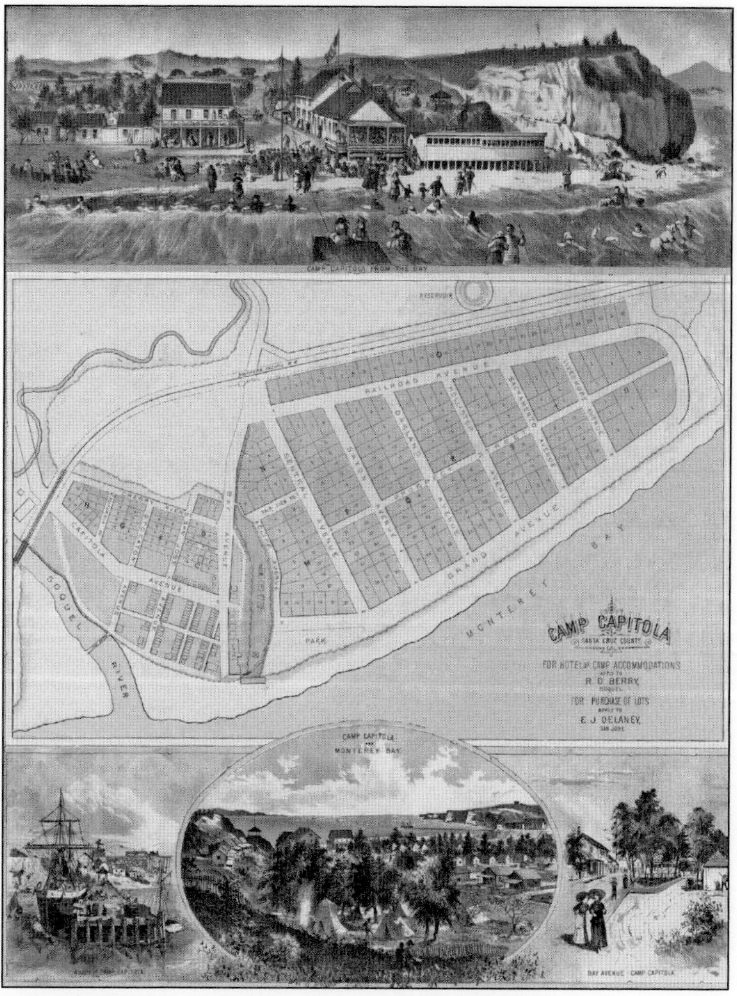

F.A. Hihn began subdividing tracts for summer homes in 1882–1883, selling parcels in the flats starting at $100. Some streets were named for the same blistering valley towns that vacationers sought to escape in summer. San Jose Avenue lots sold the quickest. Deeds granted an easement through the resort to the beach, allowing beachgoers enjoyment of "the waters of Monterey Bay."

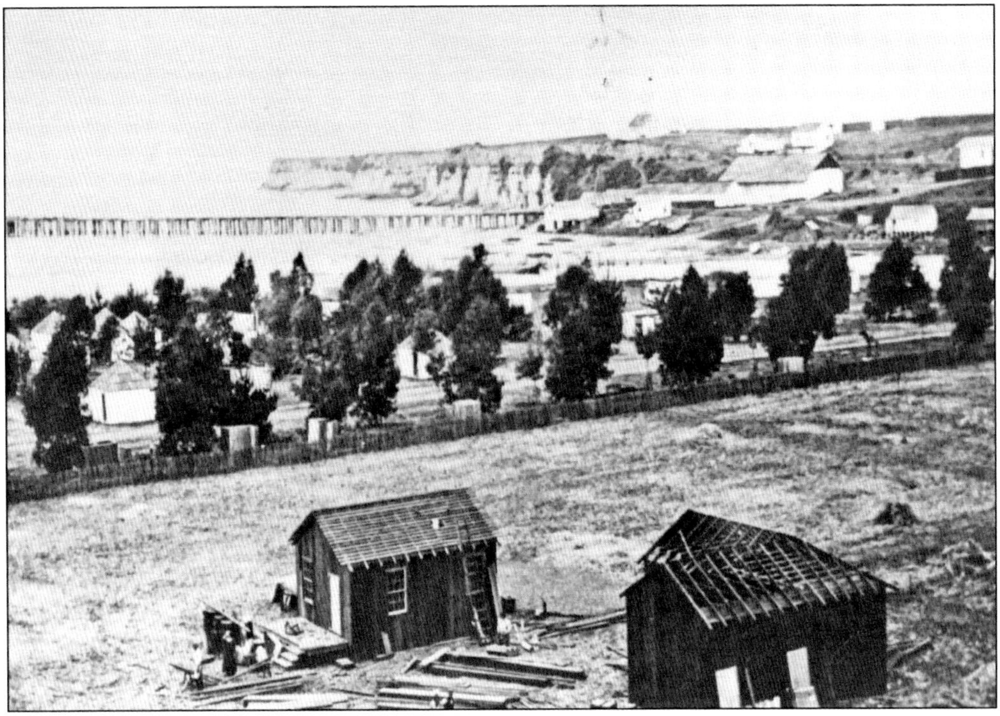

The first subdivision, today's village, was bordered by Cherry, Bay (Monterey), Capitola, and California Avenues. Lot owners built cottages or ordered them from the Hihn Company. Some pitched tents communally with relatives and friends. In the photograph above, construction is underway in 1882. The railroad depot, visible at upper right, was soon moved to the trestle's east end. Outhouses were discreetly hidden by trees along the fenced boundary at center. Below, an image from a few years later, taken in the same location, illustrates the pace of development. The house at the corner of Park Place, lower right, is still standing.

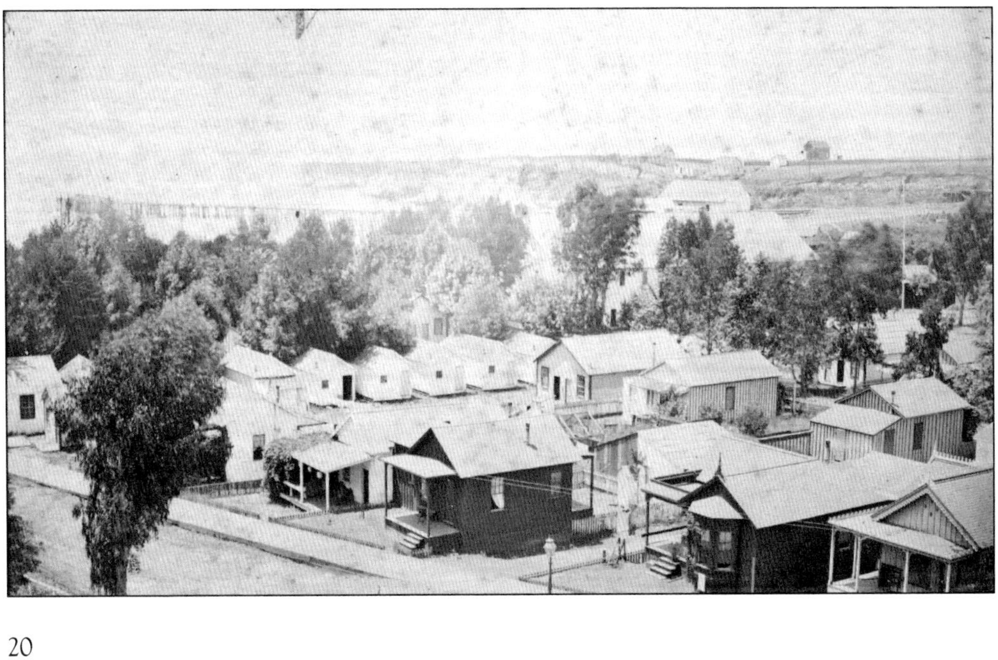

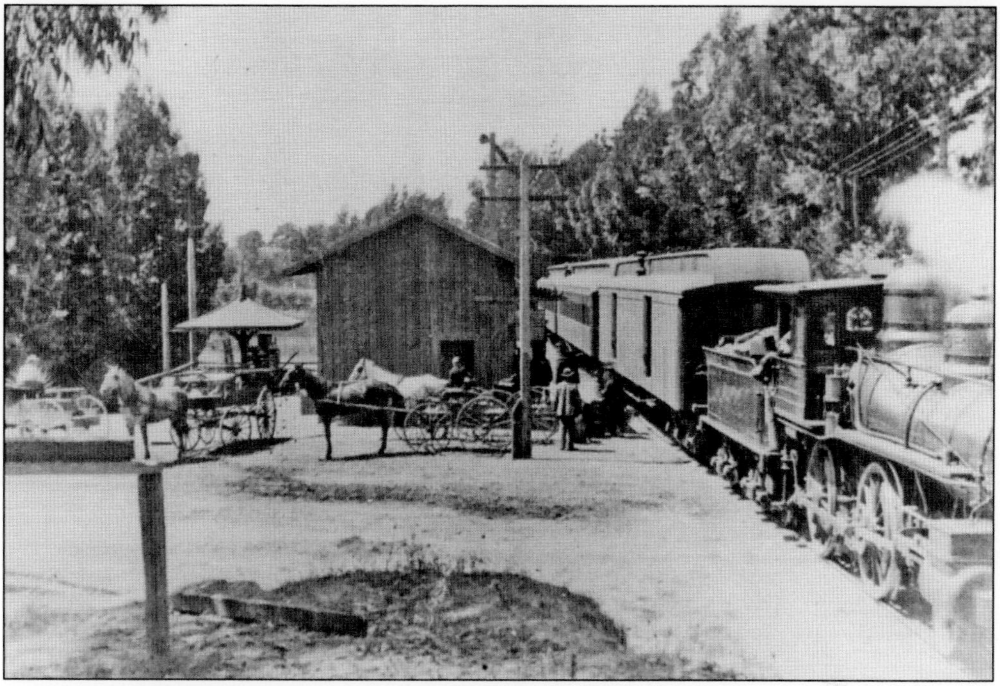

E.S. Harrison's *History of Santa Cruz County* (1892) noted that Capitola's bathing beach was one of the finest in the state. "One has but to pass through here on the train during the months of July or August to realize the fact that it is a resort of considerable importance, as he will perceive the depot and adjacent grounds thronged with people. To good-looking bachelors I will here impart the cheerful information that there is a great preponderance of the feminine element at this place during the summer season." Below, a new road built in 1888 leads from the relocated train station toward the hotel. A landslide the next winter forced the construction of retaining walls. Fossilized cliff stone was used for the embankment facing the street. (Below, courtesy of Norman Davis.)

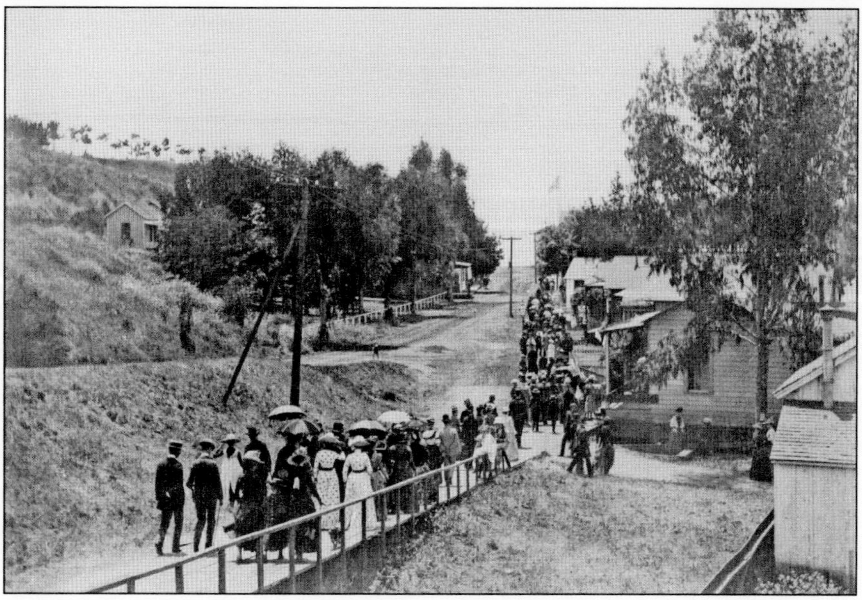

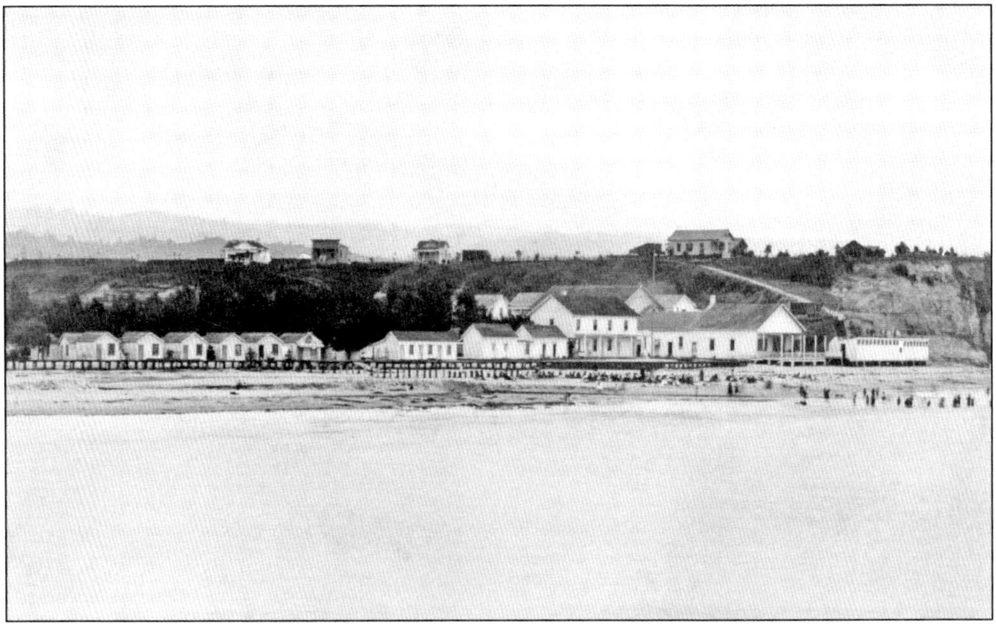

On today's Depot Hill, F.A. Hihn mapped his second subdivision in 1884. Parcels sold rapidly to German American families, many of them active in the Turn Verein, a social and athletic club. Members who were civic leaders and entrepreneurs from the Santa Clara Valley became neighbors at Capitola. A significant number of the original homes have been preserved as historic structures and are now the oldest in the city.

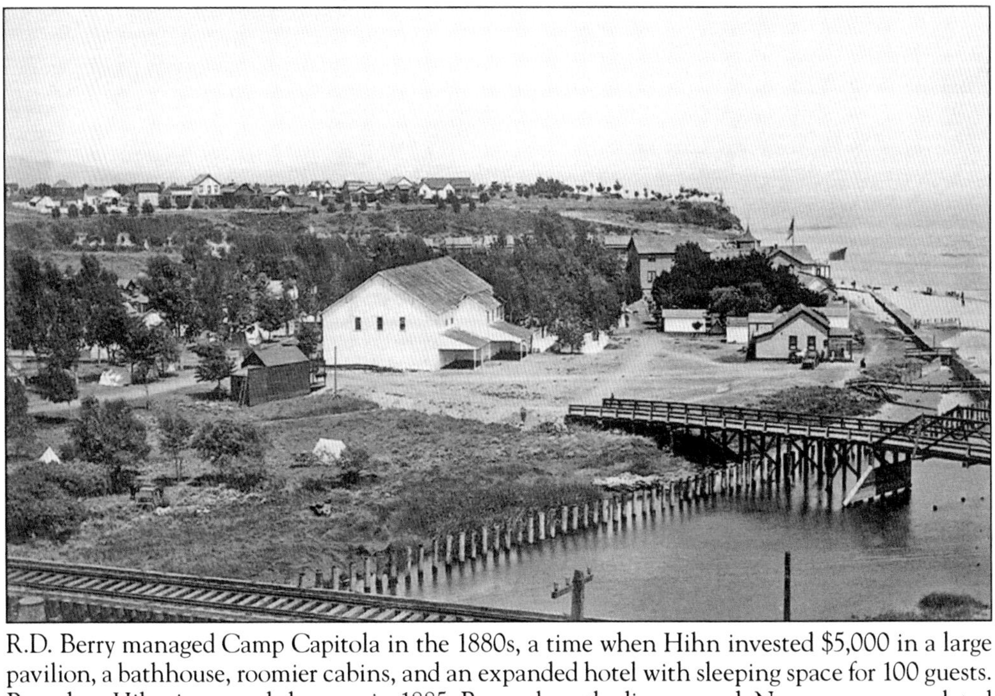

R.D. Berry managed Camp Capitola in the 1880s, a time when Hihn invested $5,000 in a large pavilion, a bathhouse, roomier cabins, and an expanded hotel with sleeping space for 100 guests. But when Hihn increased the rent in 1885, Berry abruptly disappeared. Newspapers speculated that he ran off with one of several possible women. He eventually returned, admitting that he was heavily in debt, owing $6,000 to his creditors.

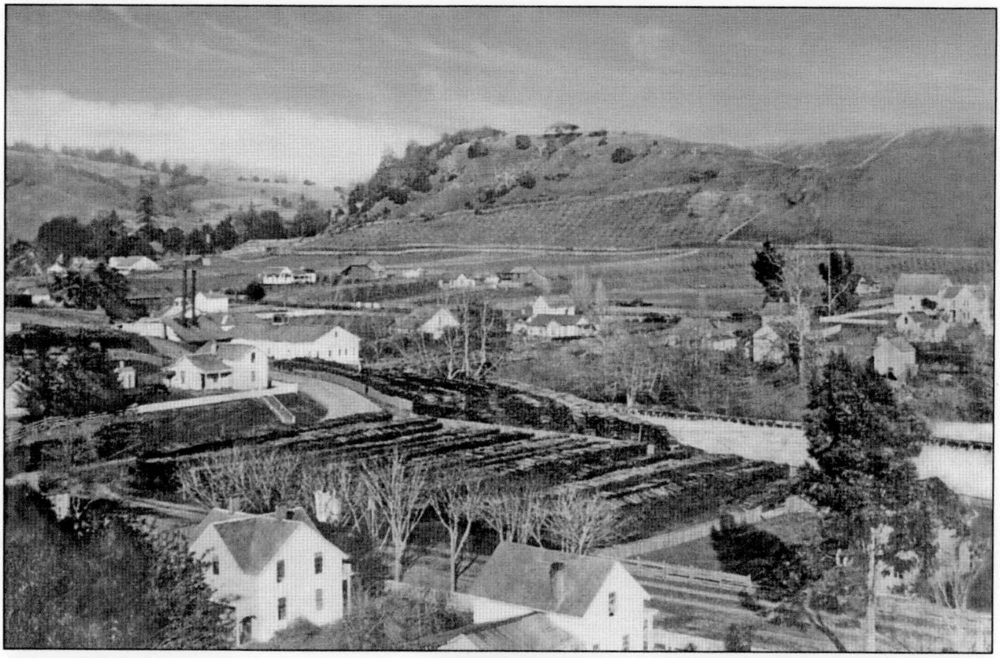

When Capitola was threatened by pollution in the mid-1880s, Hihn acted to protect his investment. Dross, rubbish, and lime from the South Coast Paper Mill, above left, were being dumped directly into Soquel Creek. Hihn negotiated with owners Edward and Frank O'Neill (O'Neil) for construction of a flume in 1885. Visible in the foreground at right, the chute ran under the bridge at the Santa Cruz–Watsonville Road (Soquel Drive) and continued along the creek for about a mile. At a point just above Capitola, near today's Riverview Terrace, the sludge was directed underground and through the camp to a 400-foot tunnel in the cliff and was then discharged into the bay down coast toward Aptos. (Both, courtesy of Richard Nutter.)

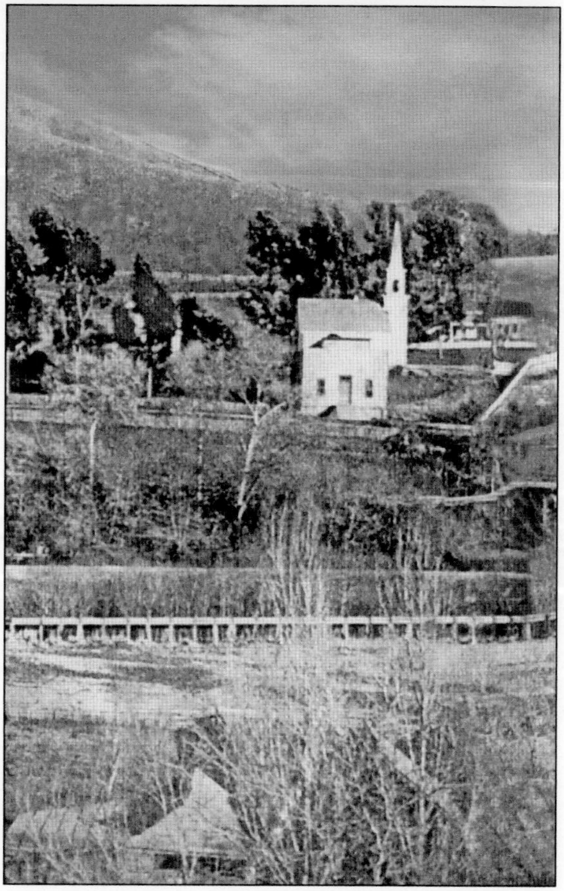

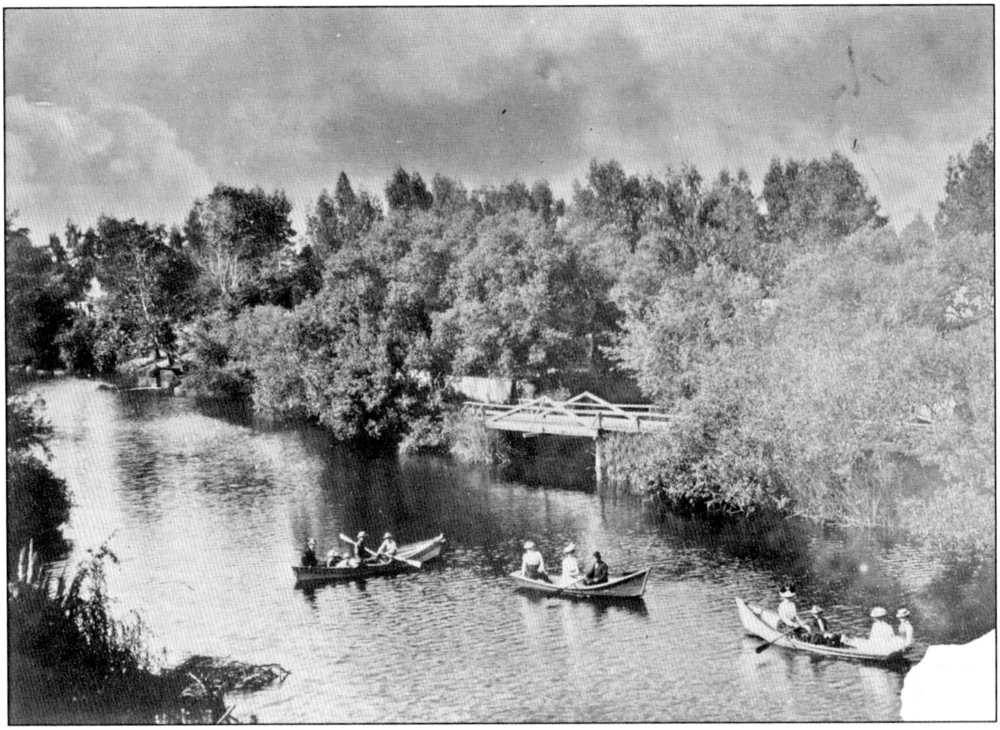

The photograph above, taken about 1900, looks toward the covered outlet where the stream from Noble Gulch empties into Soquel Creek. At a spot around the bend upstream, to the left, waste from the flume and sewage from the camp were sent inland. Capitola's publicists knew that a health-promoting climate and clean water were essential to tourism. One 1922 advertisement even claimed that a miraculous longevity had been achieved by vacationing pioneer families who drank from a "radioactive" spring flowing from the embankment near the trestle. The image below dates from the 1880s.

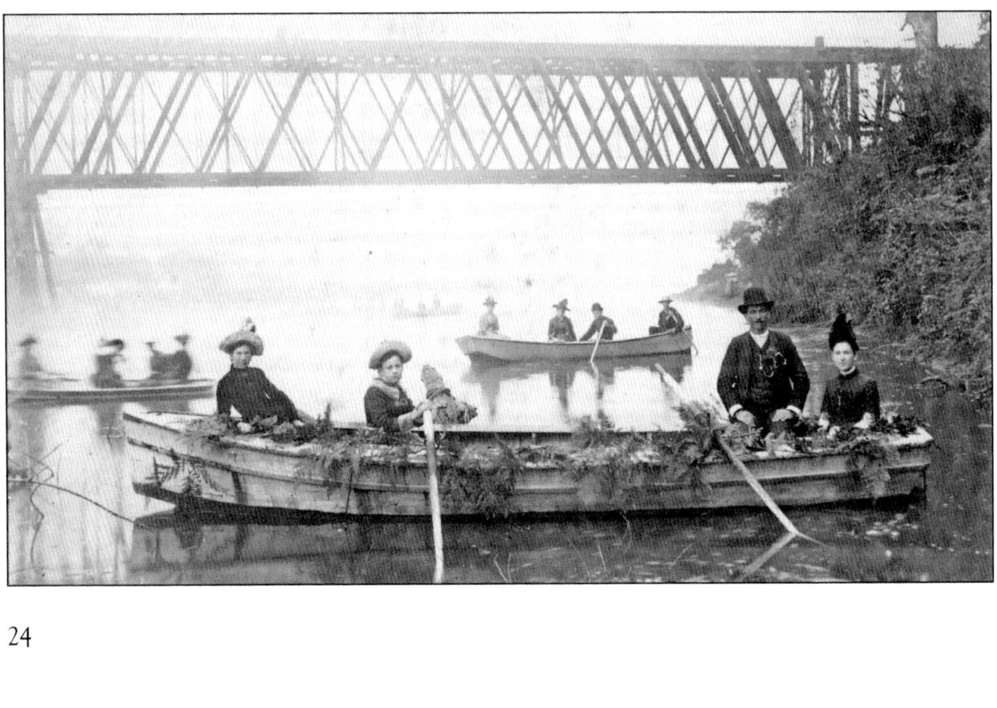

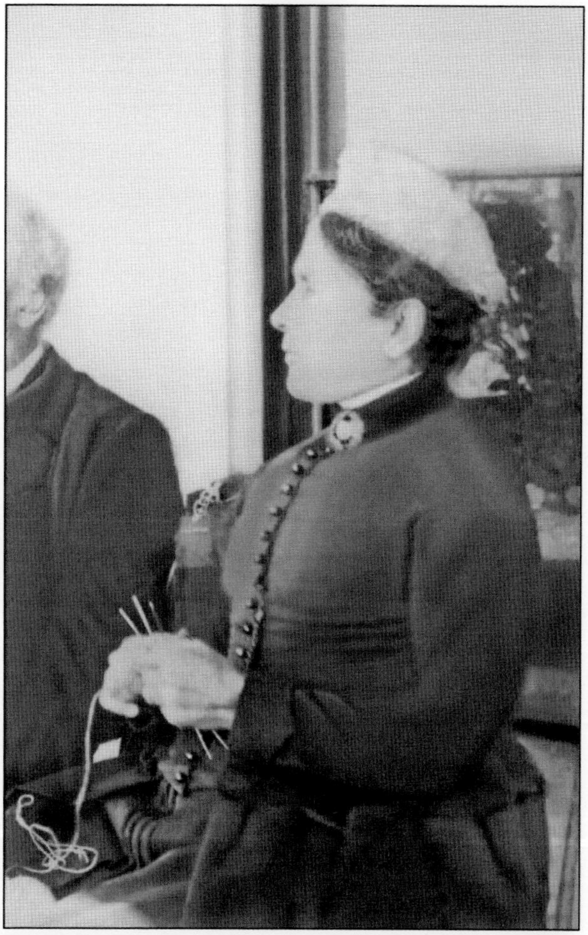

Frederick Hihn entrusted commercial enterprises to several women. Best known was Martha J. (Mrs. Frank) Lewis (1838–1923). Famed as "little Patty Reed," she was the Donner-Reed party survivor who kept a little wooden doll tucked in her dress as comfort during the tragic winter of 1847. Lewis, a widow by 1888, took charge that year of Hotel Capitola and the newly created Capitola Park Hotel east of the depot. The three-story building, below, had previously been a part of the defunct California Beet Sugar Company mill that was dismantled in 1884. (Below, courtesy of the Hihn-Younger Archive, Special Collections, University Library, University of California, Santa Cruz.)

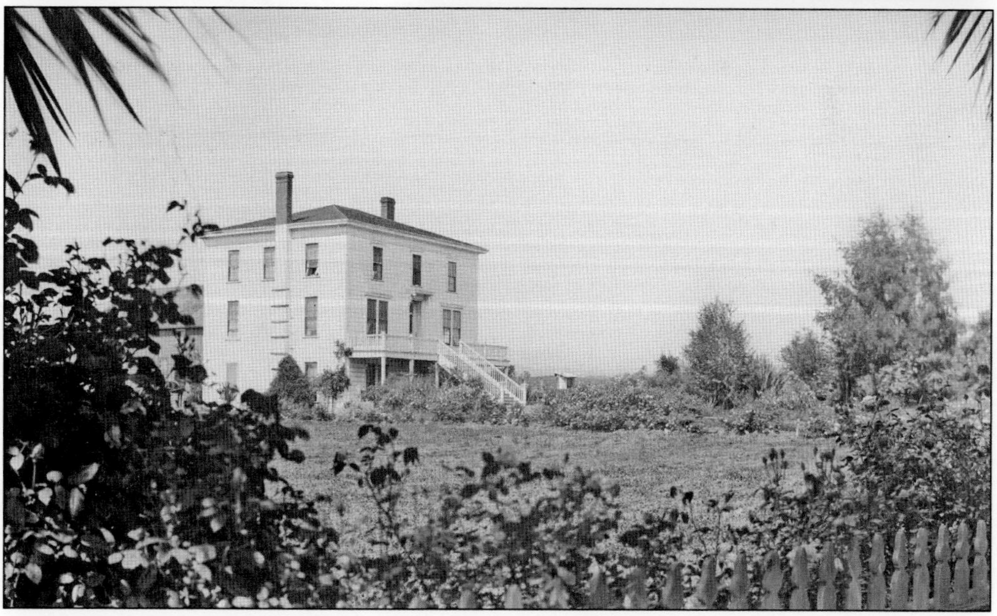

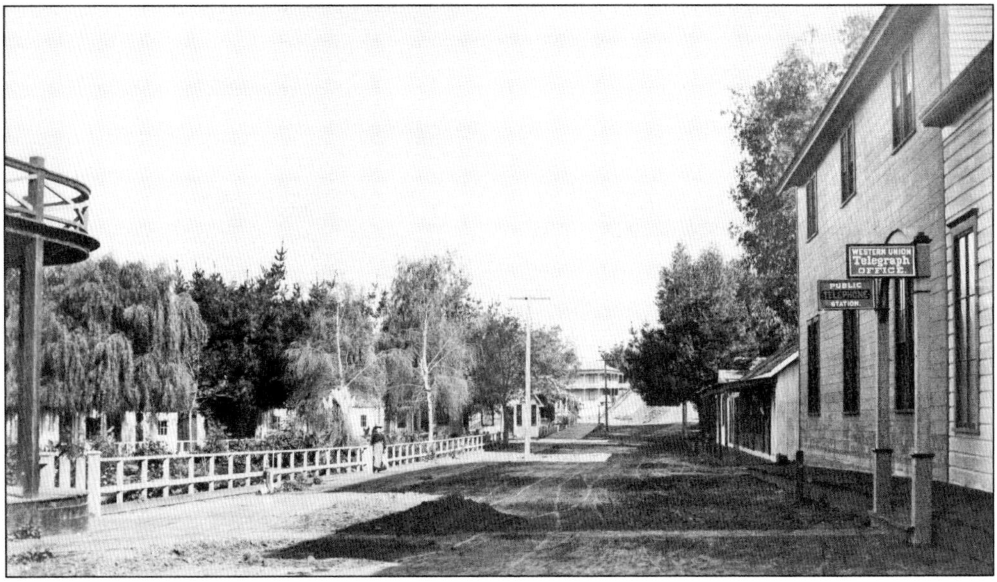

Patty Reed Lewis and her children greeted arrivals at Capitola for more than 20 years. The photographic skills of her daughter, Susan Augusta "Susie" Lewis (1873–1929), were noted while she was a teenager. These evocative images are rare. Lewis captured the street scenes shown here of the hotel and its annex on Bay (Monterey) Avenue about 1890. The hotel building, above right, had a dining room at the rear and a dance hall nearest the ocean.

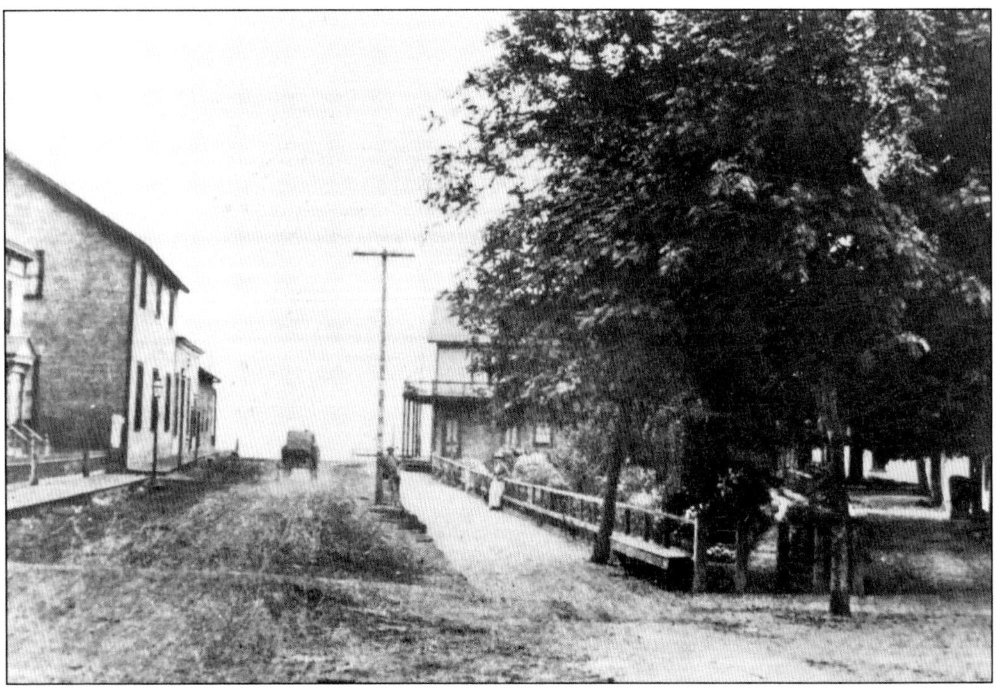

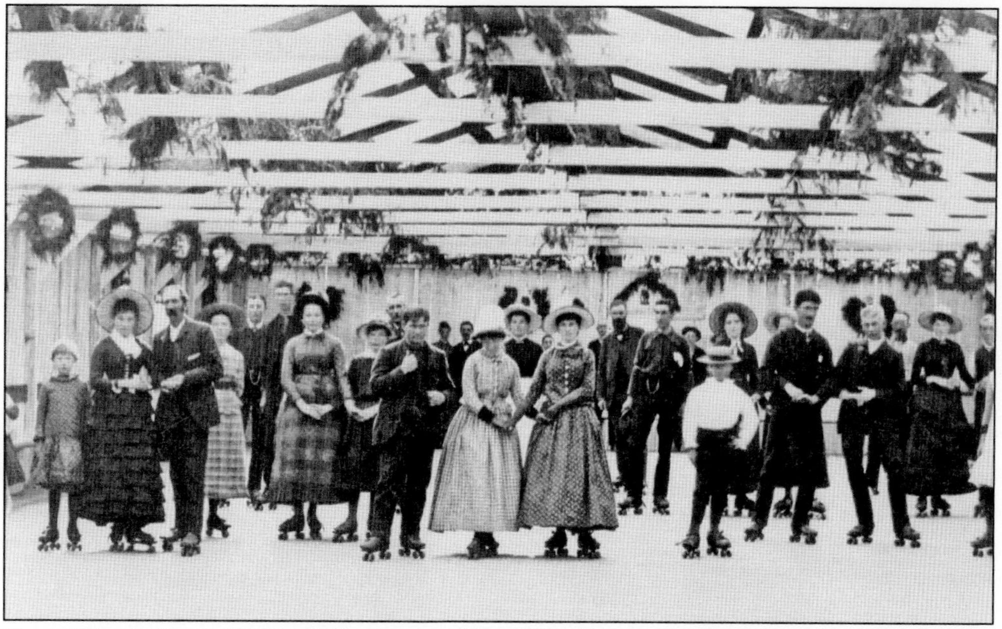

(James) Frazier Lewis (1866–1943), the son of Patty Reed Lewis, ran the telegraph and post office at the Hotel Capitola along with other Hihn resort concessions such as the skating rink and pavilion, above. In partnership with William Patterson, Lewis served up treats at the ice cream saloon, below. He eventually took over Capitola's candy store and grew famous as the creator of a nickel candy bar laced with rum, known as the Frazier Lewis Victoria Cream. In the early 1920s, the family moved to Twin Lakes, near Santa Cruz, where Frazier set up a candy factory. A walkway in downtown Santa Cruz commemorates his Victoria Cream candy.

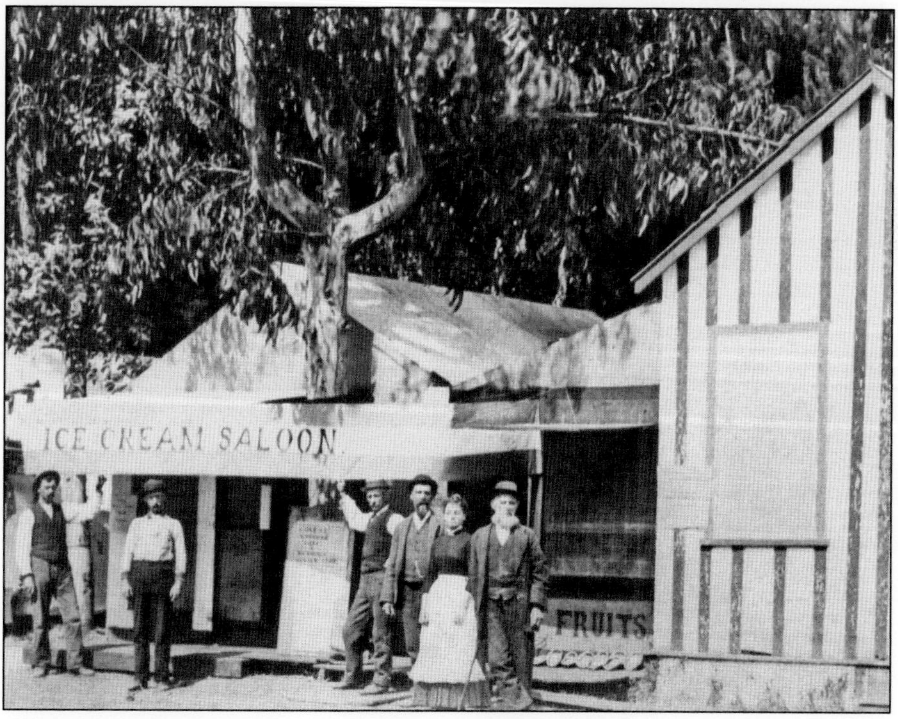

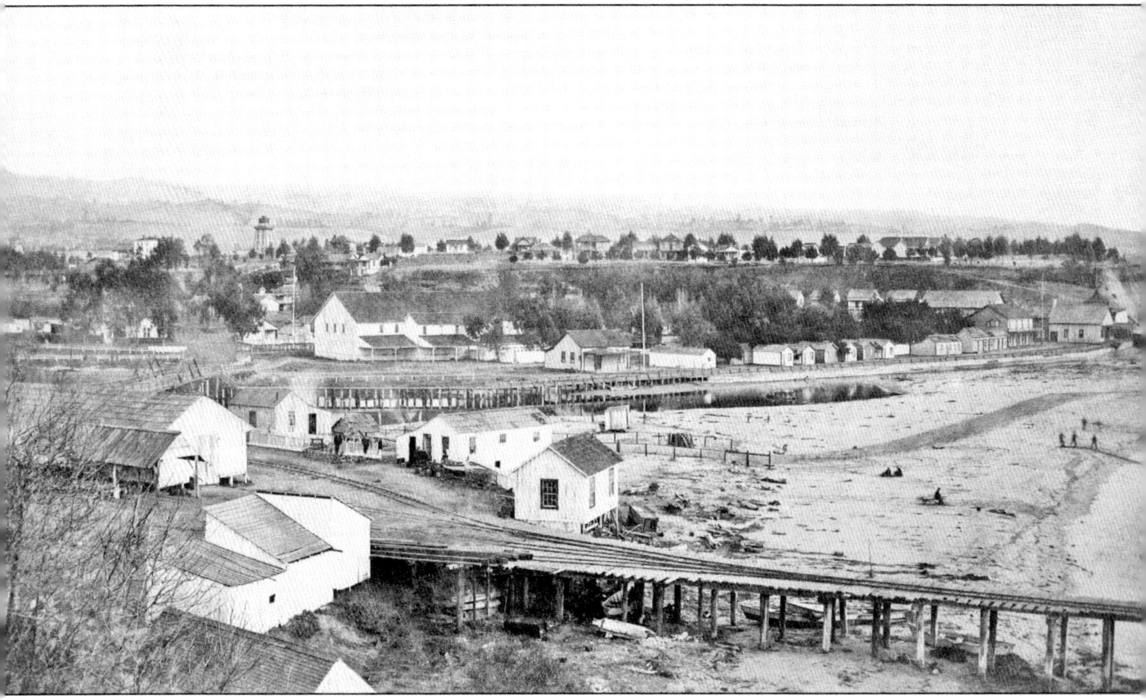

Benjamin Cahoon and his son, Edwin, built a sawmill four miles above Soquel in 1866. Once the stumps were cleared, the family established the Fern Gulch Ranch and decided to run it as a mountain resort. To learn the tourism business, Edwin spent a season or two managing Camp Capitola. One noteworthy achievement under his tenancy was the first hot-air balloon ascension in Santa Cruz County, staged over Capitola beach in 1886. In the foreground of this 1889 photograph is the fishing colony that grew around the wharf early in the decade. In the off-season, when the resort sat empty, the fishing industry spread out onto the beach.

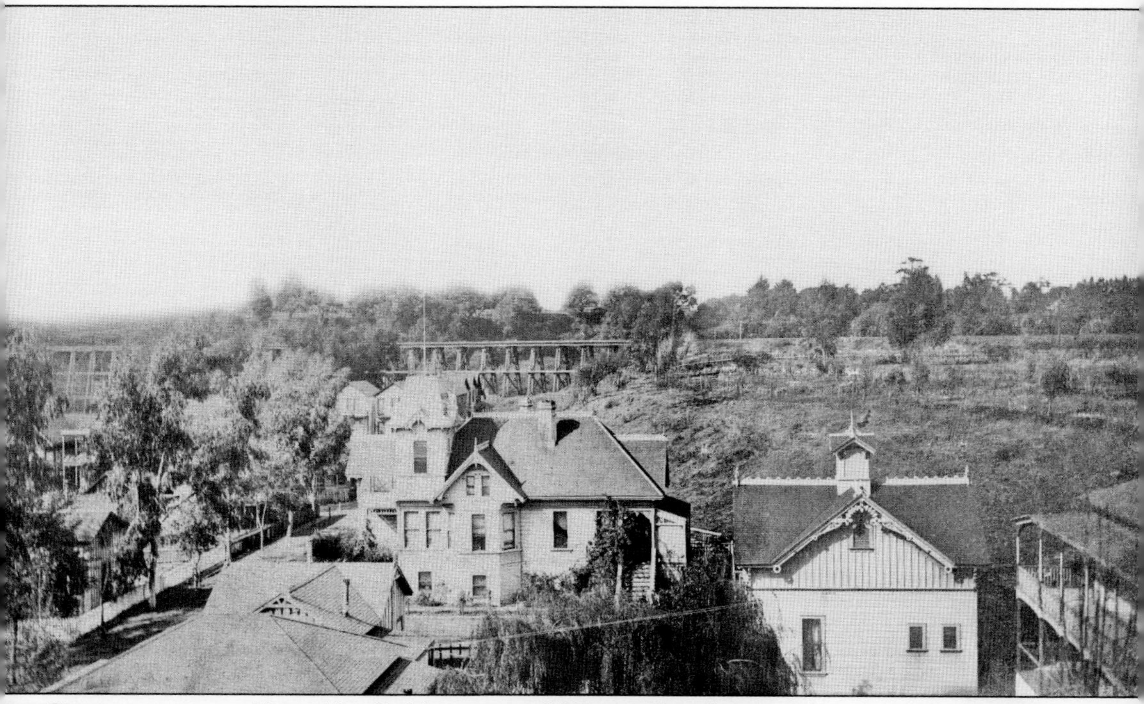

German immigrant Henry Van Syckle, a successful Santa Clara farmer and entrepreneur, bought a spacious lot on Cherry Avenue and completed an imposing Eastlake stick home costing $4,000 in 1886. The house initially had 17 rooms and a tower that was later removed. During the Great Depression, the home was converted into a boardinghouse. Even with changes made over the years, it remains the most impressive Victorian-era structure in the village and one of the first built as a permanent residence.

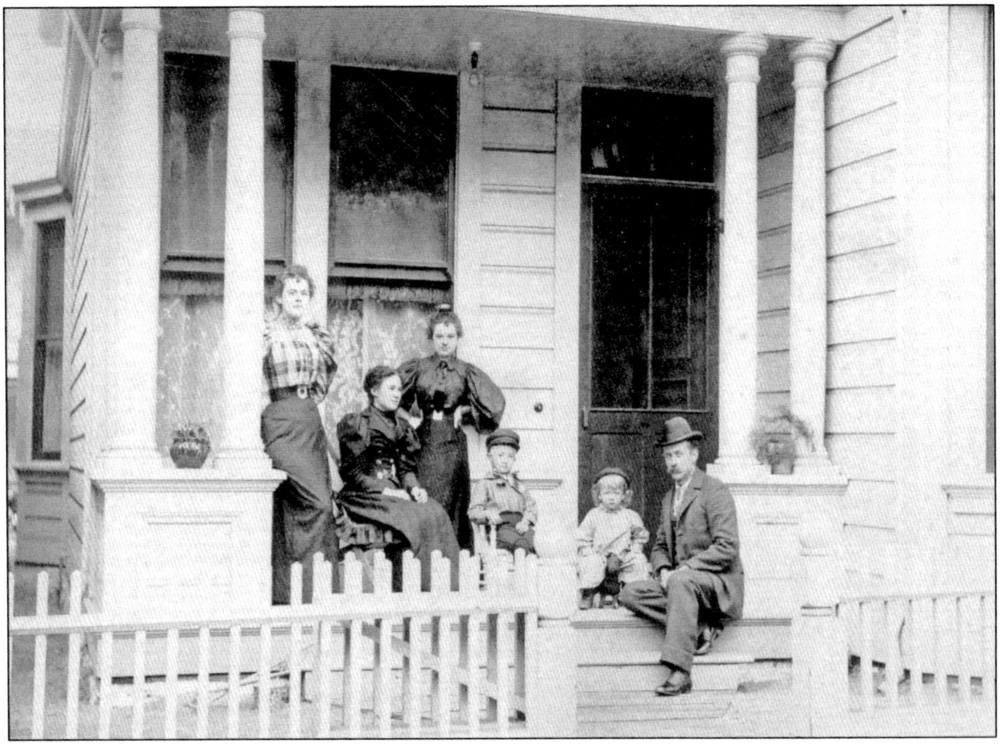

Frank Reanier, far right, moved his family into the Hihn superintendent's building at the corner of Capitola and Monterey Avenues in 1890. Below, sons Wilbur (left) and Elster Reanier are seated in a buggy beside the landmark, now listed in the National Register of Historic Places. A former Nevada County rancher, Reanier was hired by Hihn and met his employer's rigorous expectations. He remained with the company nearly 25 years, often making personal loans to help resort concessionaires in the off-season. Ultimately, Reanier was twice appointed, in 1916 and 1927, to serve on the Santa Cruz County Board of Supervisors. (Both, courtesy of the Reanier family.)

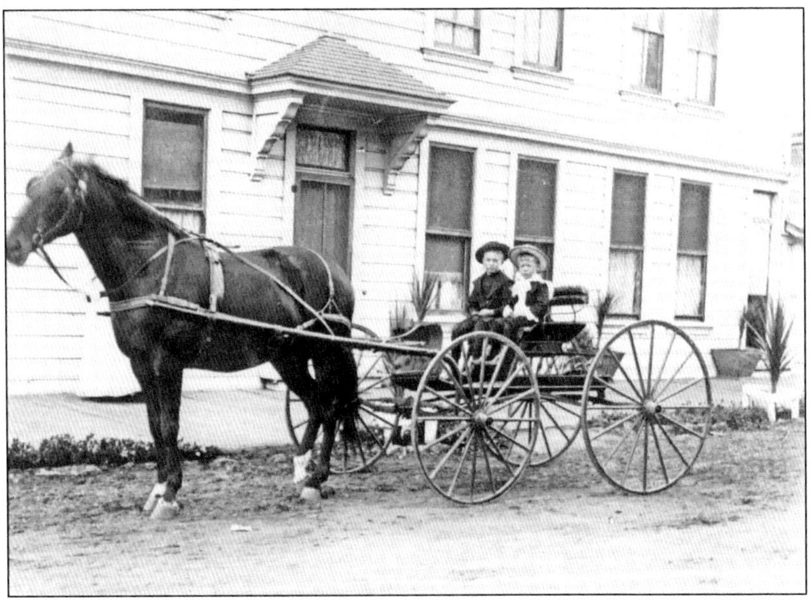

Three

Welcome to the Hotel Capitola

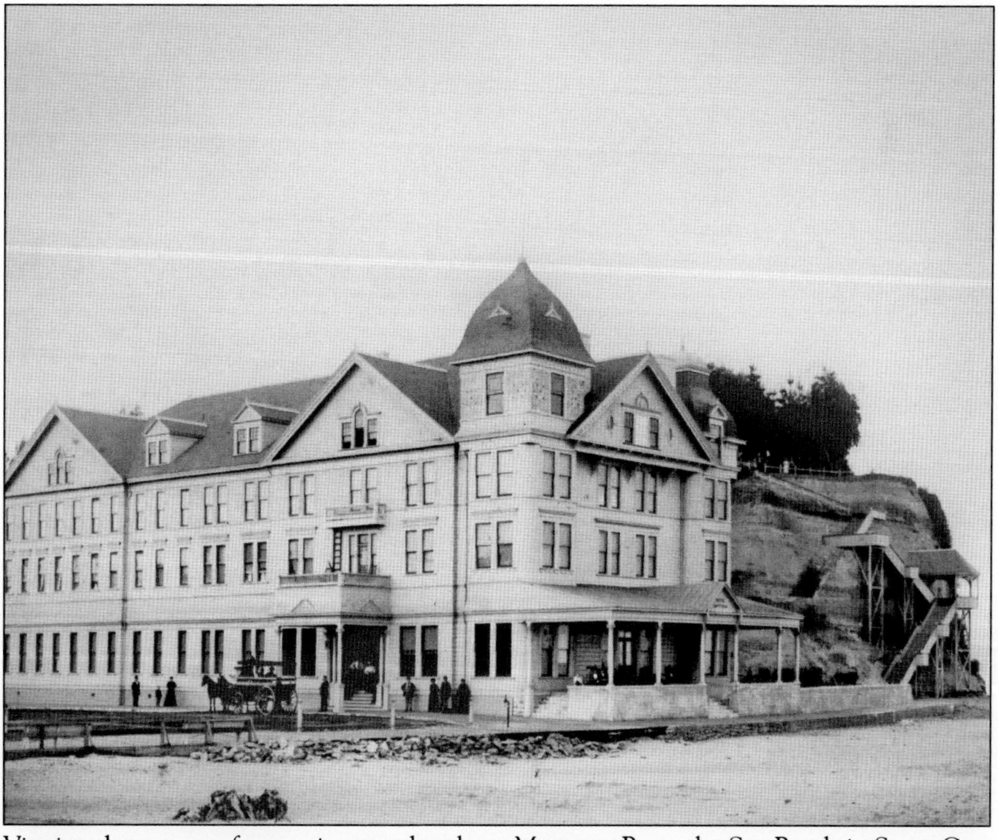

Viewing the success of two epic resort hotels on Monterey Bay—the Sea Beach in Santa Cruz and the Del Monte in Monterey—Frederick Hihn decided to build the Hotel Capitola. Architect Edward Van Cleeck (1849–1925) designed a Colonial Revival–style hotel with Queen Anne influences. The foundation was laid in December 1894, and the first guests checked in the next June. A stairway to Lover's Walk, far right, was finished at the same time.

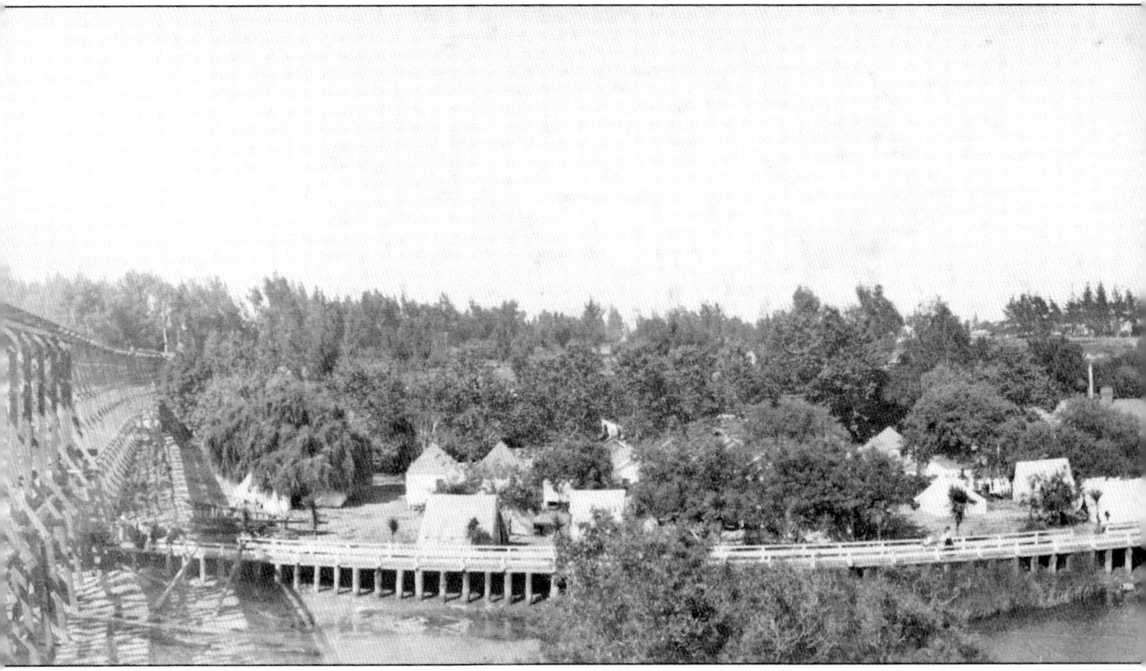

A native of New York, Edward Van Cleeck arrived in California in 1885 and within a few years opened an office at the Hihn building in downtown Santa Cruz. The architect began to draft designs for Capitola in 1891. During that decade, Van Cleeck restructured the resort as it shed

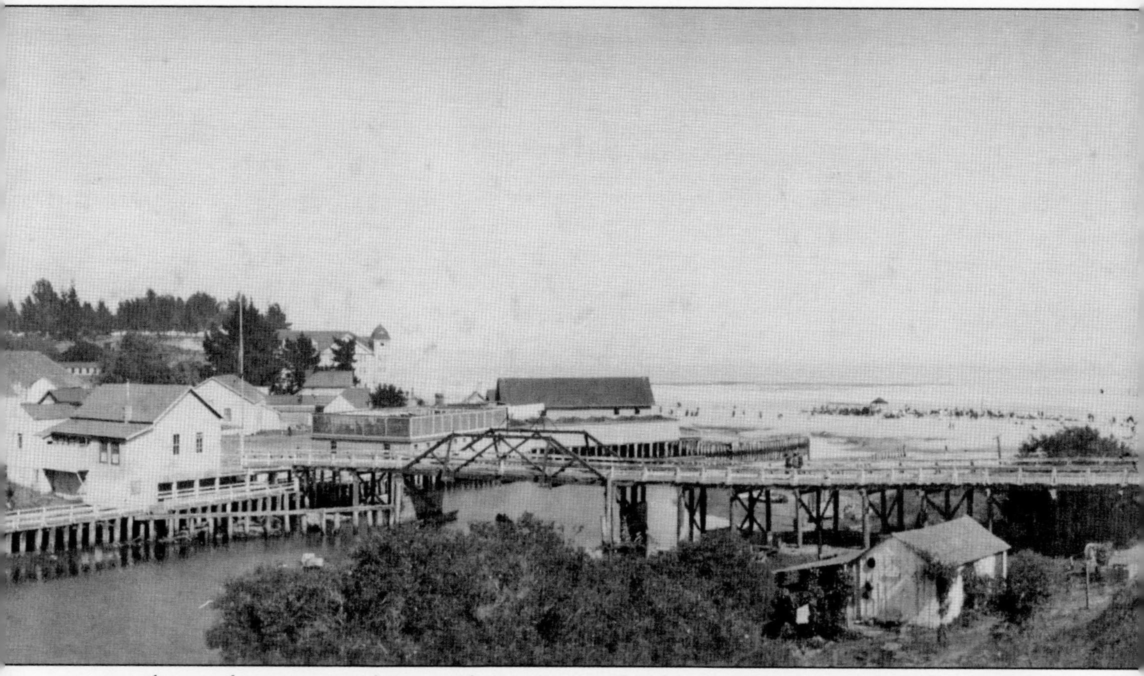

its camp identity for a more sophisticated prominence "by-the-sea." Newly completed structures are the focal point in this panoramic photograph. Hotel Capitola was described as a vacation accommodation comparable to the Del Monte Hotel but more affordable.

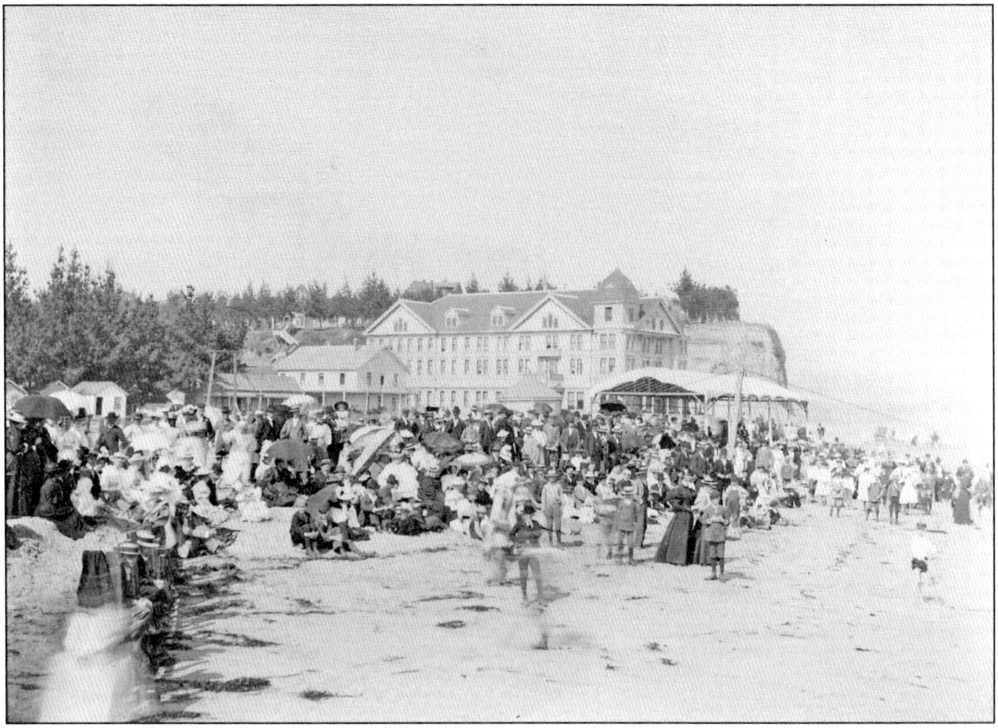

Capitola photographer Stephen West Watrous caught the crowd's attention on a breezy spring day in 1896. None of the beachgoers seem too eager for a saltwater dip. Below, a fresh fish catch is put on view at the wharf, framed in the foreground by transport rails and boat davits and distantly by the hotel and new stairway up the bluff. (Above, courtesy of the Matty/Meyer family; below, courtesy of John Nicol.)

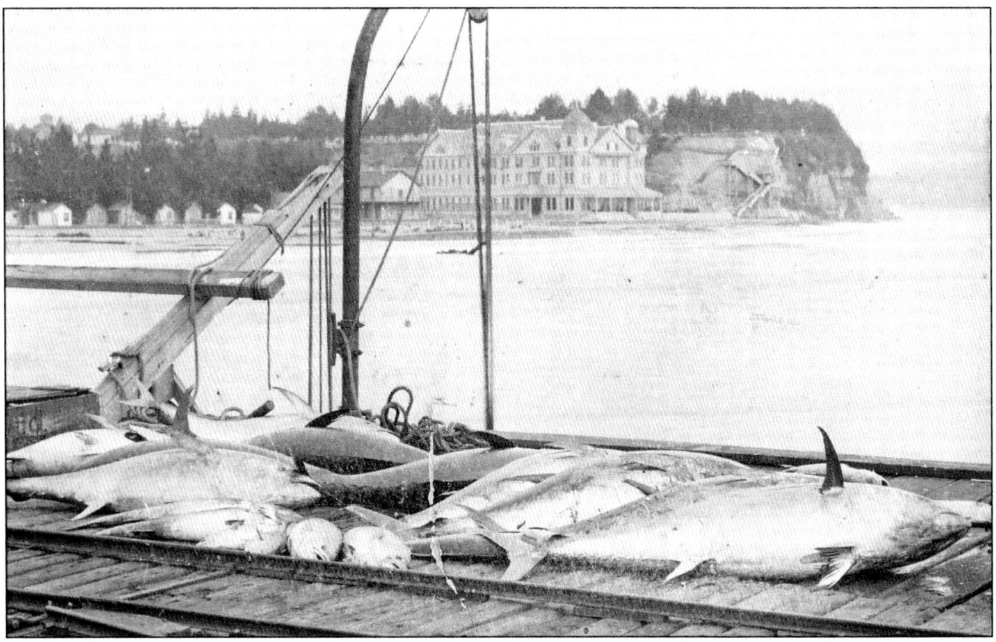

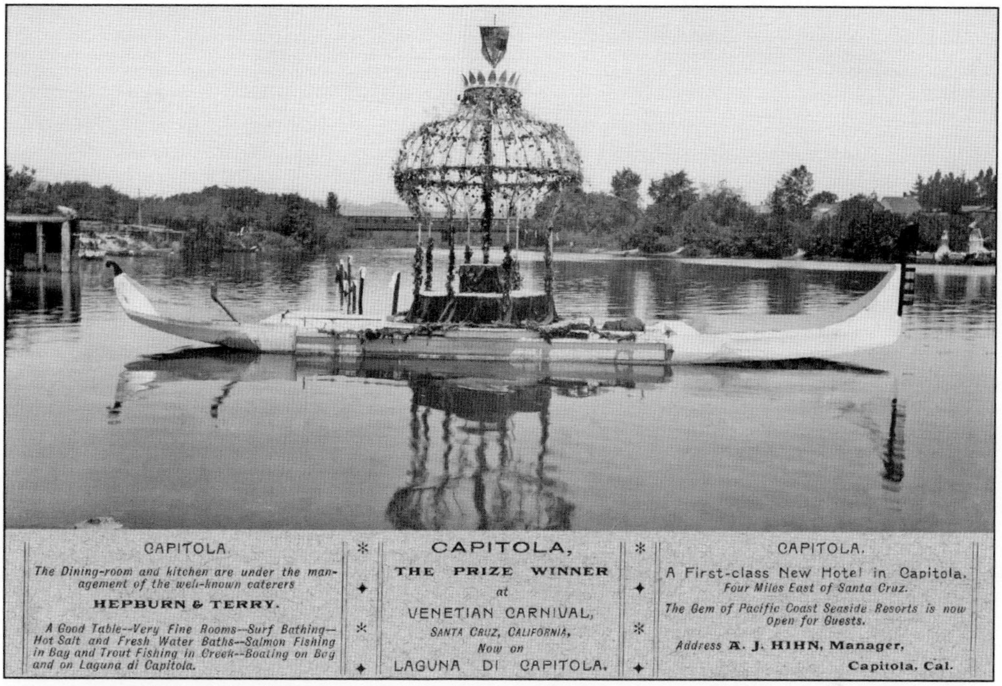

A temporary dam crossed the San Lorenzo River in Santa Cruz in 1895 for the Venetian Water Carnival, an event that dazzled spectators with aquatic floats and electric lights. F.A. Hihn—seizing the opportunity to mention a new enterprise—won first place for his "Capitola" festival entry. On the photograph, he promoted the new hotel and described Capitola as "the gem of the Pacific Coast Seaside Resorts." (Courtesy of the Hihn family.)

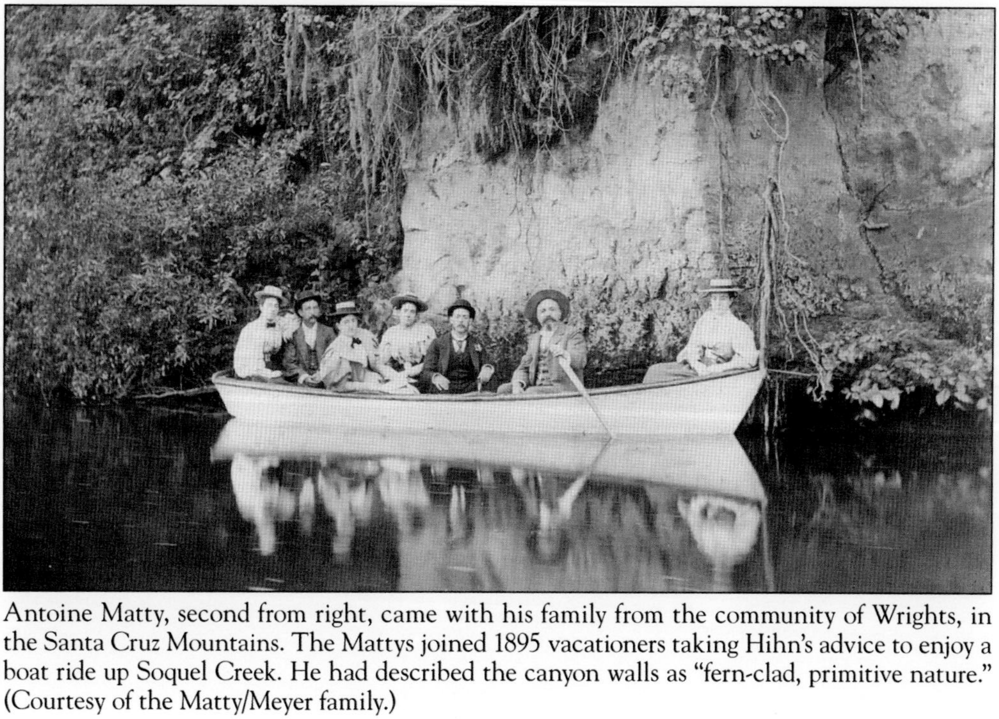

Antoine Matty, second from right, came with his family from the community of Wrights, in the Santa Cruz Mountains. The Mattys joined 1895 vacationers taking Hihn's advice to enjoy a boat ride up Soquel Creek. He had described the canyon walls as "fern-clad, primitive nature." (Courtesy of the Matty/Meyer family.)

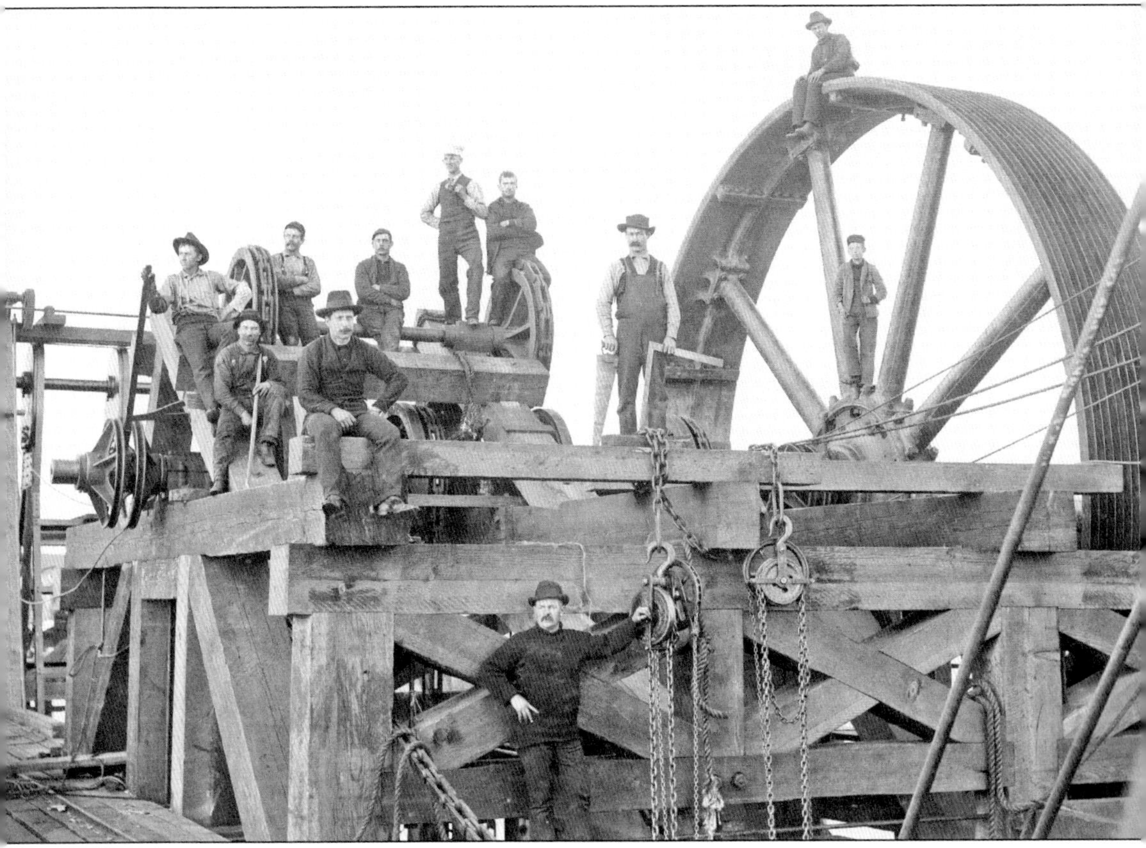

Electric power for Capitola was essential to F.A. Hihn, and he wanted it fast and economically. In 1895, he leased a section of the wharf to Emil Gerlach. Convinced that waves could be harnessed to provide energy, Gerlach designed a large-scale wave motor to generate electricity. Under his agreement with Hihn, he added 20 feet to Capitola's 750-foot wharf and constructed on its end a 30-ton, wave-powered electric generator. Its balance wheel was several stories tall, with paddles moving forward and backward through the action of the waves. The ocean experiment was expensive, using thousands of feet of lumber. The work crew, above, posed for photographer Stephen W. Watrous when the job was done.

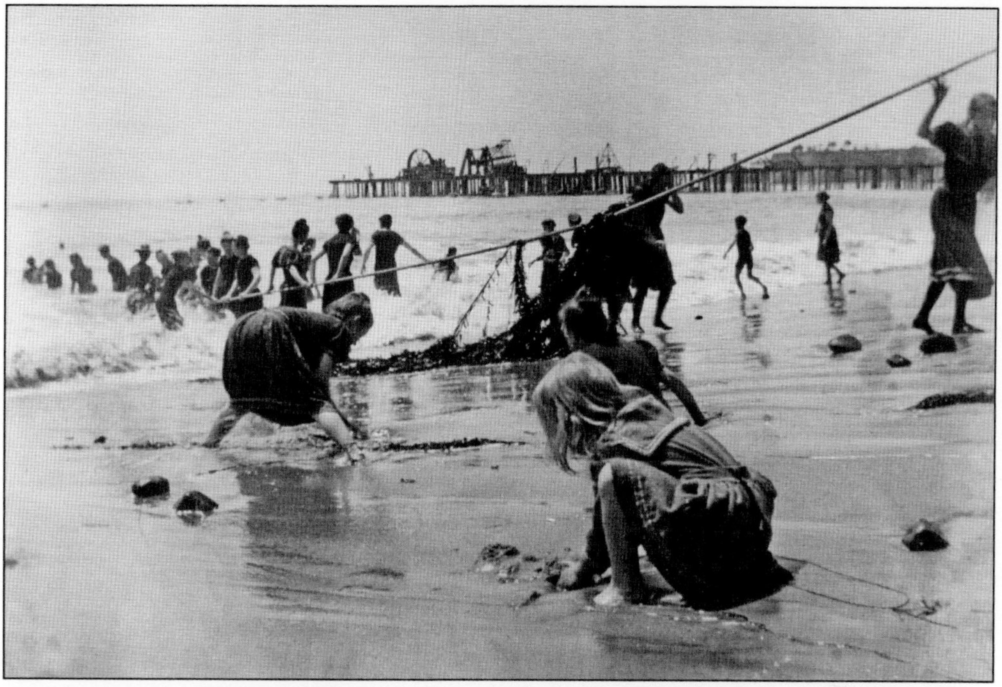

Tested and repaired early in 1896, the experiment was reviewed at the start of the summer season. Results were disappointing. The *Santa Cruz Sentinel* reported in June, "The Gerlach Wave Motor at Capitola does not allow itself to be disturbed by the waves." Within months, little trace of the machinery remained. By the time the photograph below was taken a few years later, the enormous wheel was a dim memory. (Above, courtesy of Norman Davis.)

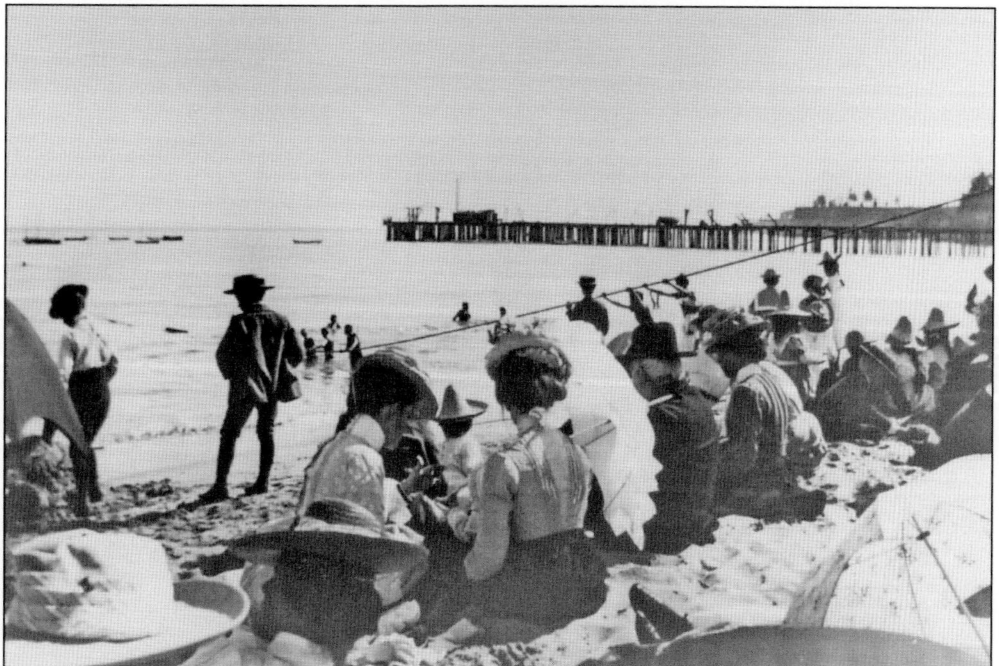

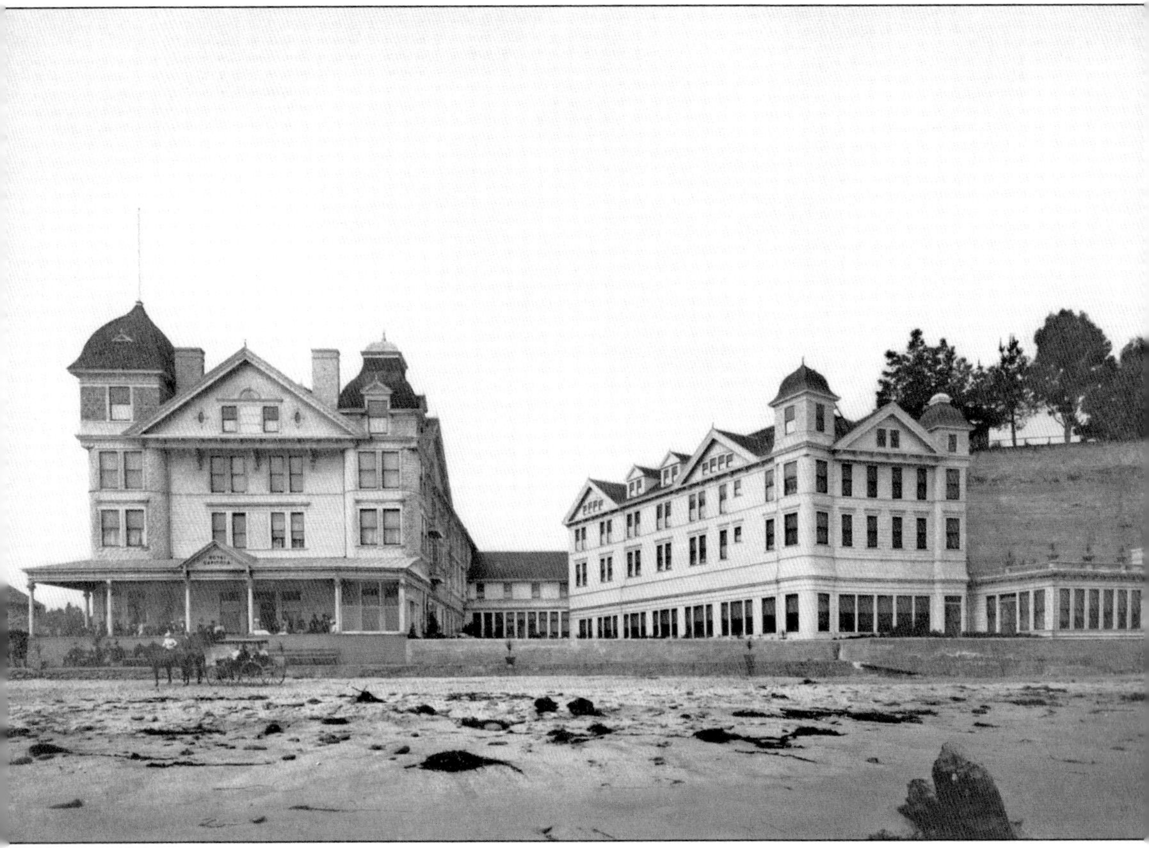

Two seasons after the observation stairway was built, Hihn decided to rip it out, shearing off the cliff face to make room for expansion. A new wing doubled the size of the hotel to 160 rooms, allowing total accommodations for 300 guests. It held a ballroom with concert stage and beachfront dining room windows that presented marine views at every table. The new wing of the hotel was joined to the old by a transverse section, thus forming an inner courtyard used for croquet. Under the cliff, at right, was a glass-enclosed clubhouse for card games and billiards. Van Cleeck was the architect. Work started in October 1897 and was finished in May 1899. (Both, courtesy of the Hihn-Younger Archive, Special Collections, University Library, University of California, Santa Cruz.)

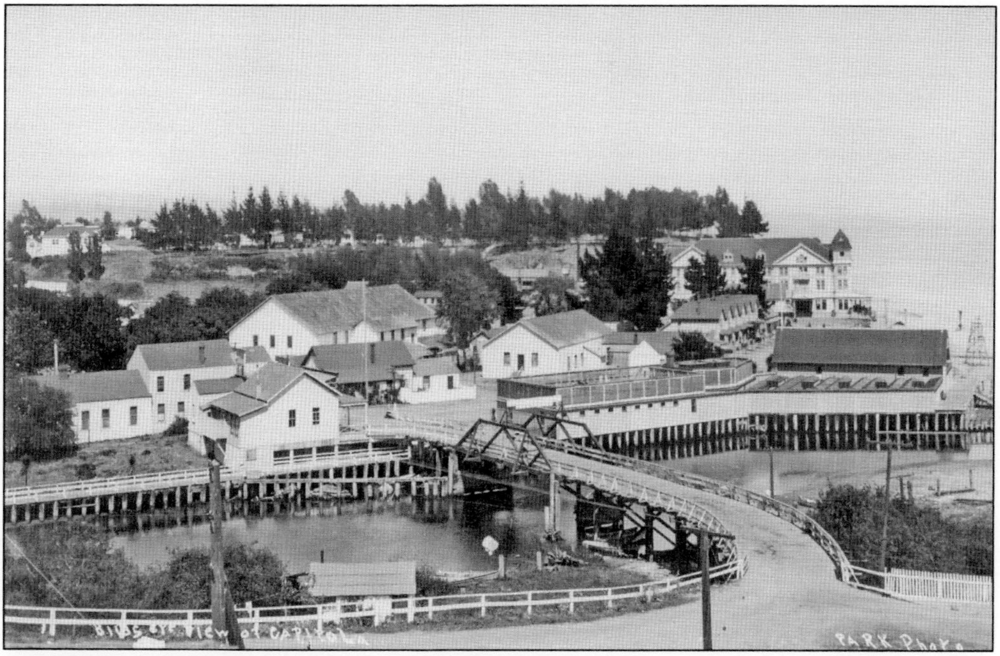

Frank Park, the photograph gallery concessionaire in 1902, shot a portrait of the Capitola village designed by Van Cleeck. The village saloon, on the left across the Stockton Bridge, was one of three taverns at the resort. Capitola's skating pavilion is the large structure at center left. Facing the lagoon are drying platforms and the office of the saltwater bathhouse. The newest buildings are Six Sisters duplexes along the Esplanade near the hotel. The distinctive style of Van Cleeck's resort architecture ended abruptly on the east bank of the creek, however. Below is an image shot from the wharf about the same time, showing rustic shacks of the fishing colony on the west side, at left.

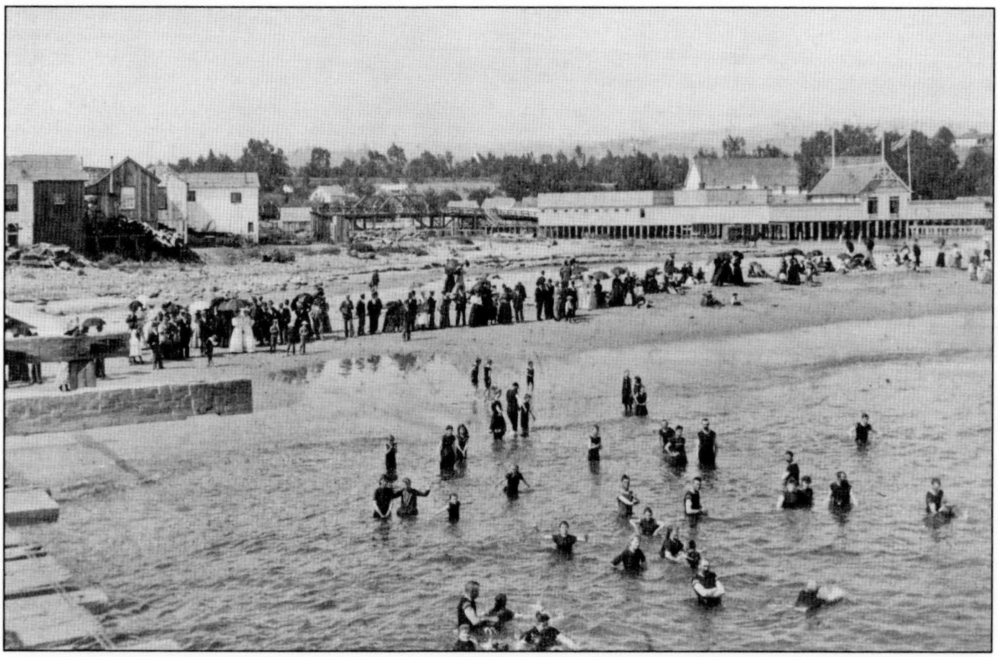

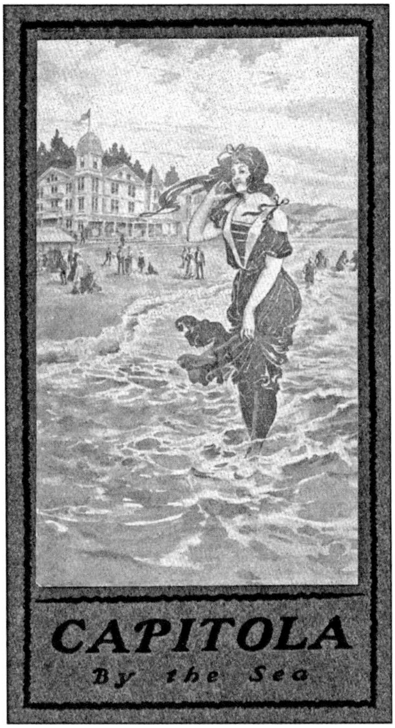

F.A. Hihn produced a brochure around 1900 introducing "Capitola By the Sea" as a modern, affordable, well-conducted seaside resort on the sunny shore of Monterey Bay. Aiming his text toward the dwellers of inland valleys and mountains, he promised that a vacation at Capitola would be a lifelong remembrance. The picture below, printed in the booklet, is a portrayal of resort life at the turn of the 20th century.

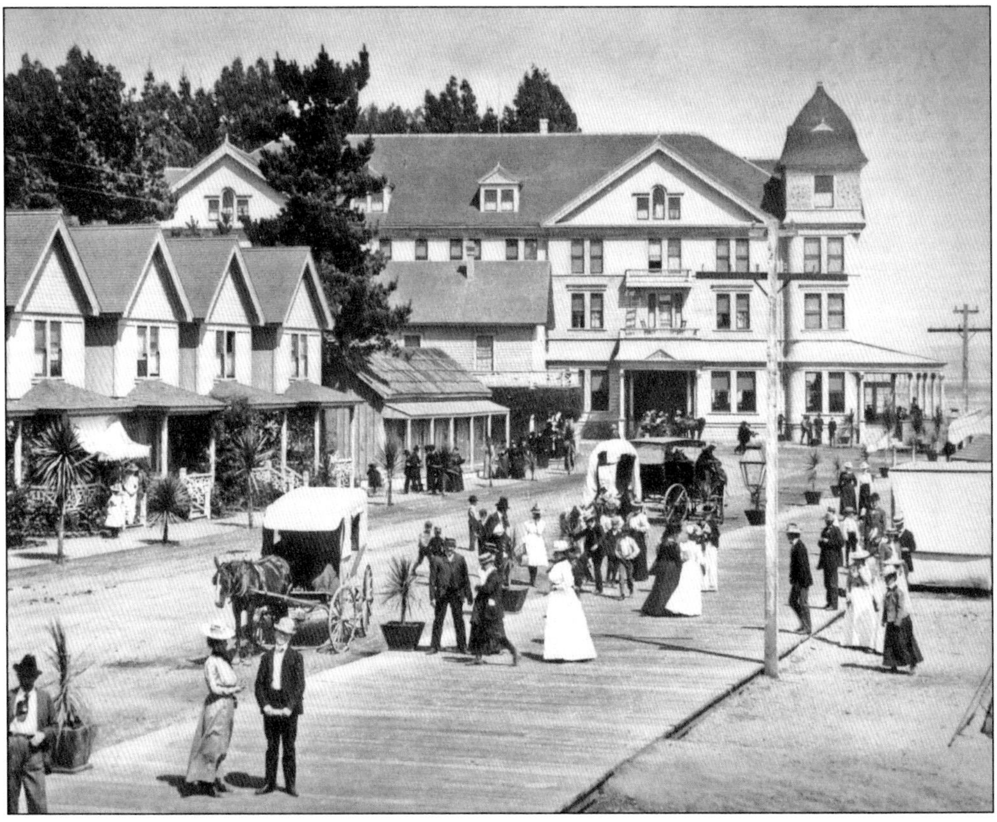

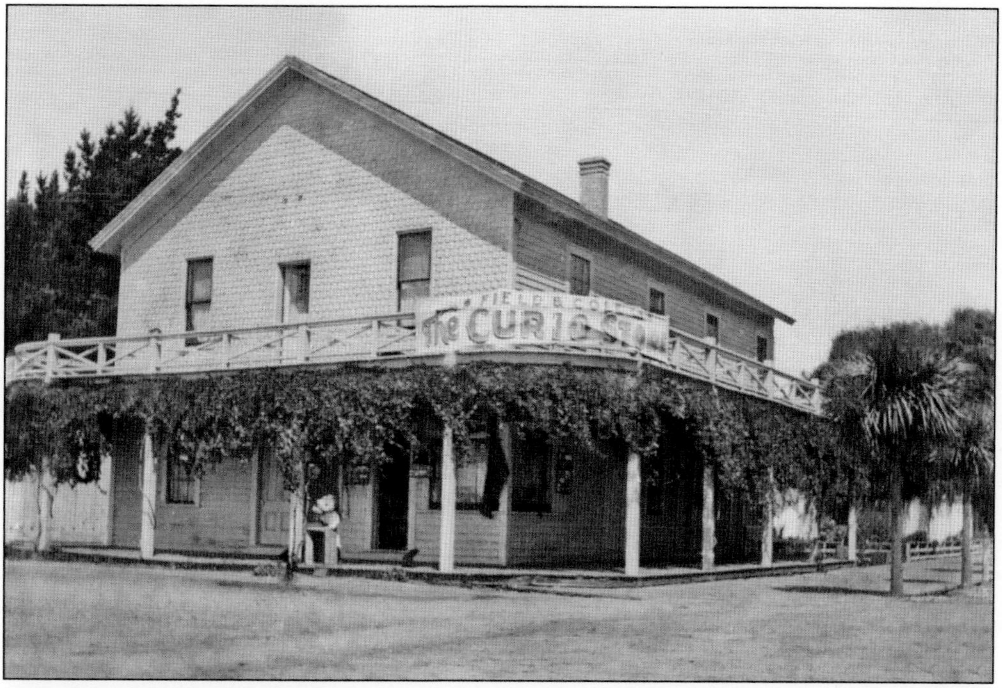

Capitola's original 1877–1878 hotel, across the road from the new one, became a branch of the Santa Cruz Field and Cole Curio Store, offering postcards and seacoast souvenirs. The Hihn Company figured by 1900 that Capitola had expanded to 100 acres of beach and bottomland. Shown below is the rear and side of the hotel near the Capitola Park subdivision, soon to be renamed Depot Hill. The vacant lot was later reshaped as a tennis court. (Both, courtesy of Lynn Baldenweek and the Arthur Ladd family.)

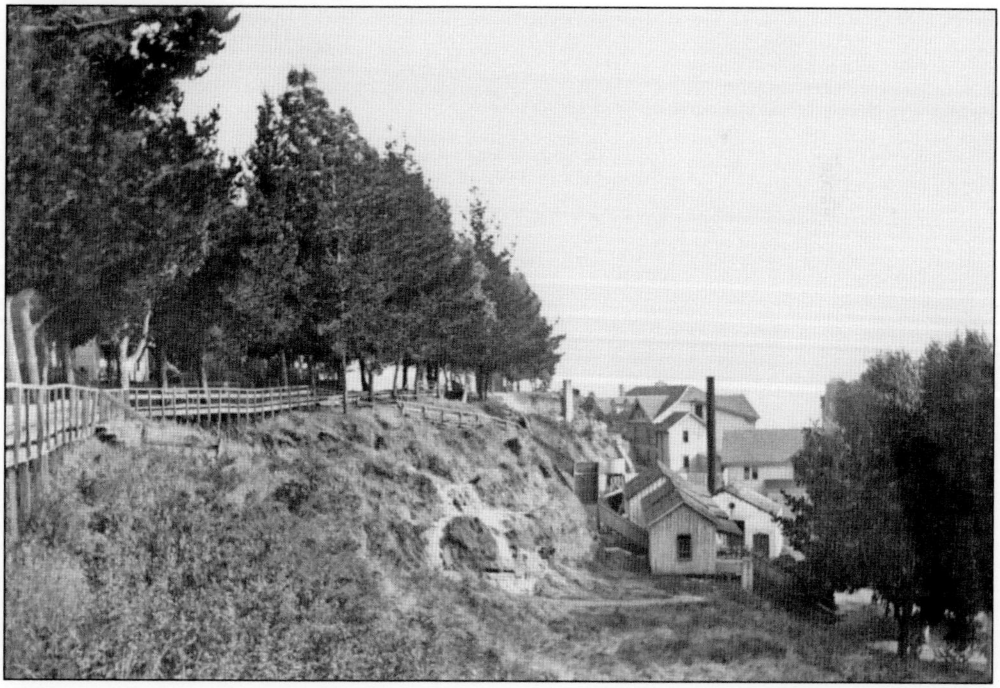

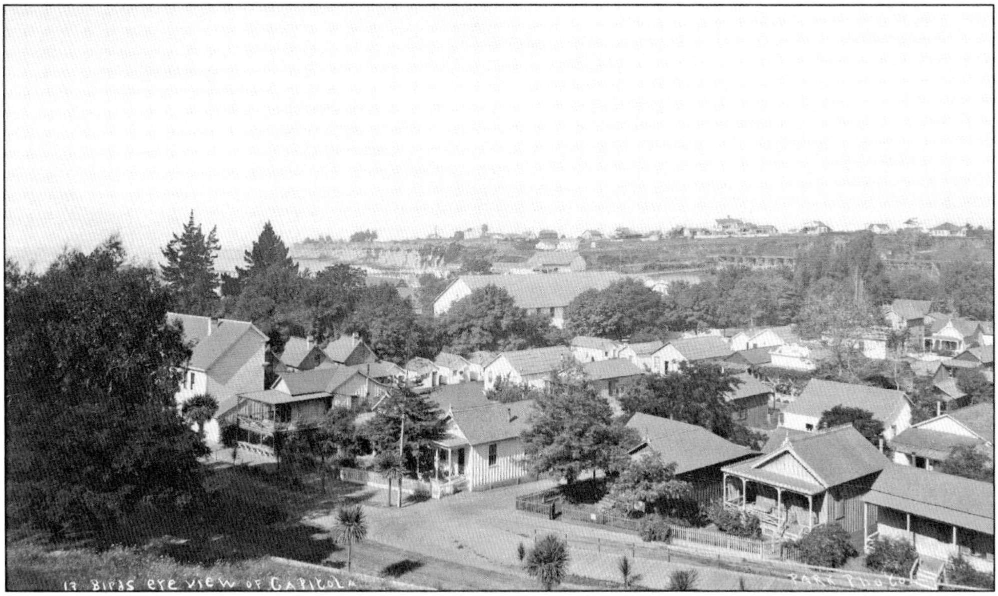

F.A. Hihn championed Capitola as a place to live year-round. "No one who has ever wintered here will go elsewhere by choice," he said. Wintertime Capitola was more appealing than Florida, the south of France, or Italy. On Hihn's list of benefits were free schooling, contented laborers, and a community of honest and intelligent people who welcomed strangers in their midst. (Courtesy of Gordon van Zuiden.)

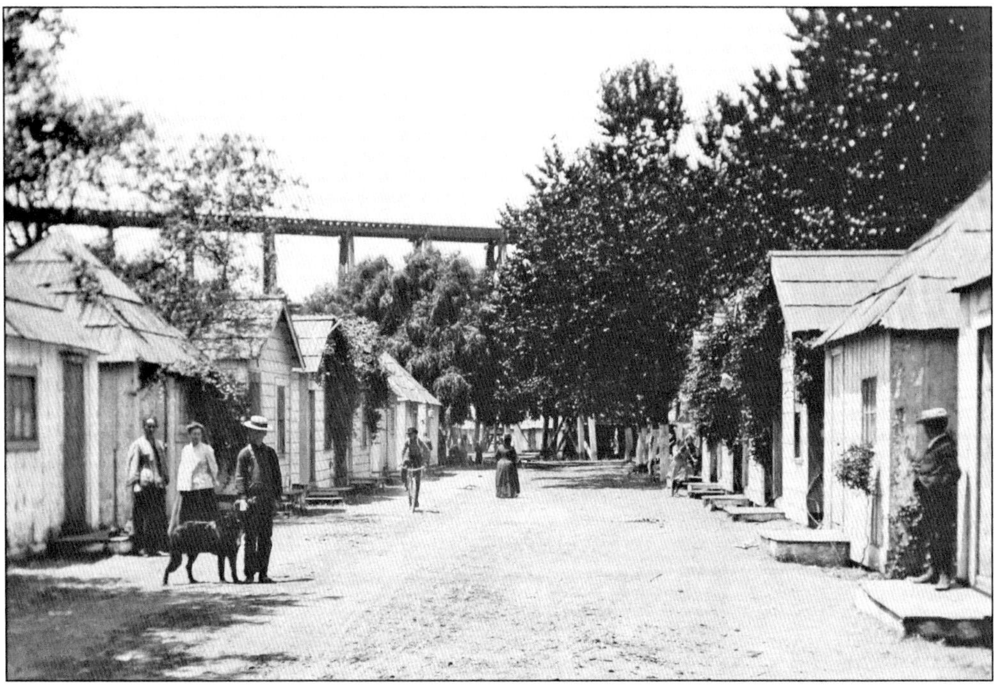

As the village expanded along with its profits, older cabins were shuffled northward, and the free tent campground was nudged up the creek past the trestle. Cottages rented from $12.50 to $60 a month at Huana Place along Riverview Avenue. Vacationers took their weekly baths in the resort tubs, which could supply hot saltwater for 250 guests a day. (Courtesy of Gordon van Zuiden.)

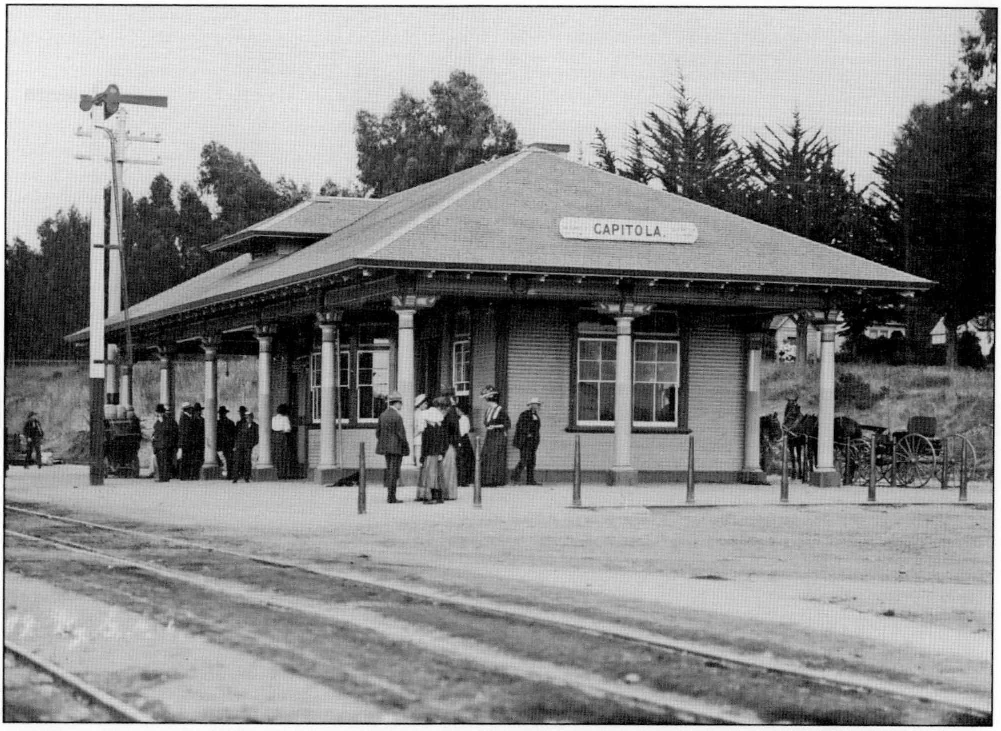

As Capitola's owner, Hihn negotiated with the Southern Pacific Railroad for a modern station built in 1903 on a site parallel to Park Avenue. In exchange for stylish architecture, he landscaped the grounds and deeded space for the rail sidings. The old depot was then shifted down the road to face the new one and used as freight storage. The picture below was taken during the departure of an encampment of the League of Cross Cadets in 1915. (Both, courtesy of Gordon van Zuiden.)

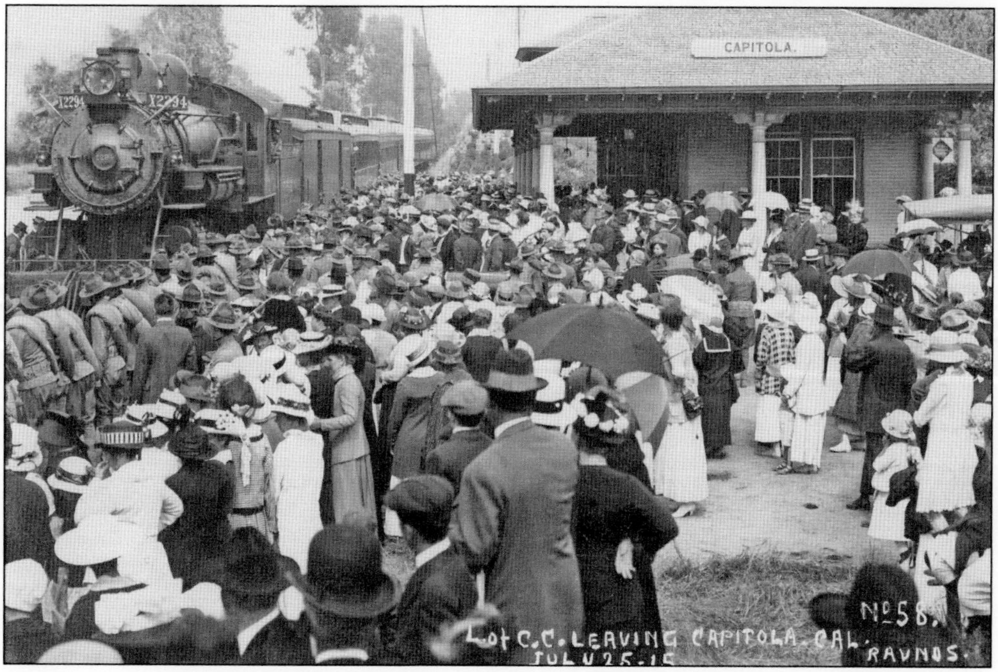

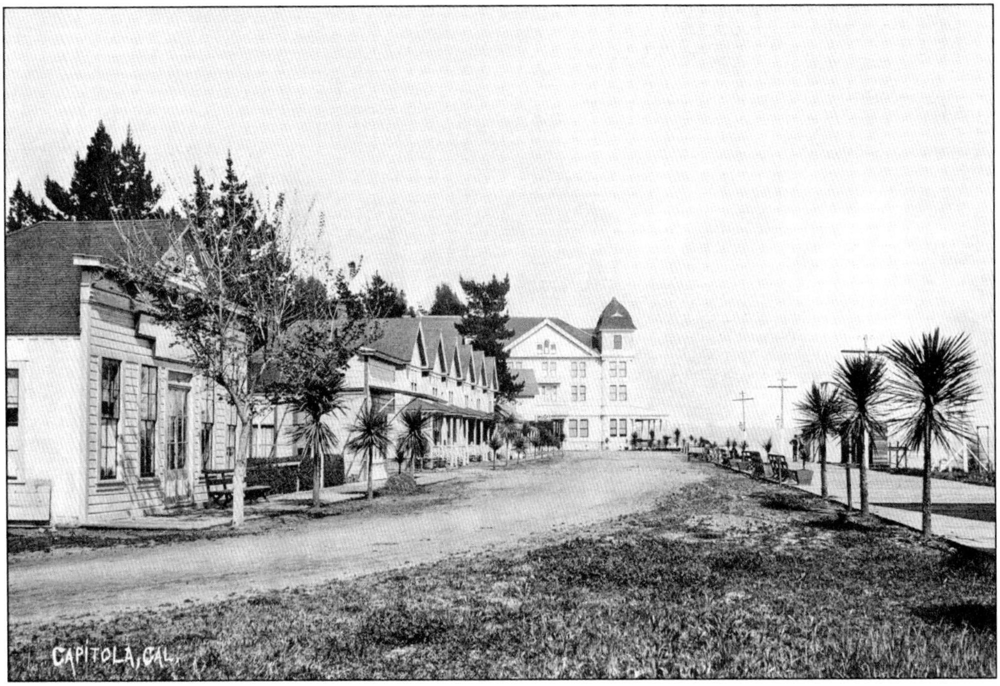

Capitola was linked in 1904 to the Santa Cruz Boardwalk by an electric railway service. Union Traction Company tracks were set down the previous year, with electric cars rolling that summer as far as the station at Opal, a brisk walk from the hill west of the village. The first trolley rounded the corner onto the Esplanade on October 4, 1904, stopping at a terminus within steps of the hotel door.

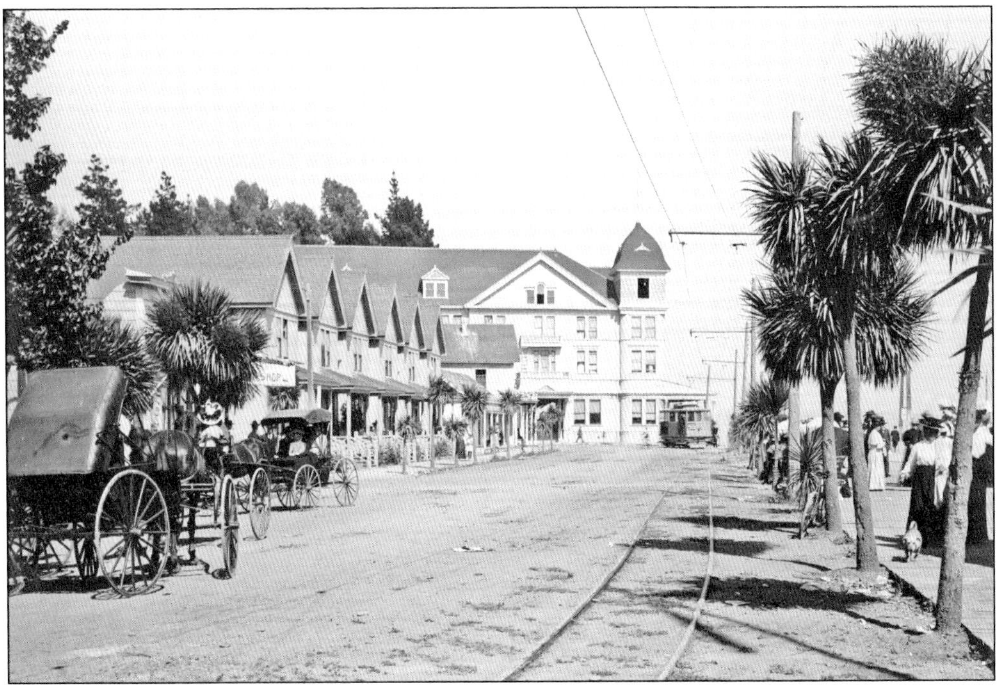

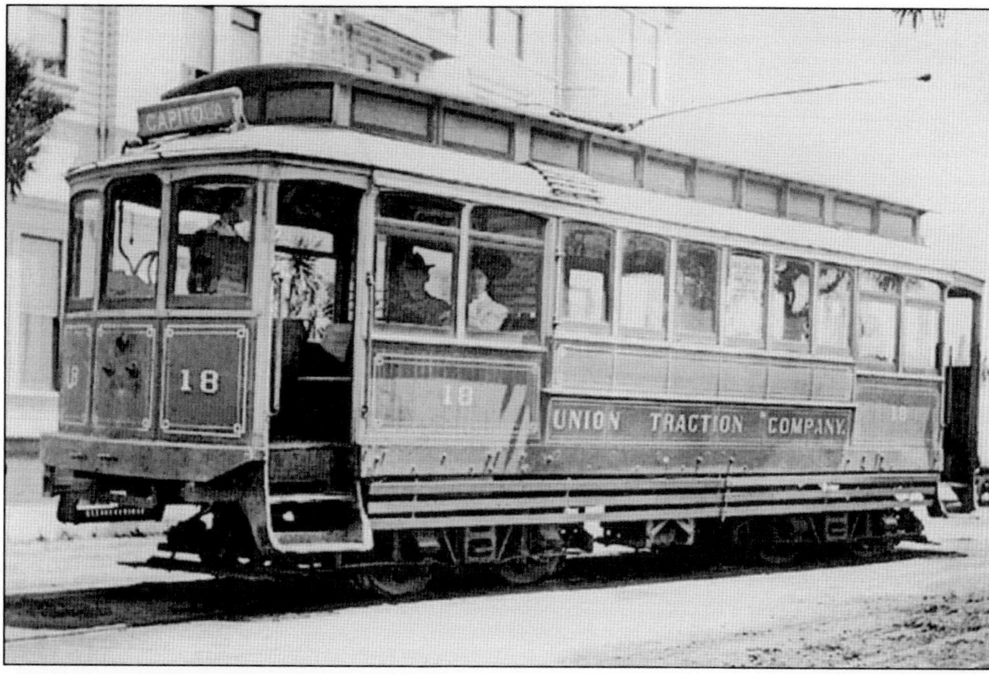

Investors believed the electric car line would eventually connect to Watsonville, but the tracks never went past Capitola. The Santa Cruz loop cost a quarter and took about an hour round-trip. Cars ran from East Santa Cruz through Twin Lakes and Live Oak along a route that is today Portola Drive. A new bridge at the mouth of Soquel Creek was the third at that site, along with the Stockton Avenue wagon bridge and the trestle. Below, the trolley is a blur as it scoots around the bend at the end of the Esplanade. (Both, courtesy of Gordon van Zuiden.)

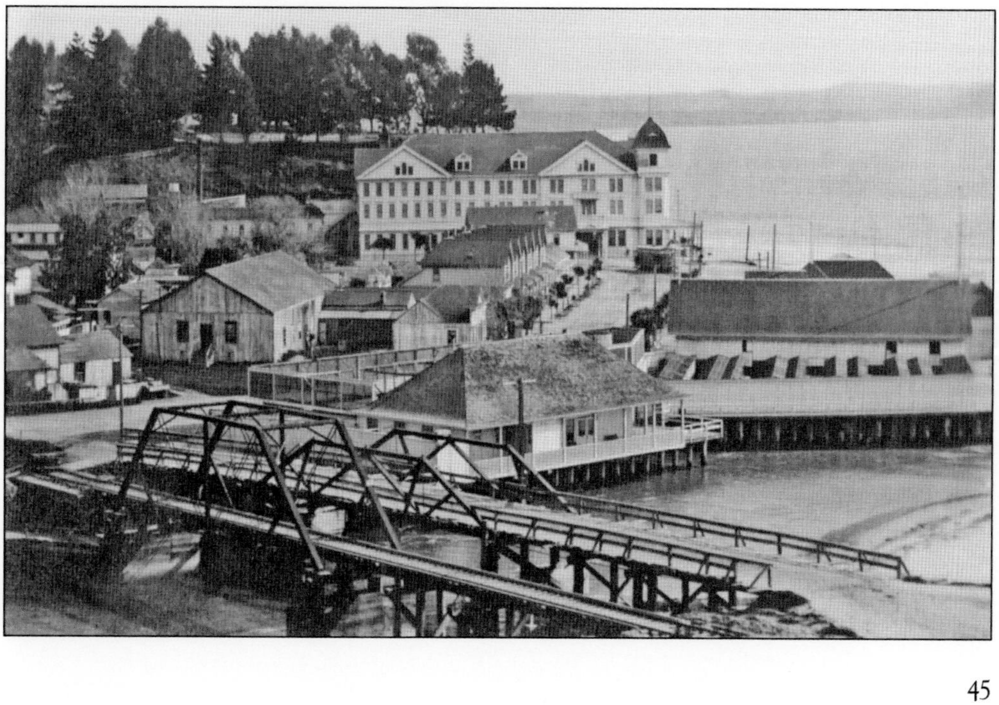

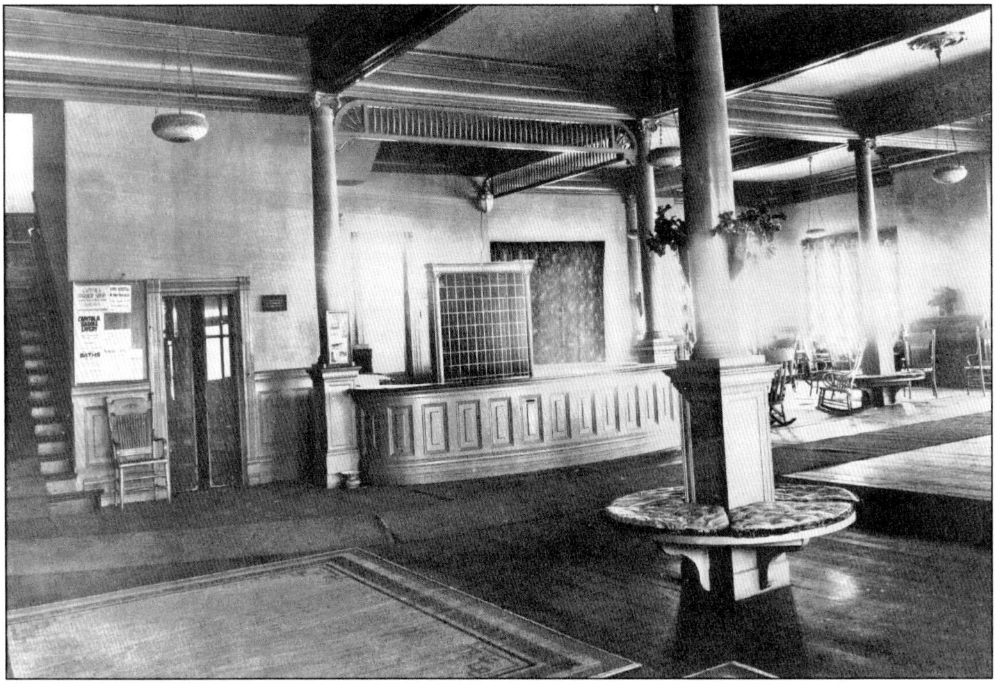

F.A. Hihn's resort enhancements coincided with a surge in tourism throughout Santa Cruz County at the turn of the century. Competing with both Santa Cruz and Monterey, Capitola's owner was determined to attract bookings for large groups. Conference registration took place in the hotel lobby, above. Guests stayed for several weeks, often attending entertainments and social events at the skating pavilion that extended the length of Capitola Avenue. (Below, courtesy of Gordon van Zuiden.)

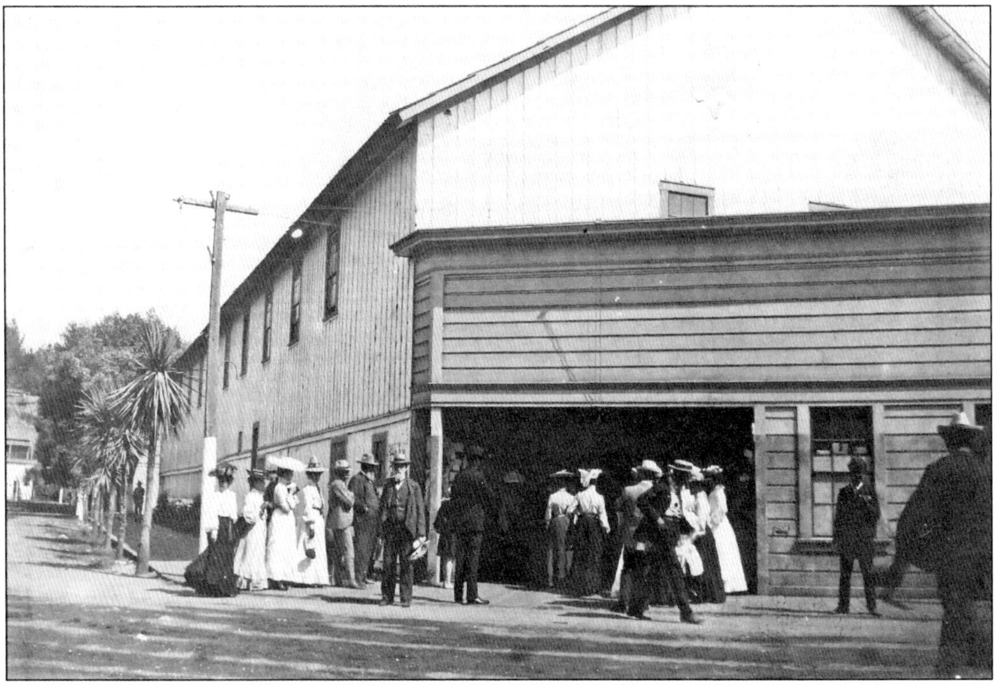

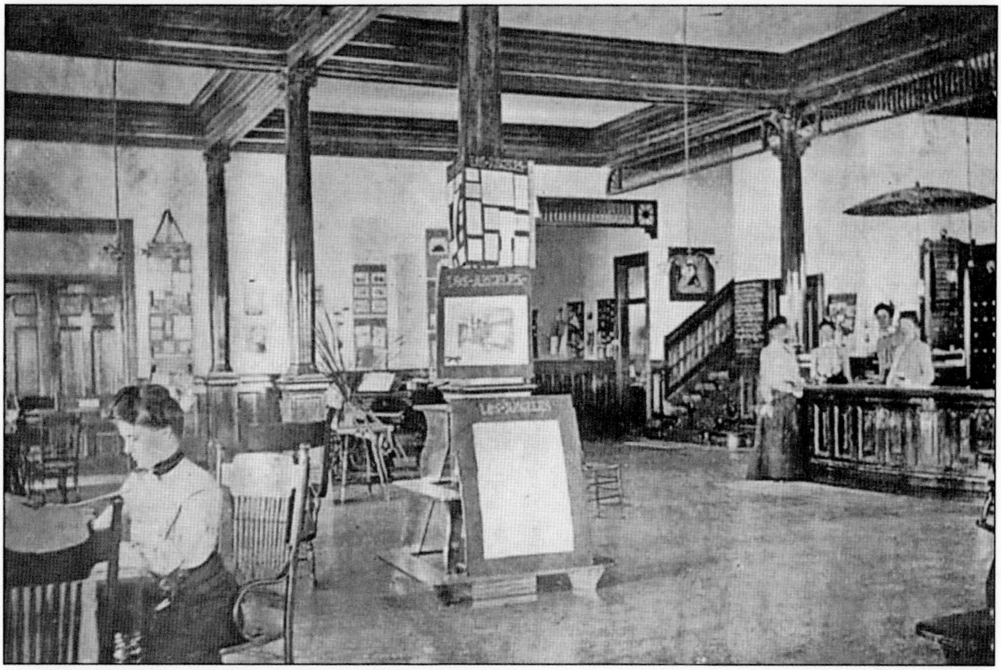

In 1903, Hihn won a bid to host the annual convention of the Young Women's Christian Association, a leading organization for working women. Above, convention attendees are shown in the hotel lobby during the conference, held May 15–25. For the YWCA convention, Capitola became known as "Guardomar." The association met here annually for 10 years, until it established the western conference center of Asilomar at Monterey in 1913. (Both, courtesy of Robert and Mary Lincoln.)

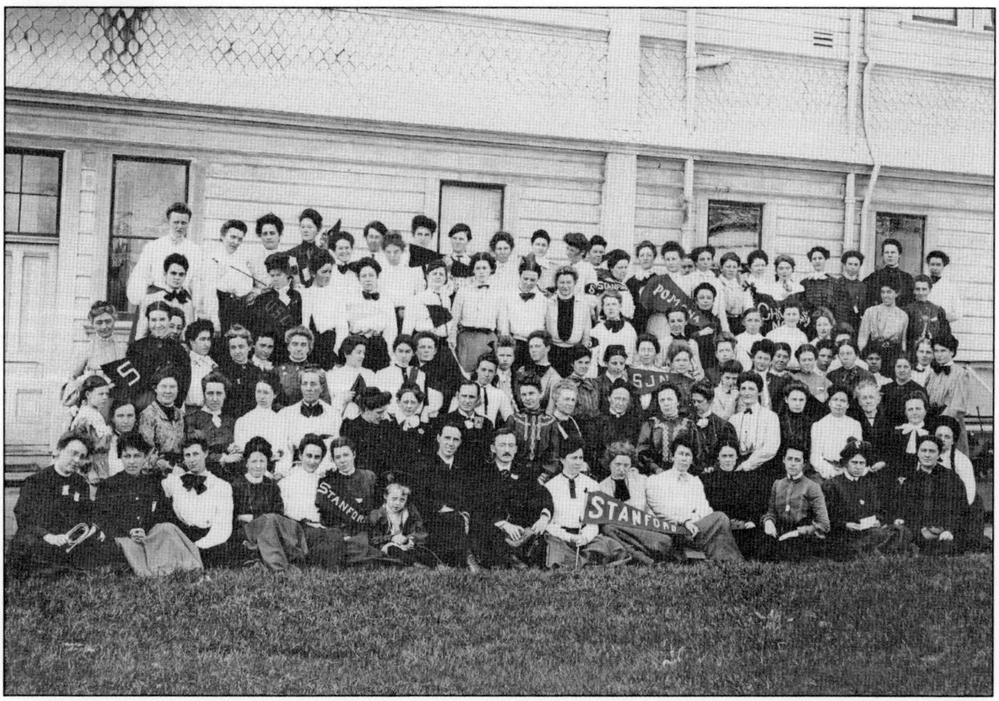

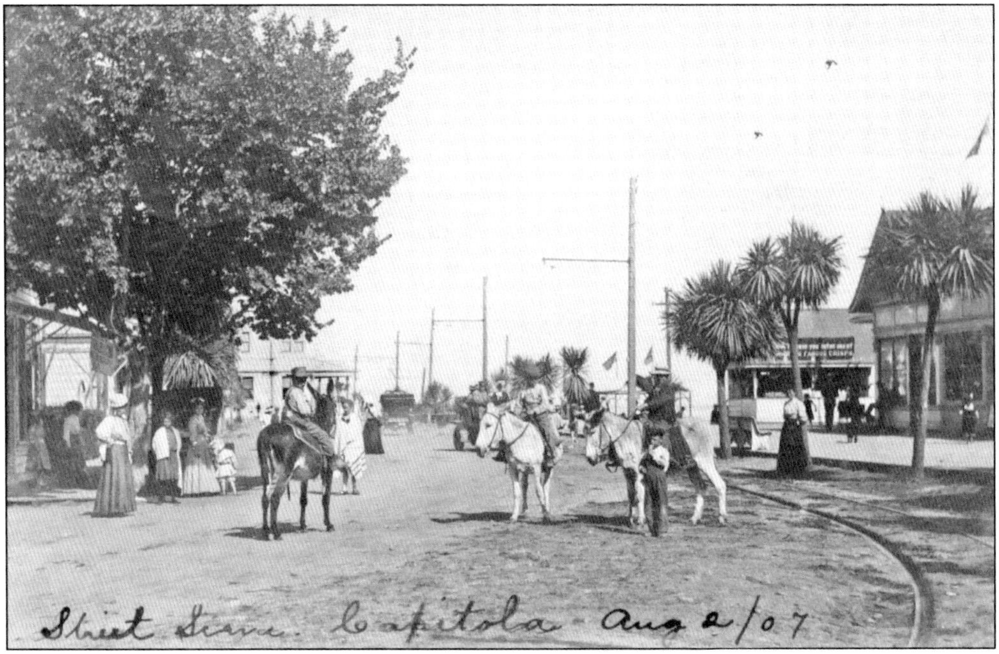

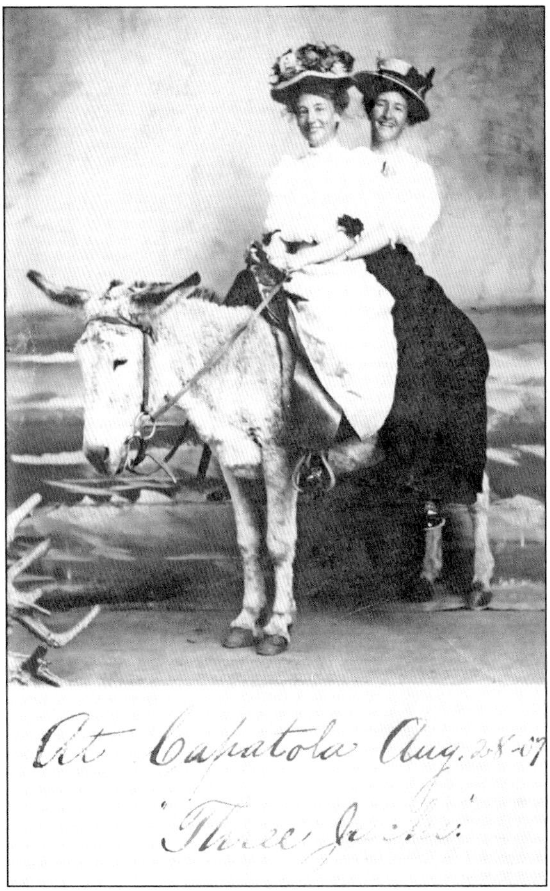

A timely juxtaposition of Capitola's past and future was photographed on Ocean Front Avenue (the Esplanade) in 1907. The youngsters are posed outside the photography studio on a trio of donkeys, which seem to be calm in spite of the mechanized contraptions puttering along behind them. In a gallery portrait taken about the same time, one of the donkeys sleepily fills his role as one of the "jacks" in the picture.

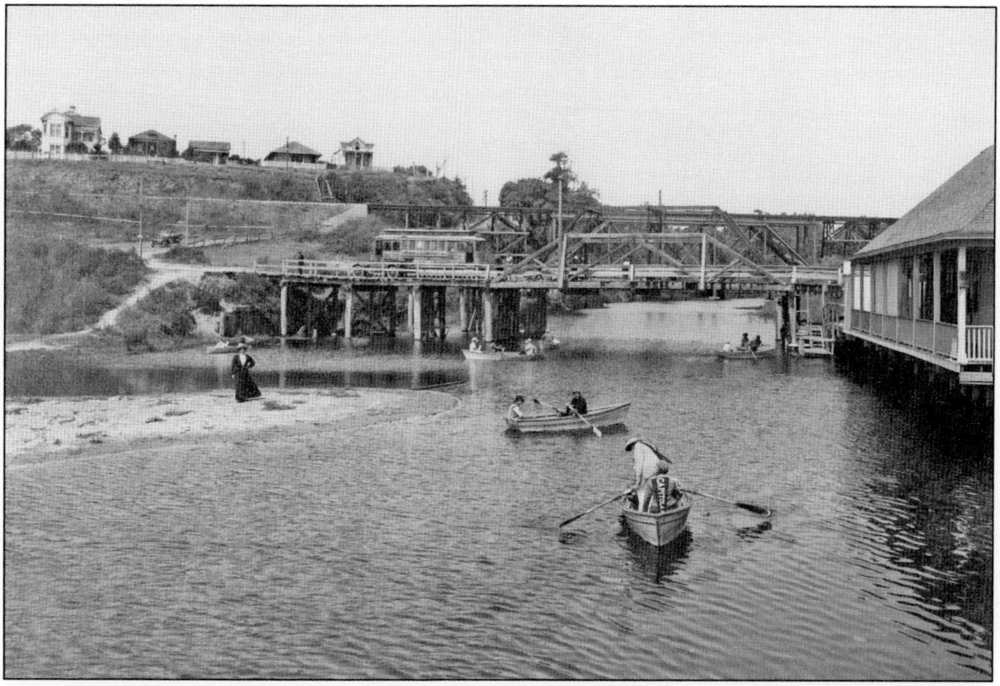

Demonstrating methods to get around and through Capitola, photographer Ole Ravnos lined up several bystanders, six boats, and at least two parked cars as he choreographed these two shots. Above, the trolley rattles across its bridge, while in the scene below, a Southern Pacific passenger train smokes across the trestle. Automobiles were rare in Santa Cruz County until Henry Ford began mass production of the Model T in 1908, about the time this picture was taken. Hihn had configured his Capitola to be served by rail. Traffic today is still a logistical challenge.

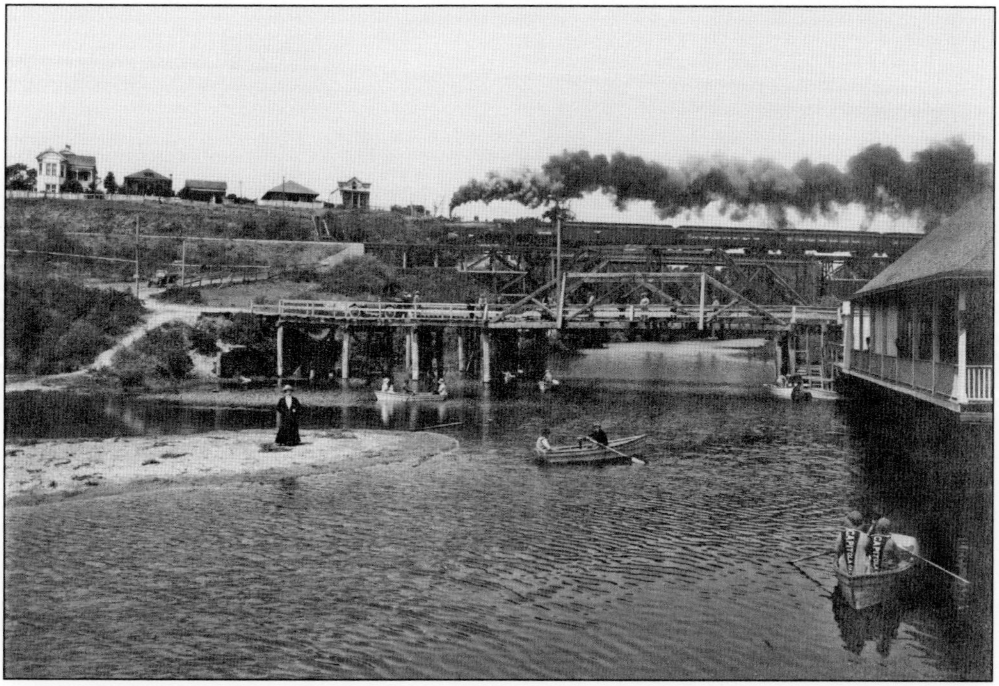

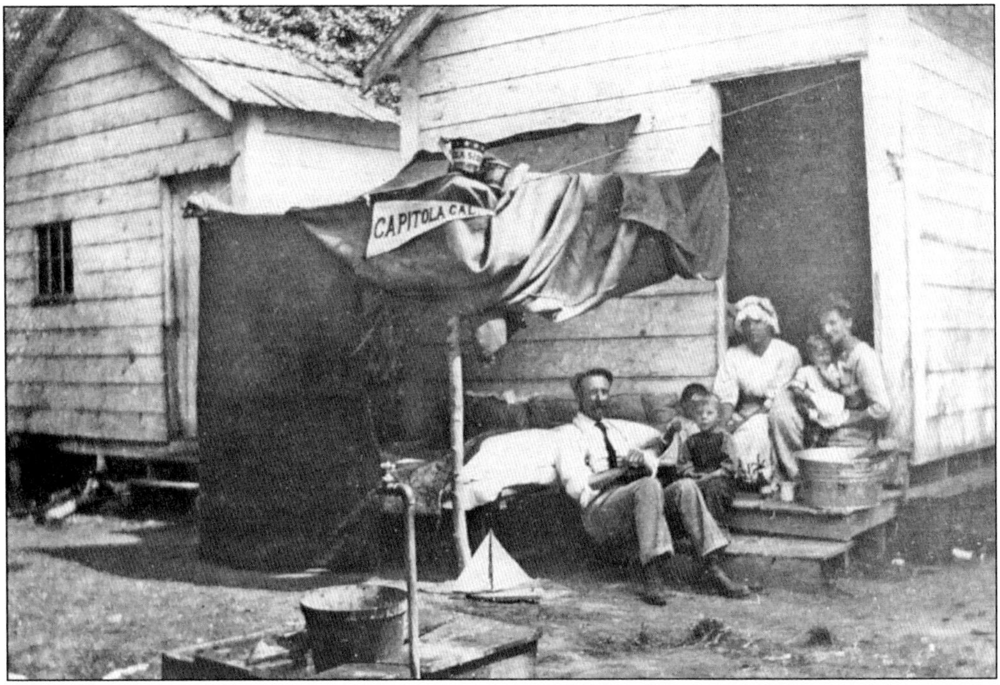

As fashionable as Capitola pretended to be once it had the well-appointed accommodations of a grand hotel, Hihn was careful to keep it affordable for vacationers of moderate means. This 1912 family postcard had a message written on the back in German. (Courtesy of Frank Perry.)

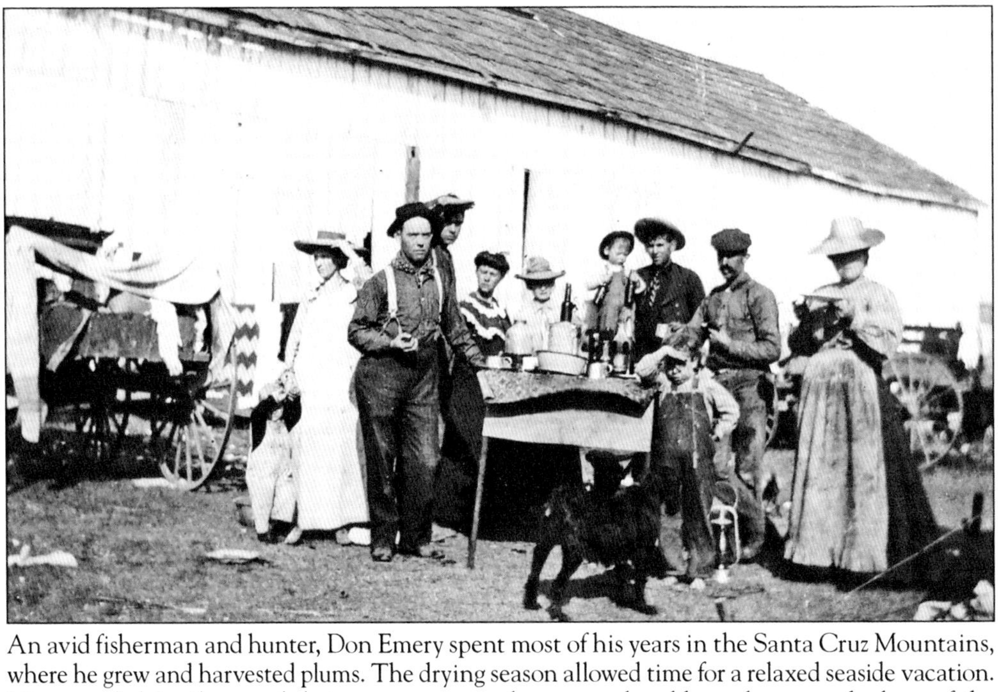

An avid fisherman and hunter, Don Emery spent most of his years in the Santa Cruz Mountains, where he grew and harvested plums. The drying season allowed time for a relaxed seaside vacation. His extended family spread their tents on grounds next to the old warehouse at the base of the wharf. Emery, third from left, later moved to Capitola and became a well-known realtor. (Courtesy of the Emery/Kooser family.)

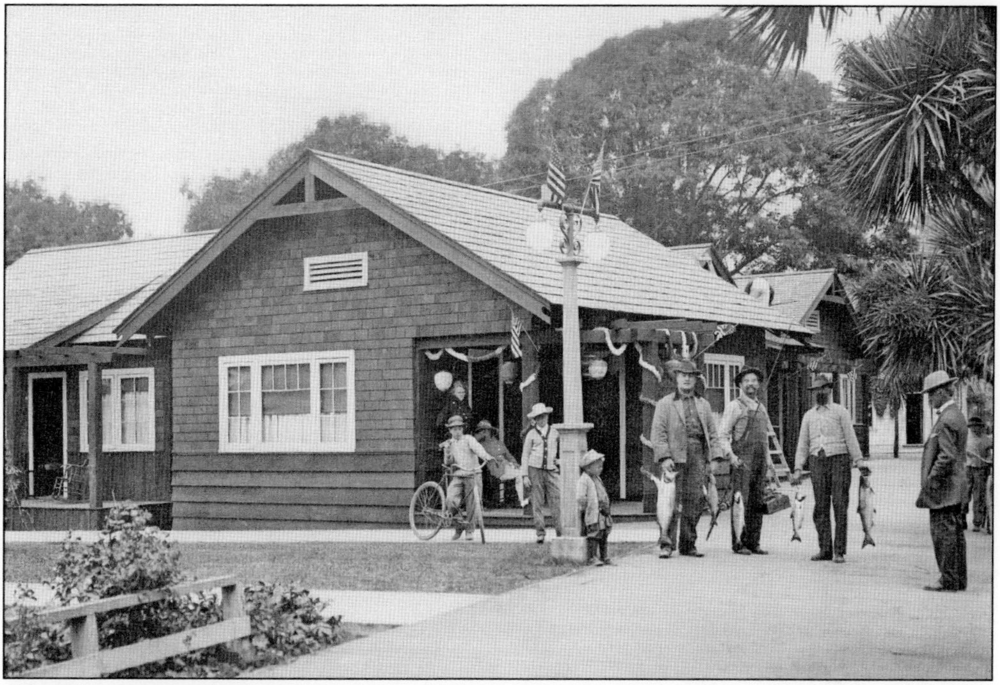

F.A. Hihn oversaw his last Capitola development in 1911. Lawn Way consisted of old and new cottages set along a grassy thoroughfare a block from the beach. The photograph above was taken on the Fourth of July. Below is a scene looking from San Jose Avenue down to the hotel. The manicured green patch is maintained today by the city.

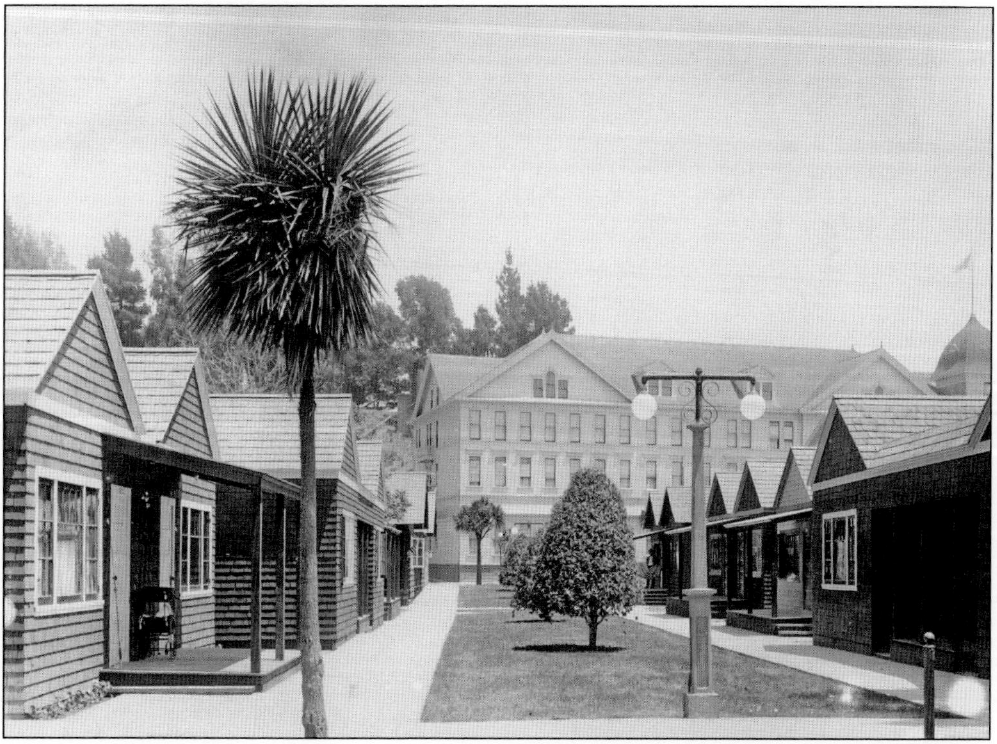

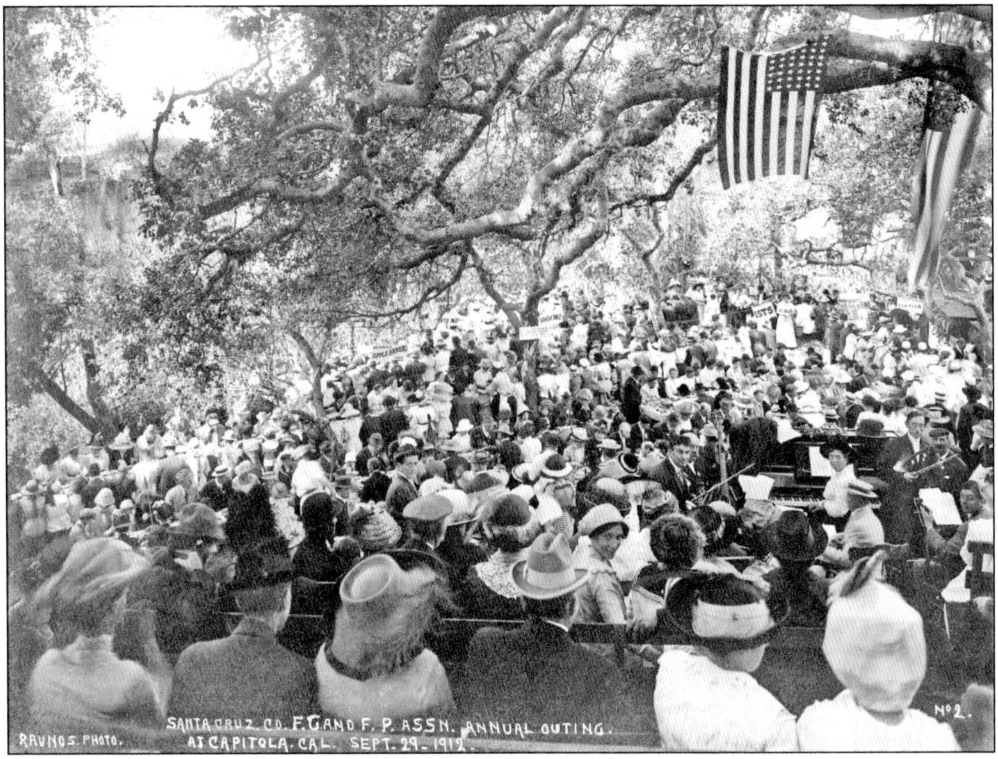

One corner of the resort that was a Hihn favorite was the oak-studded setting he referred to as Capitola Grove, later known as Glen Beulah. The picnic ground was the site of bull's head barbecues and annual outings like the Santa Cruz County Fish, Game, and Forest Protective Association's luncheon in September 1912. A music ensemble—including a full-sized piano—provided entertainment. Today, Glen Beulah is a metered city parking lot. Below, a band in front of the hotel is ready to march on the Fourth of July. Both images were taken by resort photographer Ole Ravnos.

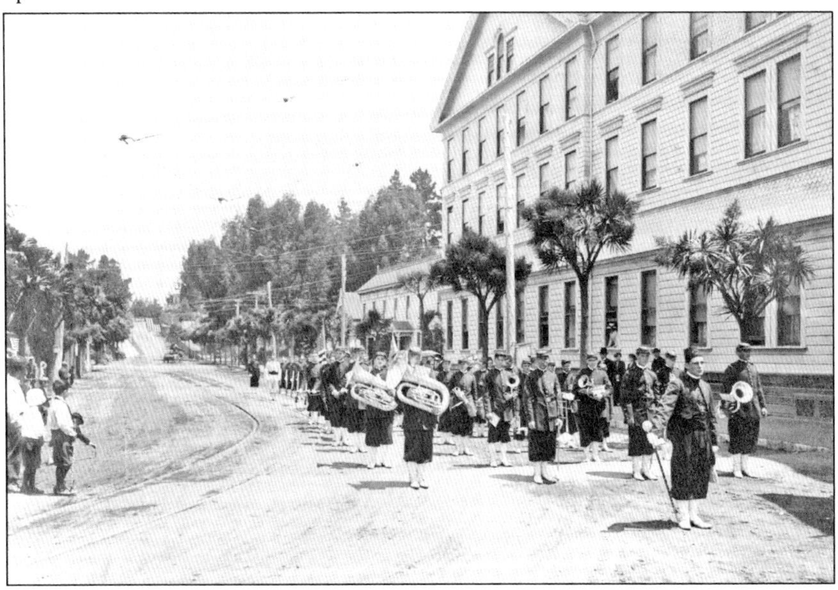

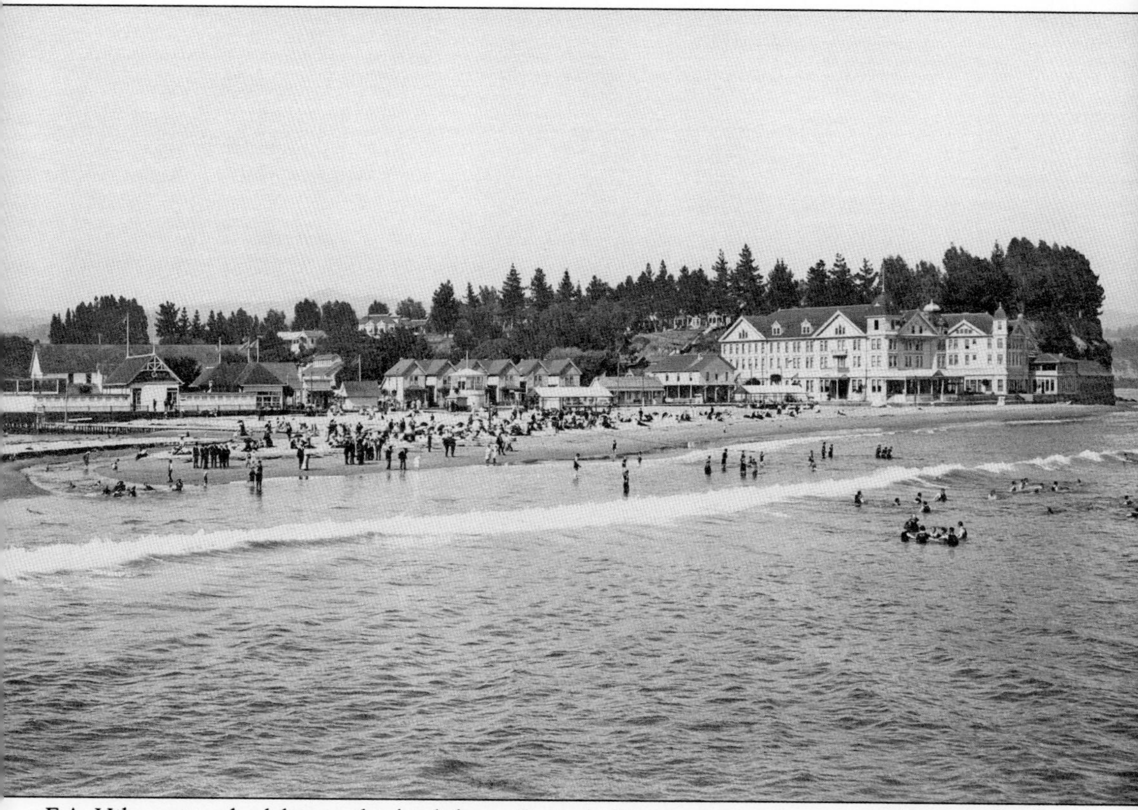

F.A. Hihn enjoyed celebrating his birthday at Capitola. His summer party was a traditional affair, a seasonal high point combined now and again with events of the Society of California Pioneers of Santa Cruz County, an organization Hihn had championed as president since its founding in 1881. Guests from all over the county looked forward to the Capitola festivities. It was a surprise even to Hihn when he caught a cold on his 84th birthday and failed to recover. He died of pneumonia at his Santa Cruz home a week later, on August 23, 1913.

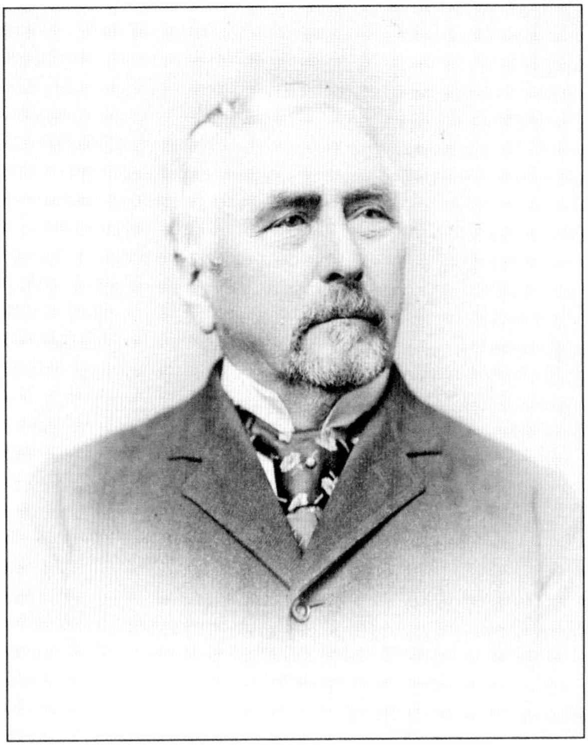

Frederick Hihn was once described as a tenacious man who took a personal interest in the most trivial detail. Predictably, authors of his obituary struggled to give Hihn's life a summary that was equally painstaking. "When confronted with obstacles which seemed to hedge him about he pushed forward, and blazed a path in the financial and commercial arena of California that few men have done," one wrote.

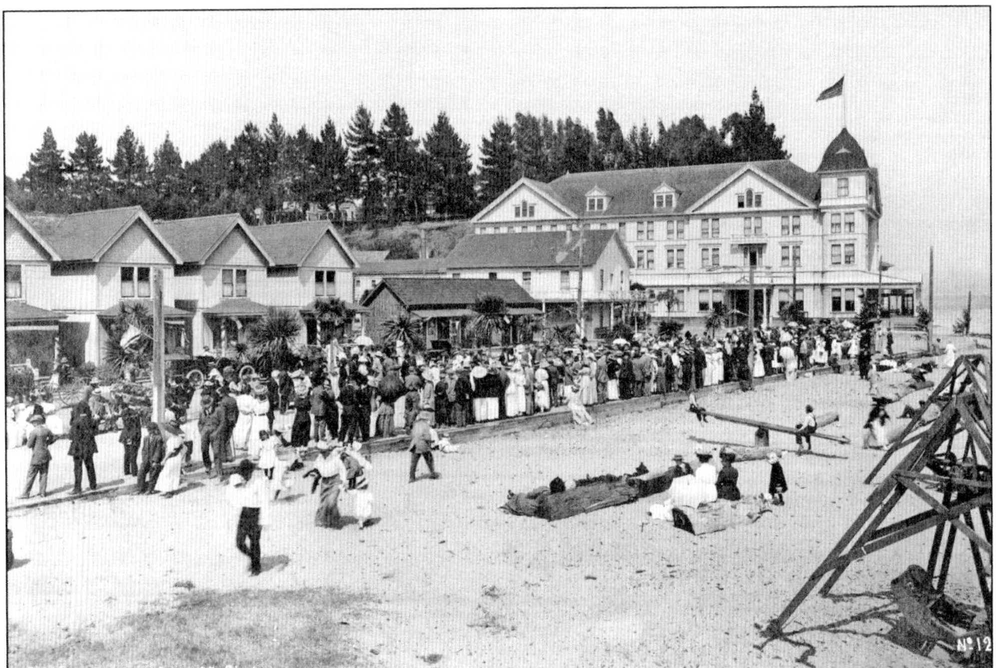

A Fourth of July parade photographed about 1913 exemplified Capitola's spirit on a holiday that today is still one of its favorites. When Frederick Hihn died, the resort lost some of its character along with the accustomed guardianship that had directed its growth for more than 40 years. From 1913 onward, Capitola began its shift away from private ownership.

Four

Neighbors, Friends, and Local Heroes

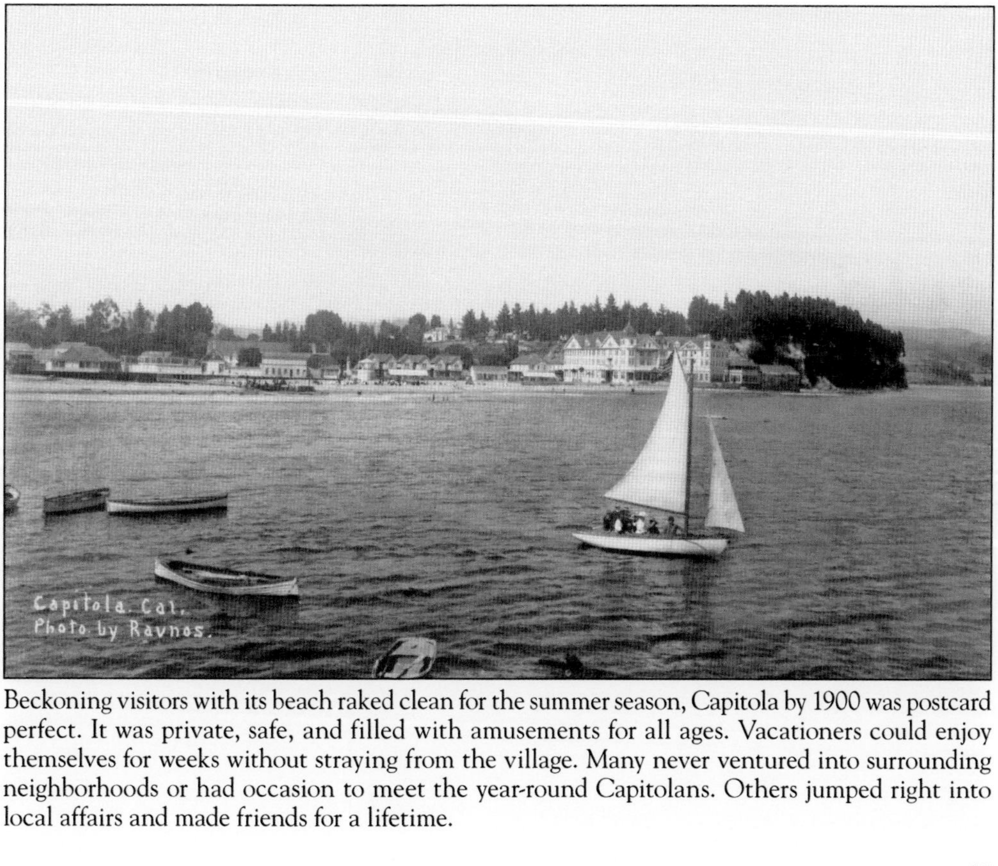

Beckoning visitors with its beach raked clean for the summer season, Capitola by 1900 was postcard perfect. It was private, safe, and filled with amusements for all ages. Vacationers could enjoy themselves for weeks without straying from the village. Many never ventured into surrounding neighborhoods or had occasion to meet the year-round Capitolans. Others jumped right into local affairs and made friends for a lifetime.

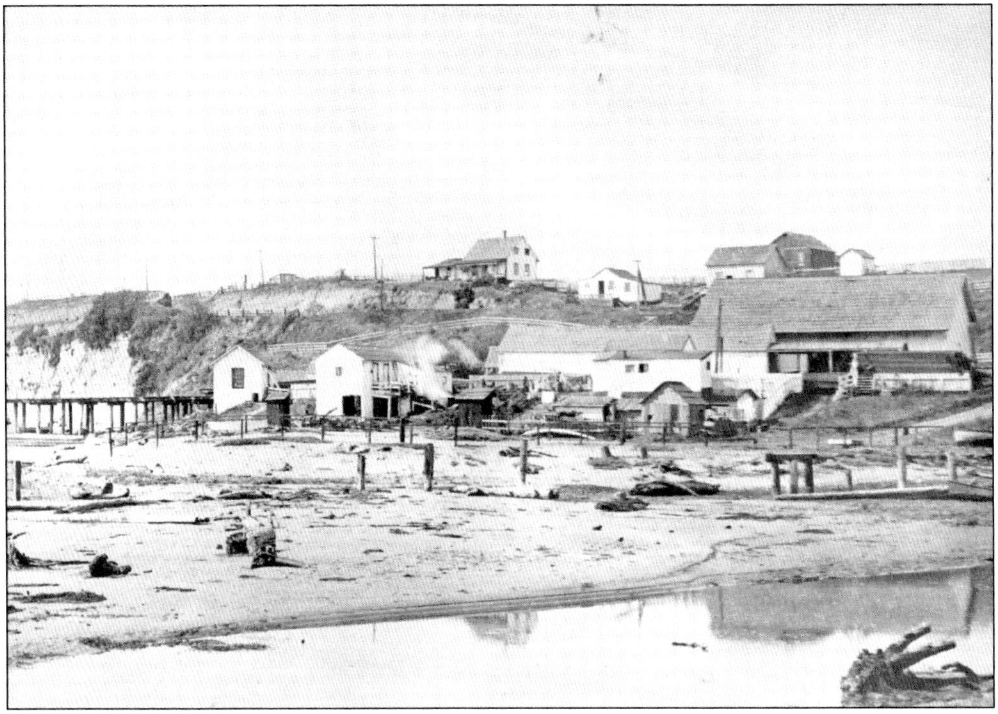

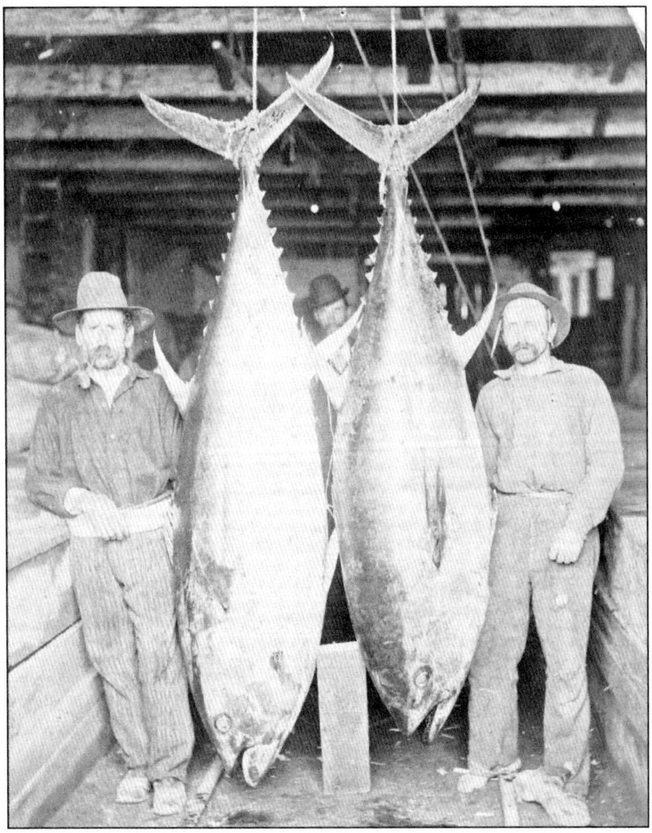

As long as people lived along Soquel Creek and its channel at the ocean, they fished. For centuries, native inhabitants took all they could get from the water. Rancho grantees and their descendants did the same. Capt. John Davenport (1818–1892) ran an on-shore whaling company in Monterey and then shifted his rendering pots to Soquel Landing. Davenport fished and, without much success, hunted whales for two years before moving farther up the coast. A fishing camp began to take shape in the 1870s, when a row of lopsided shacks appeared near the wharf entrance, shown above. Once the railroad offered a timely delivery to San Francisco markets, the colony settled in. (Left, courtesy of R.O. Lincoln.)

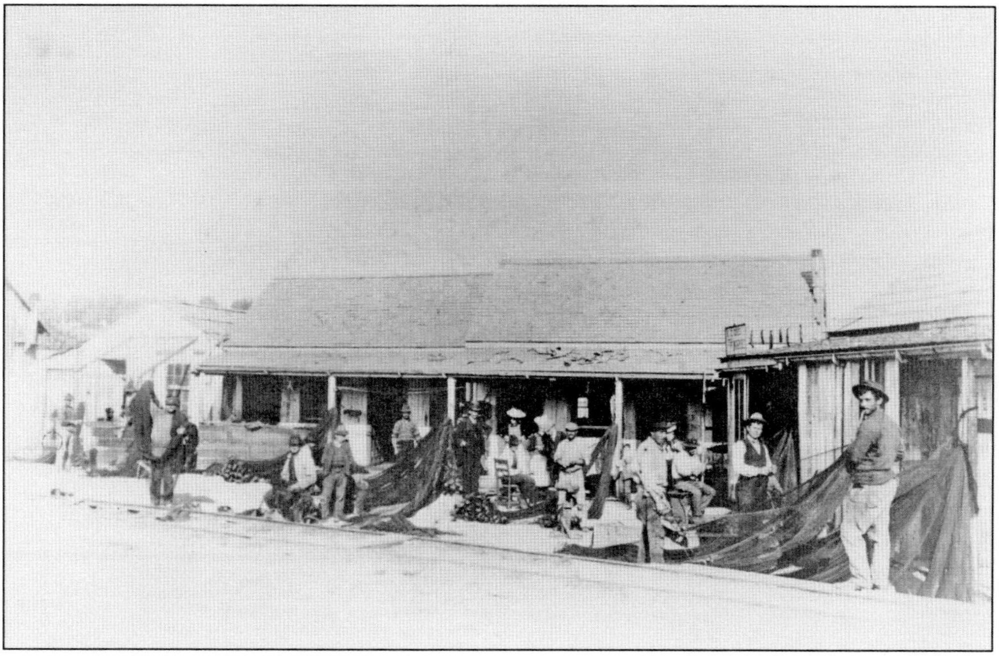

As the fishing colony expanded, Hihn set up lease agreements. A majority of tenants by 1900 were Italians from Riva Trigoso, a remote community on the Ligurian coast. Domenico Canepa and his wife, Nicoletta, were among the first to settle at Capitola in 1890. Other longtime residents were from different regions of Italy and from Ireland, Portugal, and Germany. Herman Gehring, who grew up fishing at Capitola with his brothers, later kept a small fleet of excursion boats and ran the fish market. He sold fish of all sizes to neighboring locals for as little as a dime. Above and below, fishermen check and repair their handmade nets. (Below, courtesy of John Nicol.)

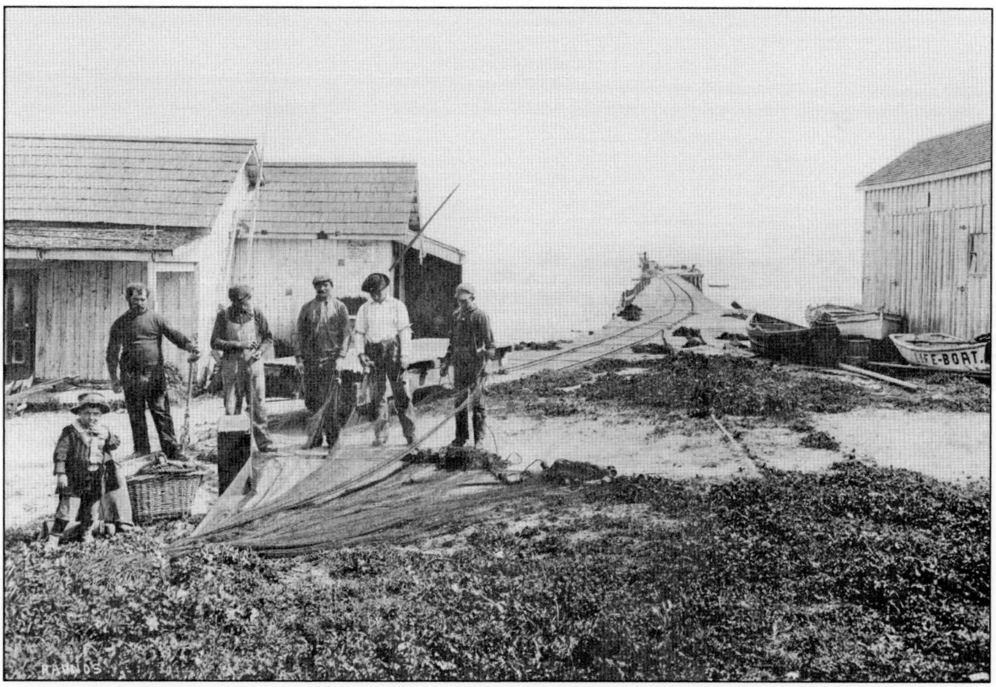

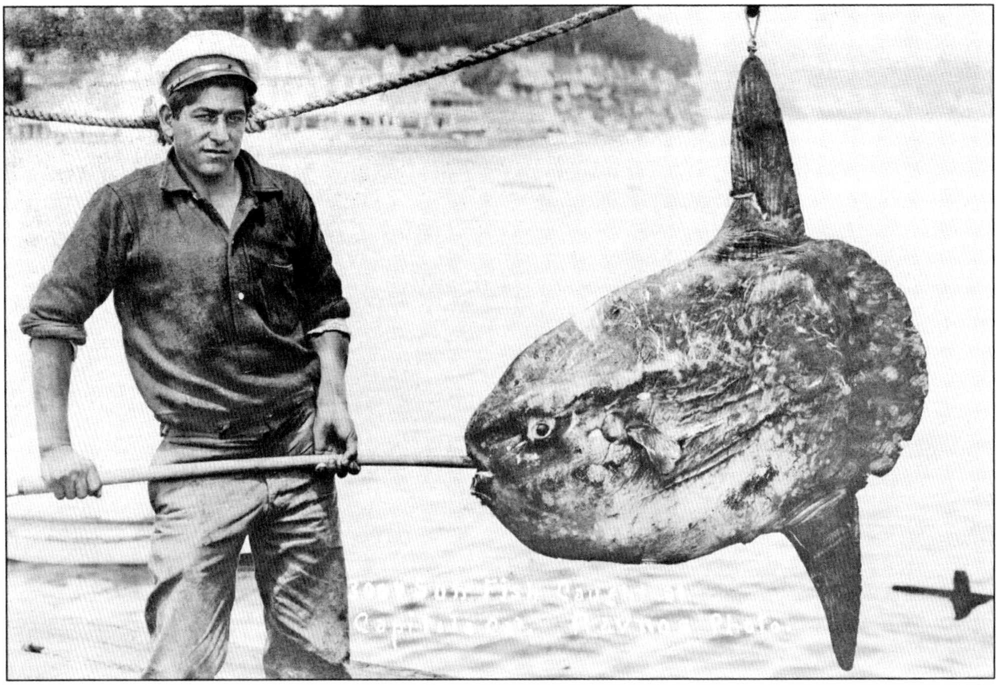

Fishermen worked a fleet of 20 to 25 boats. Pictured above is the uncommon capture of a 300-pound ocean sunfish, or Mola mola, one of the largest of the bony fishes. Catches such as this one typically became sightseer attractions for several days, or for as long as the odor permitted. (Courtesy of Gordon van Zuiden.)

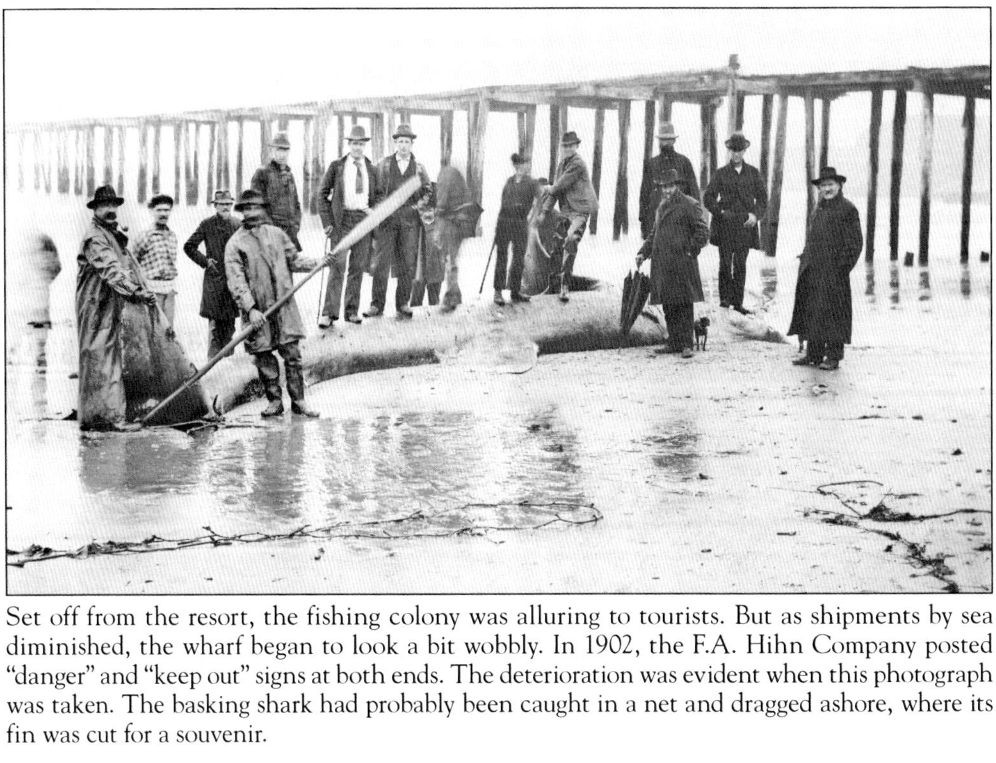

Set off from the resort, the fishing colony was alluring to tourists. But as shipments by sea diminished, the wharf began to look a bit wobbly. In 1902, the F.A. Hihn Company posted "danger" and "keep out" signs at both ends. The deterioration was evident when this photograph was taken. The basking shark had probably been caught in a net and dragged ashore, where its fin was cut for a souvenir.

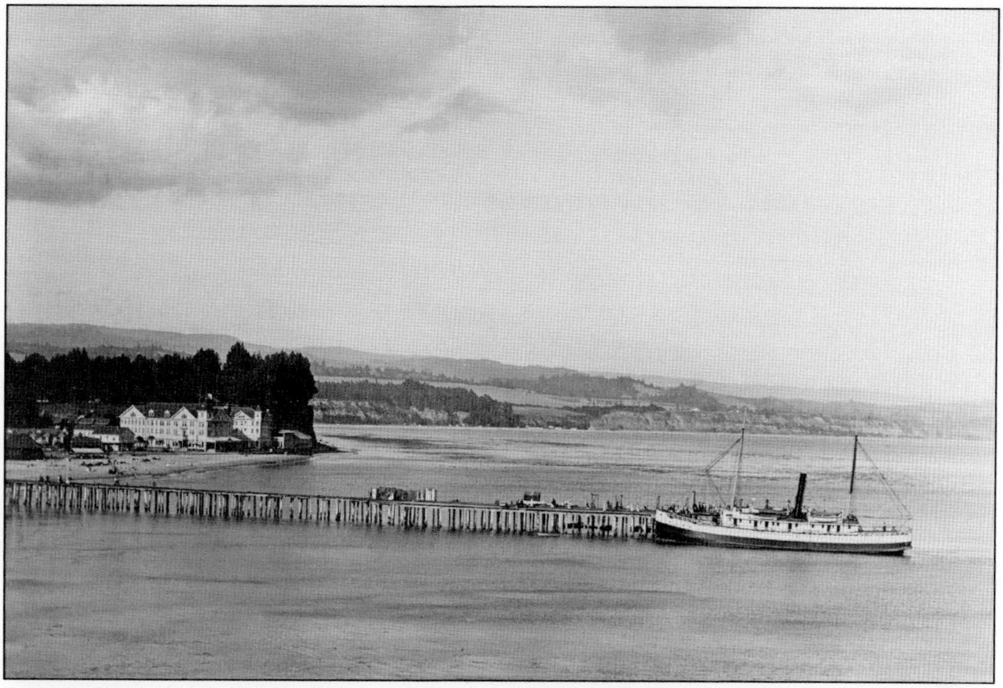

Steam schooners moored regularly at Capitola from the time it was known as Soquel Landing, before the railroad. Pacific Coast Steamship freighters such as the one above transported massive quantities of lumber, leather, grain, and manufactured products, including chairs and paper from Soquel factories. Best remembered was one of the later boats, the *Gipsy*, which stopped at the wharf from 1886 until it was wrecked on the rocks off Monterey in September 1905.

George Elmer Mitchell managed excursion party boats from 1894 until his retirement in 1945. He had a fleet of skiffs and two launches, the *Capitola* and the *Bessie*, for fishing and pleasure trips. Mitchell eventually acquired ownership of the wharf fishing business and became the wharfinger. He once recalled that his best season in 40 years was the time 764 salmon were brought in. (Courtesy of Gordon van Zuiden.)

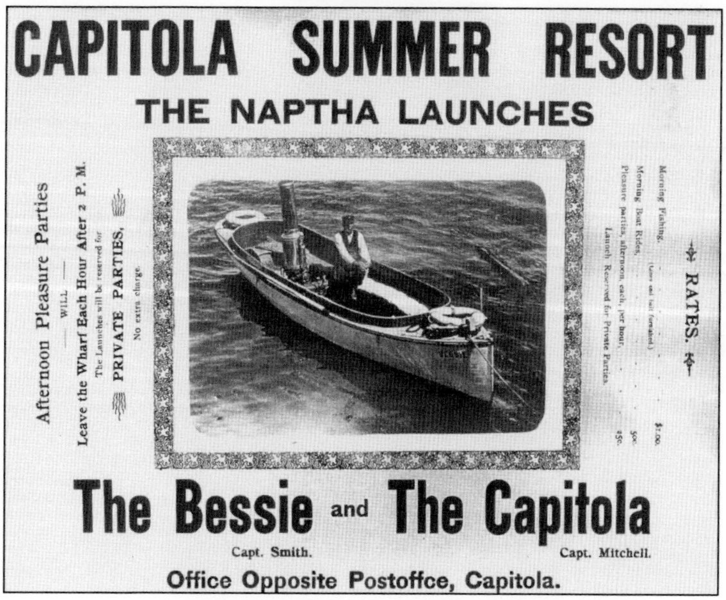

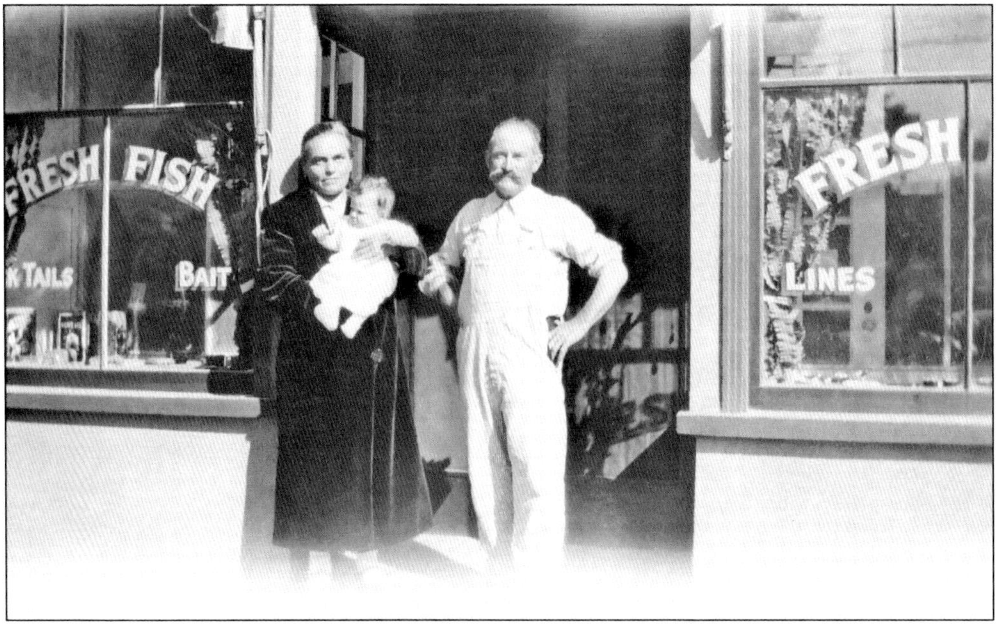

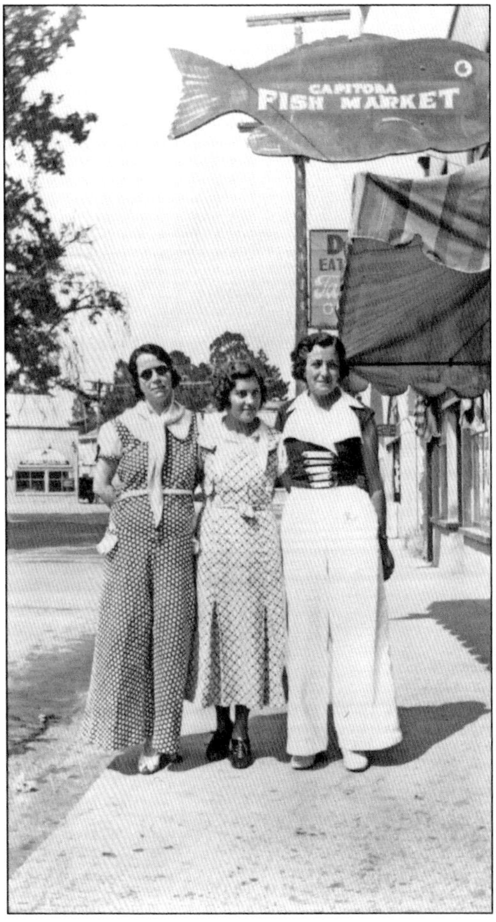

Luigi and Luigia Canepa, above, were among the first to leave Capitola's fishing colony once demolition was imminent after 1919. Shifting the family home up to the Fairview Tract above the wharf, the Canepas started a business back down in the village. Working with his sons, Augustine and Battiste, Luigi set up a market with upstairs apartments on the corner of Stockton Avenue and the Esplanade. Capitola Fish Market opened in 1928. A trio of relatives and friends stopped outside for a snapshot in the 1930s. (Above, courtesy of Jeff Canepa; left, courtesy of Karen Nevis.)

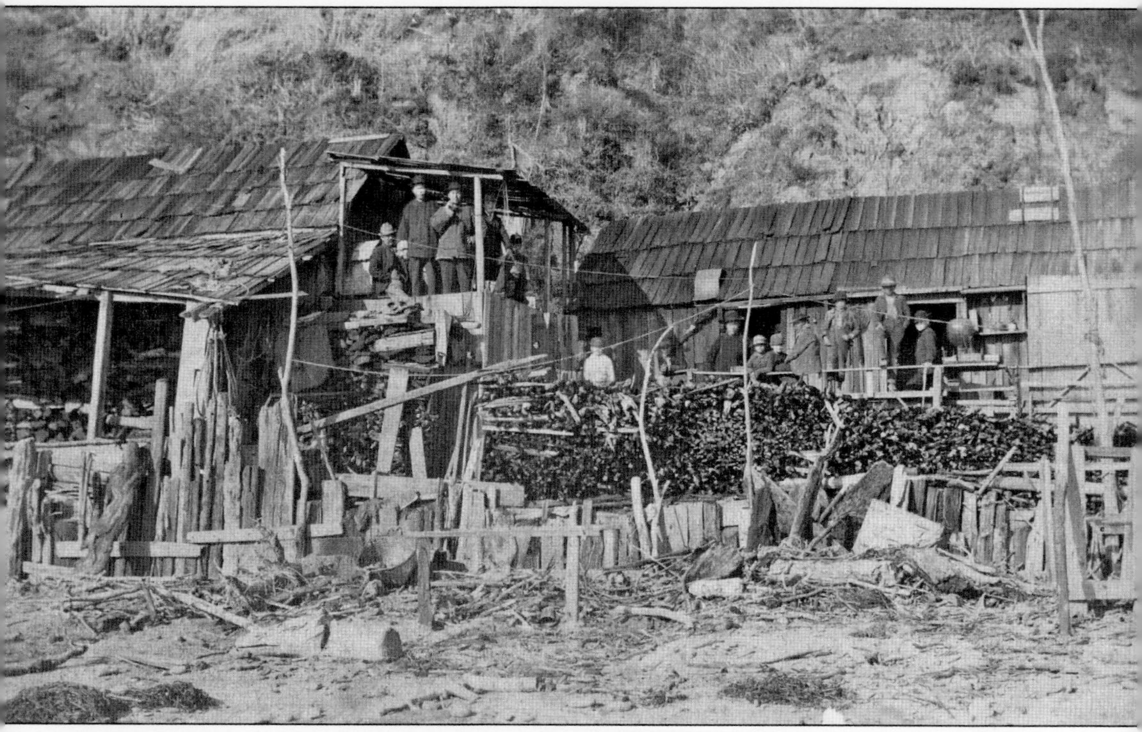

Aware of the potential yield of seine-net fishing along the shallow coastline east of Soquel Landing, Chinese fishermen built a camp along a stretch of sand that is sometimes referred to, even today, as China Beach. Once they were able to ship boxes of fresh fish by rail, it was estimated that more than half the fish caught in the county were taken by the Chinese at Capitola. A writer for the *Daily Alta California* noted in 1876 a great variety of fish and then added, "But more delicious than all is the celebrated pompano, a fish that readily sells in the San Francisco market for almost its weight in gold." The 1880 census counted 29 single Chinese men living at the camp, working with up to 10 sampans that were crafted by hand.

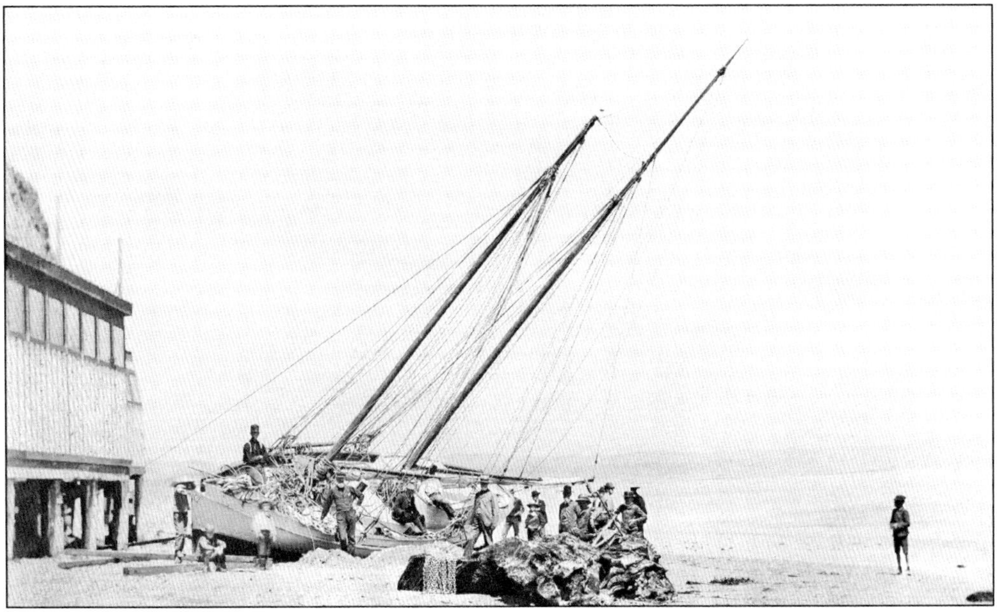

Repairs were made to this boat after it was brought ashore and careened about 1890, anchored near the old hotel bathhouse below the cliff of today's Depot Hill. The photograph is from the collection of Capt. Thomas Lindsay, a native of Ireland, who arrived in the United States in 1879 after a life at sea. Lindsay spent 45 years fishing on Monterey Bay and was described at the end of his days as a man who only had friends.

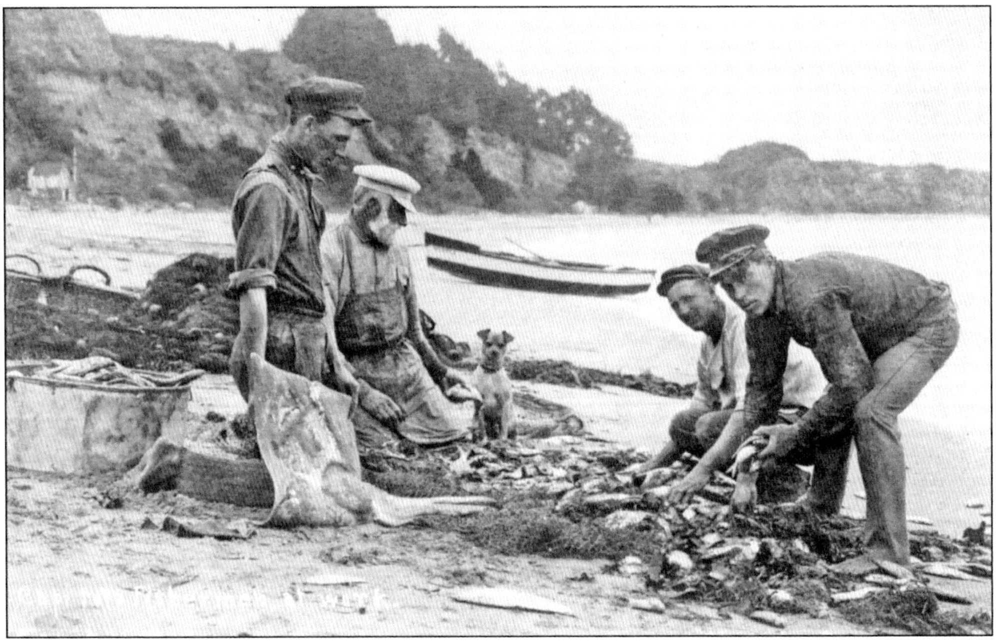

Captain Lindsay became part of the local fishing community and oversaw wharf maintenance through the 1880s. When the Chinese fishermen were pressured to leave their camp east of Capitola a few years later, Lindsay moved his boats to China Beach. He established the Soquel Seining Company in 1894. Lindsay, second from left, is sorting fish from a seine net with the help of his crew and mascot about 1912.

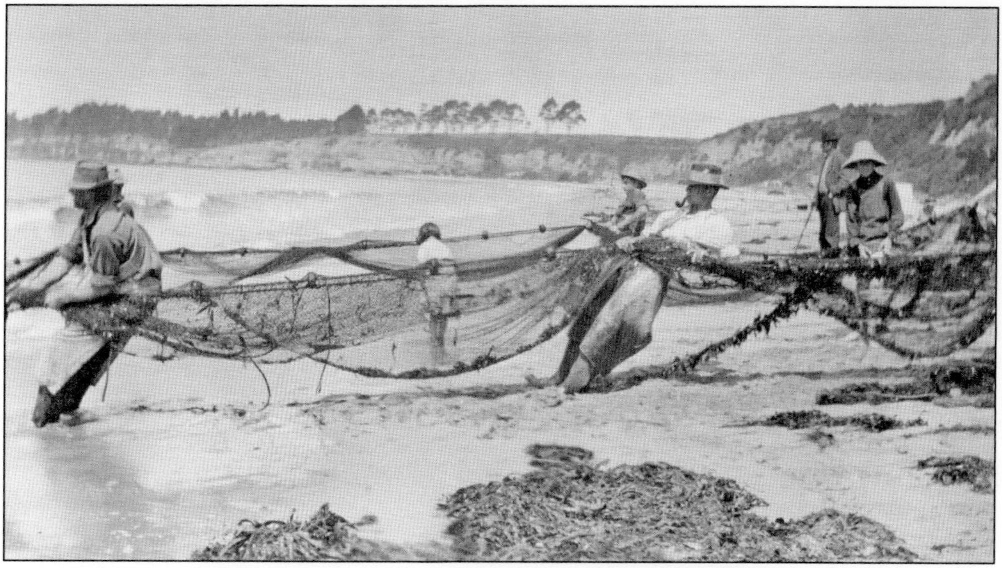

Captain Lindsay ran the seining company in later years with his son, Athol Thomas "Tom" Lindsay. Over time, both men built cabins below the bluffs at China Beach. These were used by fishing crews and campers on summer holiday. The younger Lindsay continued seine fishing until restrictions against the use of fine mesh nets were enforced by the California Division of Fish and Game. Below, Lindsay relatives Harold and Harriet Daubenbis visited the family cabins in the 1930s with their son, Stanley, and niece, Daphne Crossen. (Above, courtesy of Lee Lester; below, courtesy of Alice Daubenbis.)

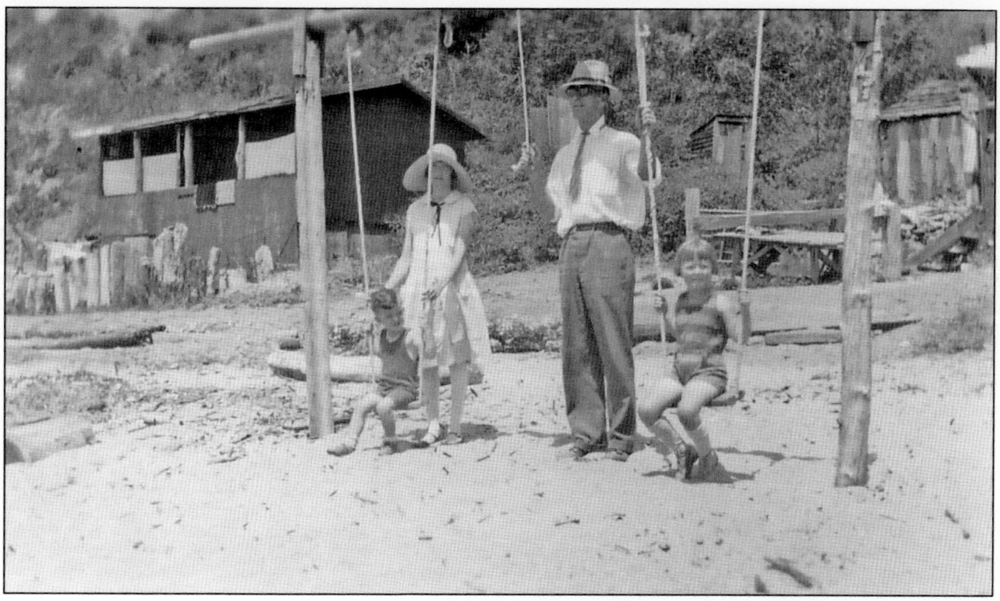

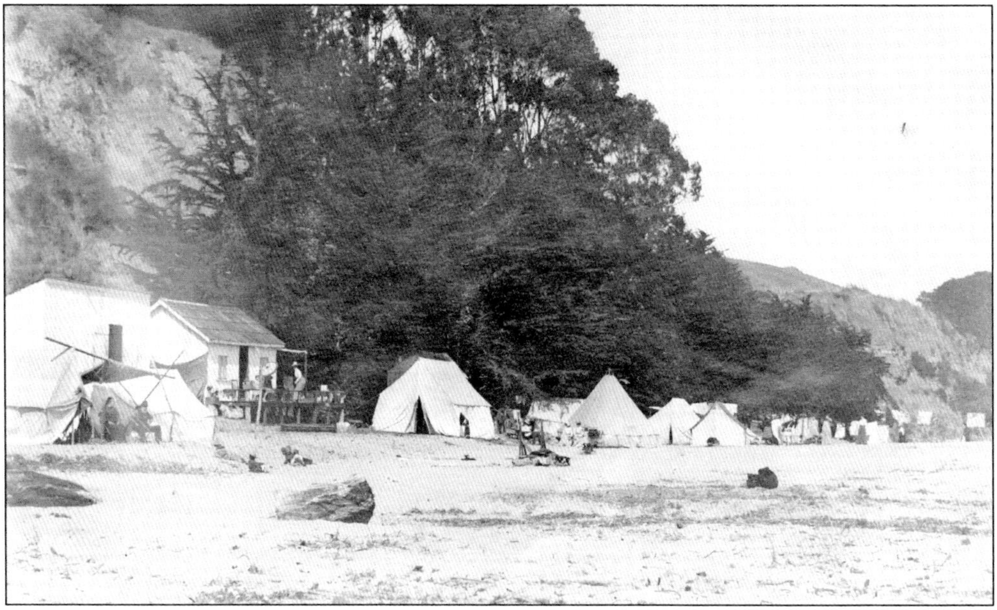

Thomas Fallon, a former San Jose mayor and Martina Castro Lodge's son-in-law, owned the coastal land between China Beach and Aptos. Observing that Camp Capitola was surviving as a favorite of Santa Clara Valley vacationers, he decided in 1878 to establish Camp San Jose. He planted the terrace with pines, cypress, and eucalyptus to enhance the setting. Fallon later built a hotel named New Brighton, and that name was eventually transferred to the beach. However, Fallon's resort was never successful. The beach became known as Pot Belly after 1933, when New Brighton Beach State Park was established at adjoining China Beach. About 1915, in the photograph below, several fully-dressed women dig into the sport of burying themselves in the sand. (Both, courtesy of Diane Hodges Emigh.)

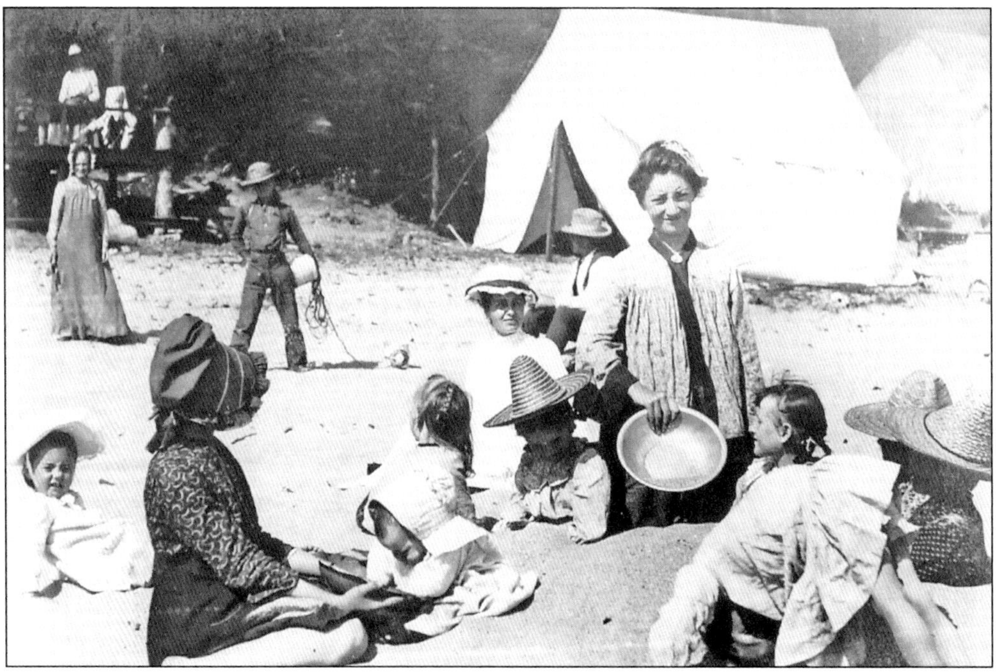

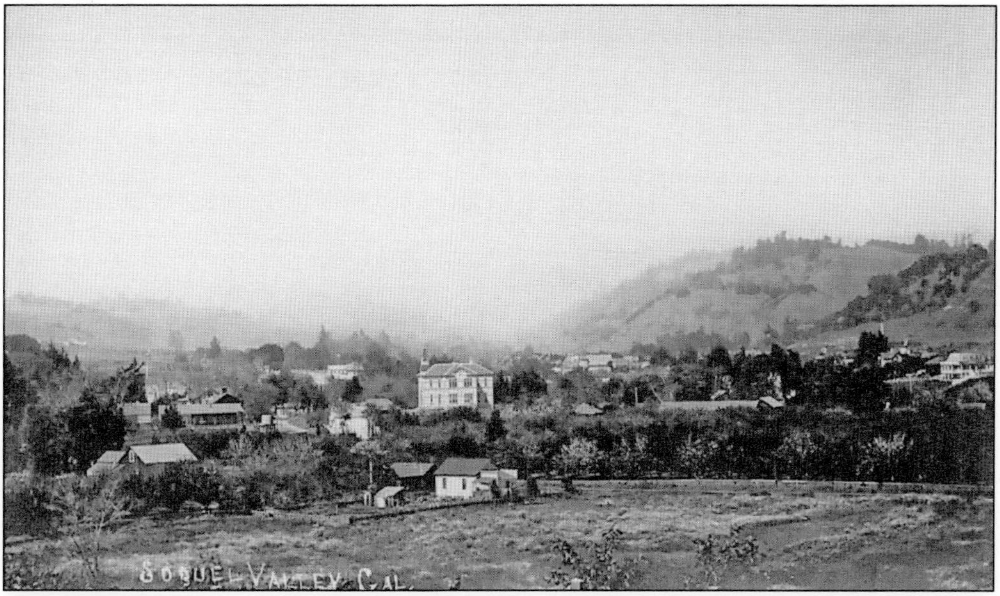

Capitola children went to school in Soquel, a distance that in the winter required pupils either to walk a mile into town or to risk a hazardous crossing of Soquel Creek. Frederick Hihn donated land for the Capitola School in 1898, but the attendance was so low that it closed in 1914. The above photograph offers a view from Wharf Road toward Soquel School, at center. Farther up the road was Pawla's Violet Gardens, one of the few specialty violet growers in the nation. Edith Pawla and daughter Emily collected more than 100 violet varieties and sold plants by mail-order catalog. In the 1920 photograph below, Emily poses with one of the English sheepdogs they raised. Edith is on the horse. Their car was custom-ordered in a violet color. (Below, courtesy of Shirley Coleman.)

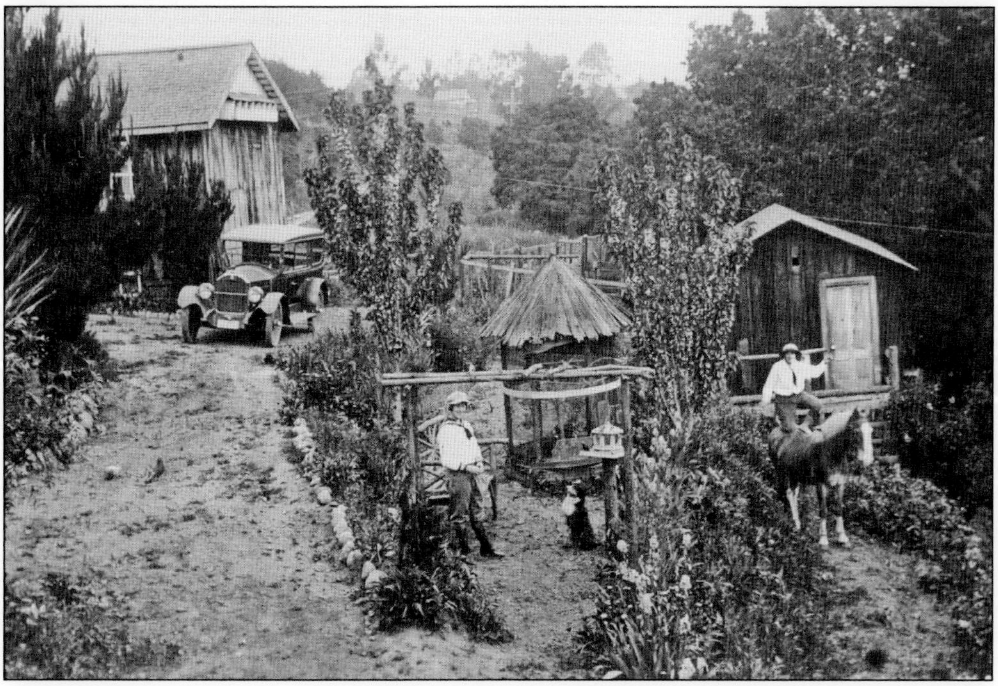

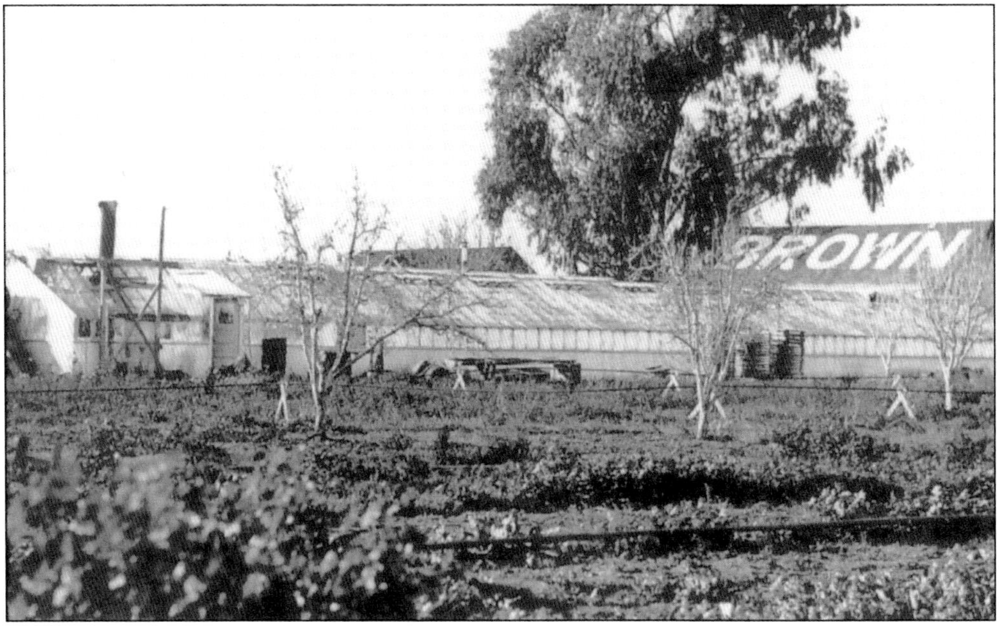

James and Rura Brown bought a tract along Forty-First Avenue in 1911. Starting with strawberries, they shifted to bulbs and by 1921 were worldwide producers of the tuberous begonia. To supply fertilizer for the bulbs, Brown bought registered heifers and a bull and raised one of the state's finest Guernsey herds. By the late 1920s, the family dairy bottled and delivered milk for sale and produced ice cream under the label "Moo Cow." A tour of the plant is in progress below in the 1930s. For decades, the Browns provided begonia blossoms for the annual Capitola Begonia Festival. Now organized as the Golden State Bulb Growers Inc., the enterprise still donates flowers for the festival that are picked from growing fields near Marina Beach. (Both, courtesy of the Brown family.)

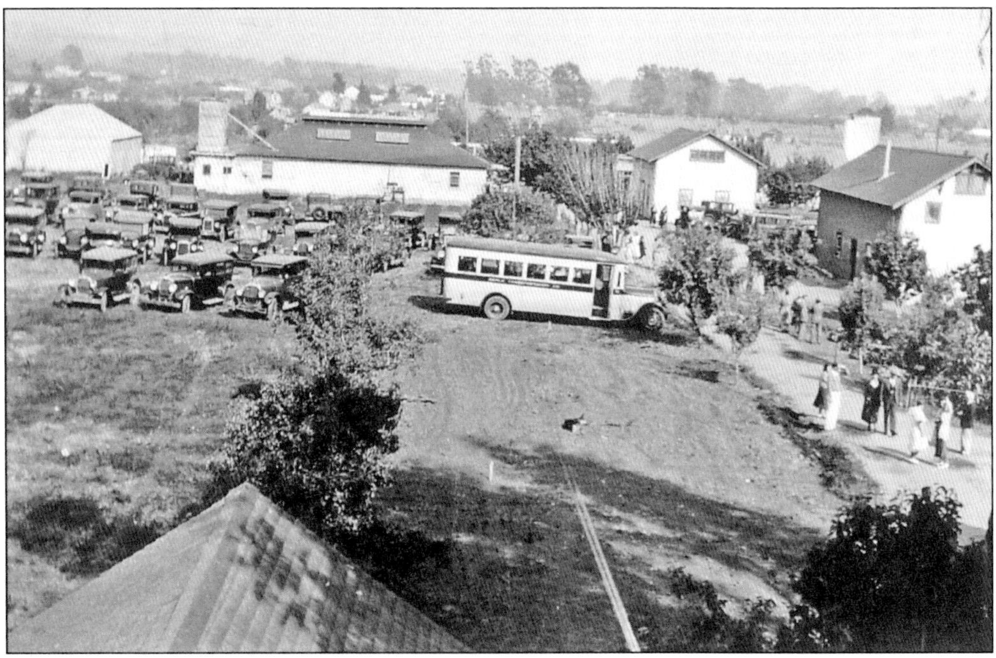

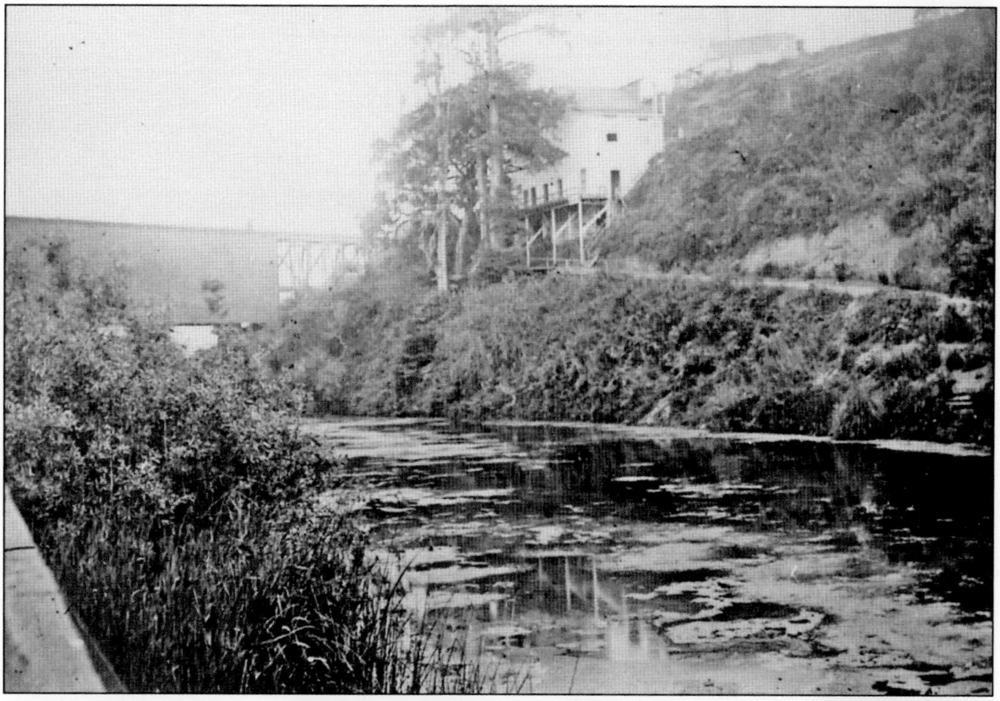

Soquel pioneers Henry and Ann Britton moved to Capitola about 1890 and, with their son, Frank, built the Ivy Cottage Saloon along Wharf Road. Although the hillside tavern closed with the start of Prohibition in 1919, the family stayed in Capitola, moving their home to the top of the hill. Both Henry and Ann Britton were skilled anglers. She had her favorite spot in the lagoon for bait fishing, supplying trout at 50¢ a dozen to customers that included the resort hotels. At right, Britton family members grab an outdoor shower to wash the sand out of their wool swim suits before heading home. (Both, courtesy of the Britton and Hayford families.)

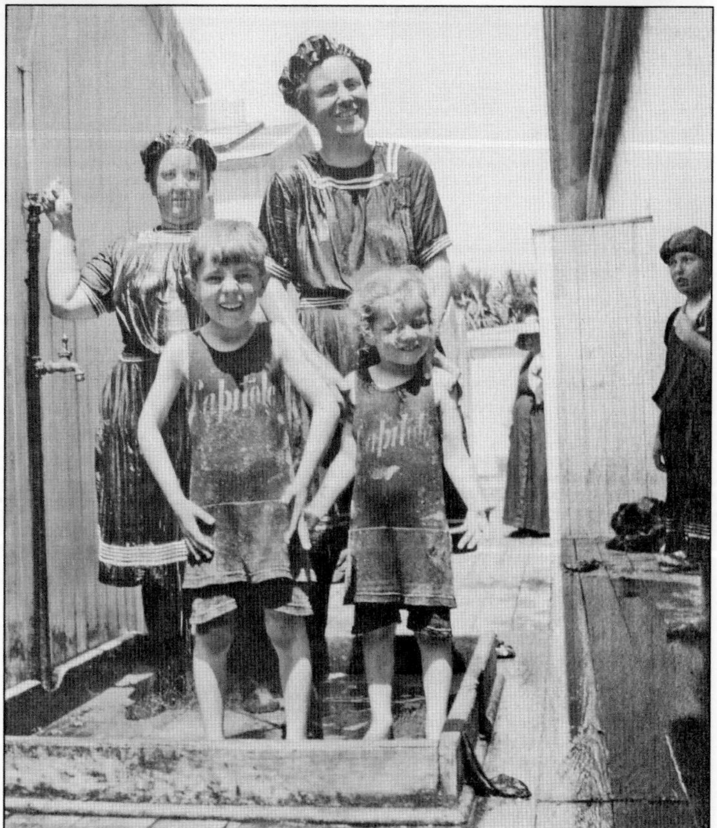

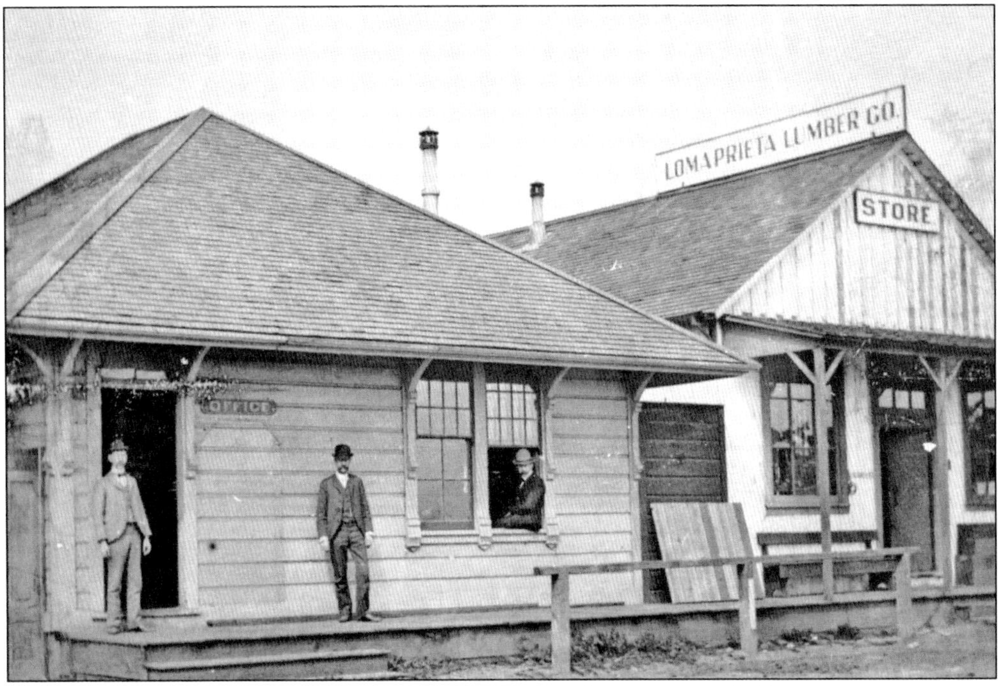

Frederick Hihn leased land to the Loma Prieta Lumber Company in 1884 for a train stop known as Opal, west of Capitola. Lumber from the mills above Aptos was stored at the yard, which had a planing mill and store. Stationmaster Albretto Stoodley, standing at the doorway in this 1906 photograph, was a nearby resident. At least three train accidents occurred at the Opal spur before the site was abandoned in 1931.

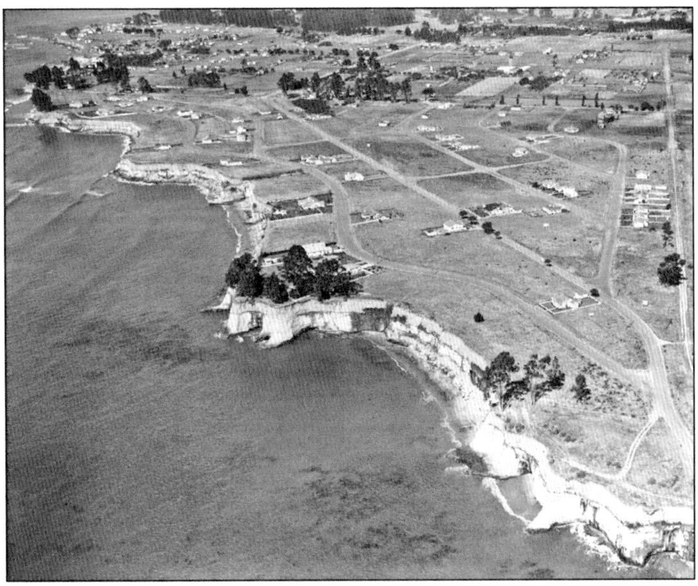
Kathryn McGeoghegan, the widow of F.A. Hihn's grandson Eulice Hihn, subdivided the Opal Cliffs Tract in 1923 above the railroad stop and lumberyard. Developer Harry McBain is credited with the creation of the residential neighborhood after he purchased the 40-acre tract in 1936. Shown in a 1940s aerial photograph is the Opal Cliffs neighborhood and the former path of the electric car line, now the route of Portola Drive.

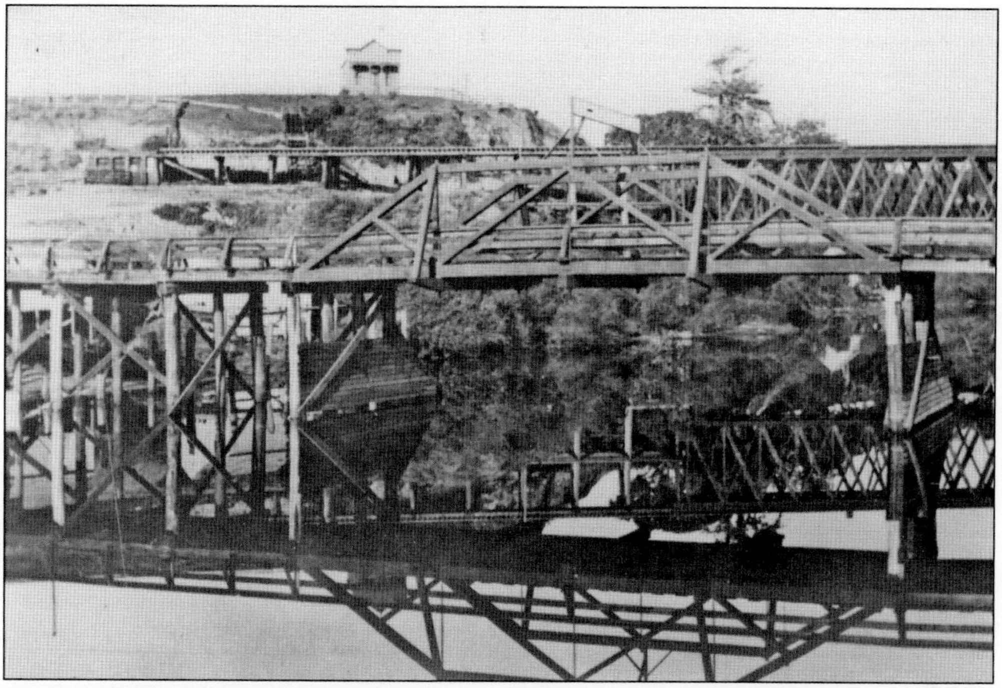

Dennis C. Feeley, a Santa Clara rancher, obtained title to 20 acres on the west hill above Capitola in 1870. Once Frederick Hihn began to sell lots for summer homes, Feeley decided to do the same, opening Camp Fairview in 1886. One of the first cottages, set on the bluff above Wharf Road, was built for year-round resident Charles Cleal, the night watchman at the wharf.

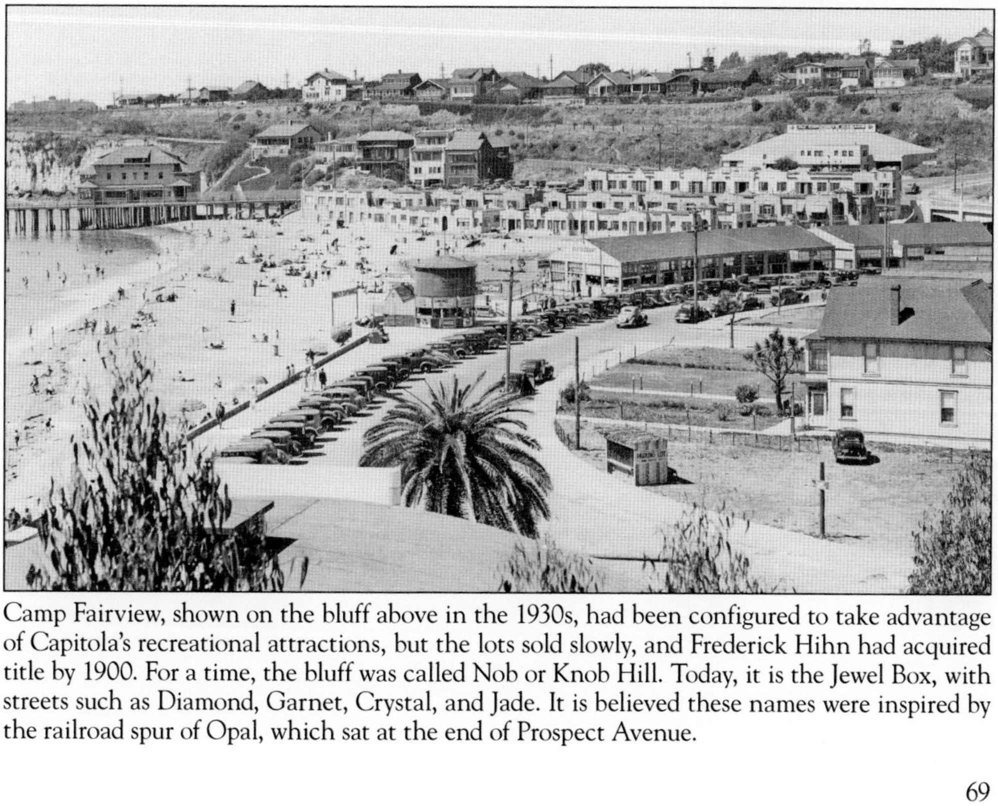

Camp Fairview, shown on the bluff above in the 1930s, had been configured to take advantage of Capitola's recreational attractions, but the lots sold slowly, and Frederick Hihn had acquired title by 1900. For a time, the bluff was called Nob or Knob Hill. Today, it is the Jewel Box, with streets such as Diamond, Garnet, Crystal, and Jade. It is believed these names were inspired by the railroad spur of Opal, which sat at the end of Prospect Avenue.

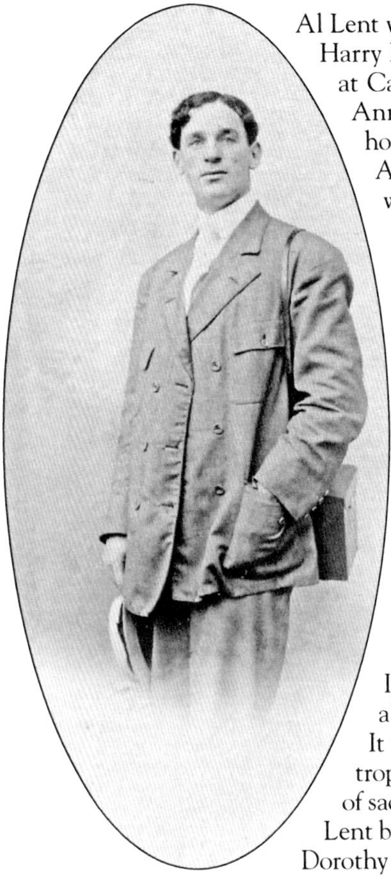

Al Lent was playing on a semi-professional team with baseball star Harry Hooper when he was convinced by his friend to join him at Capitola. Lent bought the hilltop cottage of Charles and Anna Cleal, and in 1915, he built a new Arts and Crafts–style home that gradually became a favorite landmark on Prospect Avenue. As an avid fisherman, hunter, and horseman, Lent was one of the resort's best-known personalities.

In the mid-1920s, Lent acquired a right-of-way along the cliff, allowing him to add an octagonal-shaped bay to the house. It was filled inside with western relics, fishing and hunting trophies, polished guns, fishing tackle, and a peerless collection of saddles and gear. A collection of hats included those given to Lent by Will Rogers, Jack London, and Bing Crosby. (Courtesy of Dorothy Lent Washam.)

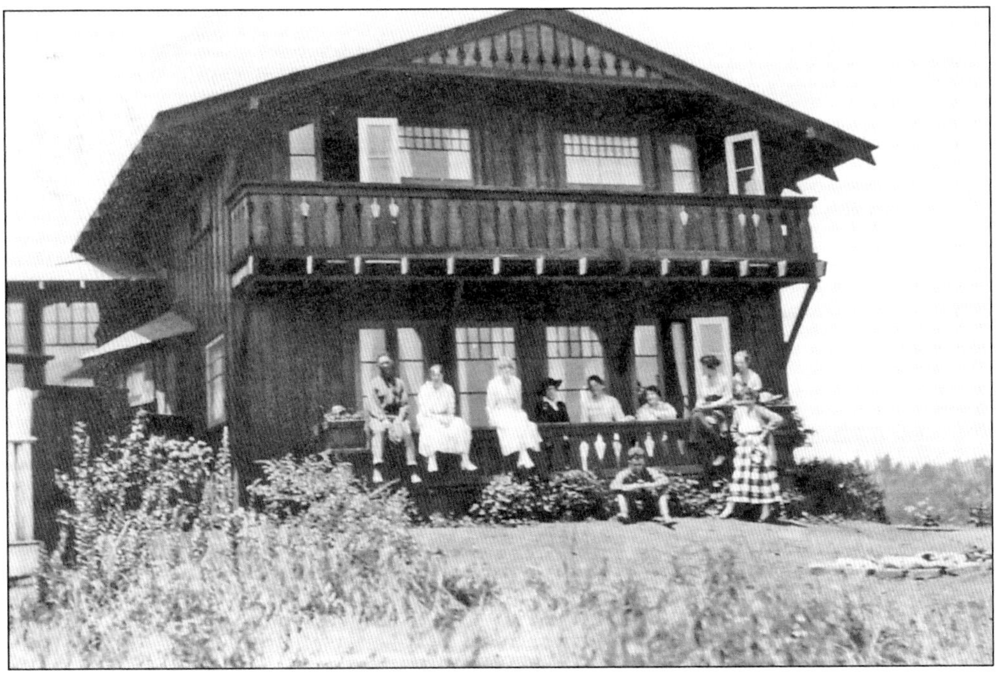

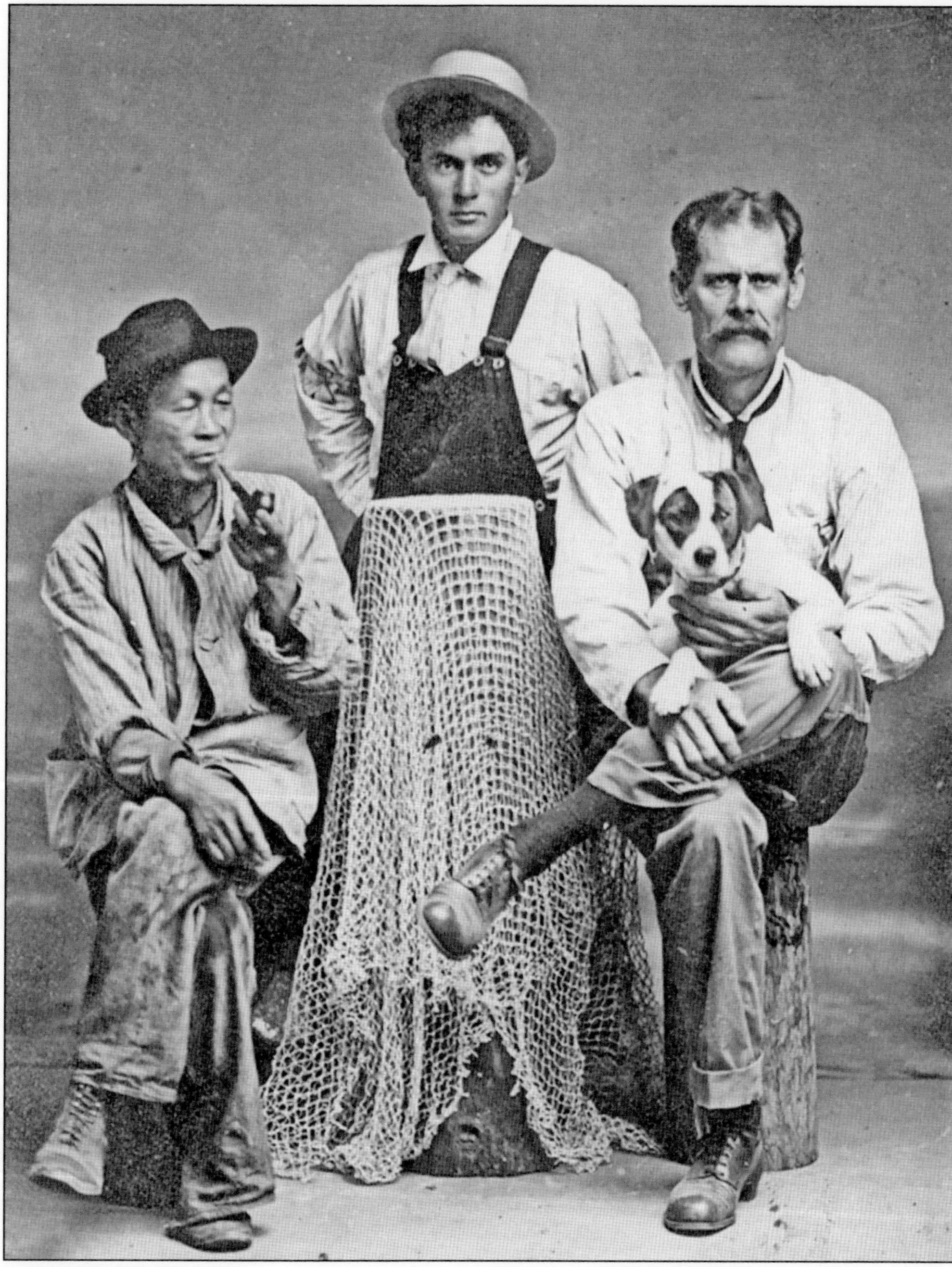

For many years, Capitola was open to whites exclusively. Individuals considered to be non-white were restricted from buying subdivision lots and could live and work within the boundaries of the resort only as servants or concessionaires tending the needs of vacationers. Workers who lived nearby seldom spent time enjoying summertime entertainments in the village. This rare image was taken while the photograph studio was still open for the season. From left to right, Song Lee relaxes with his neighbor Jack Bostwick, standing in a workman's apron, and an unidentified friend with a puppy. For decades, Lee ran a laundry situated on Capitola Avenue just outside the resort, where the Capitola City Hall complex is today. (Courtesy of John Nicol.)

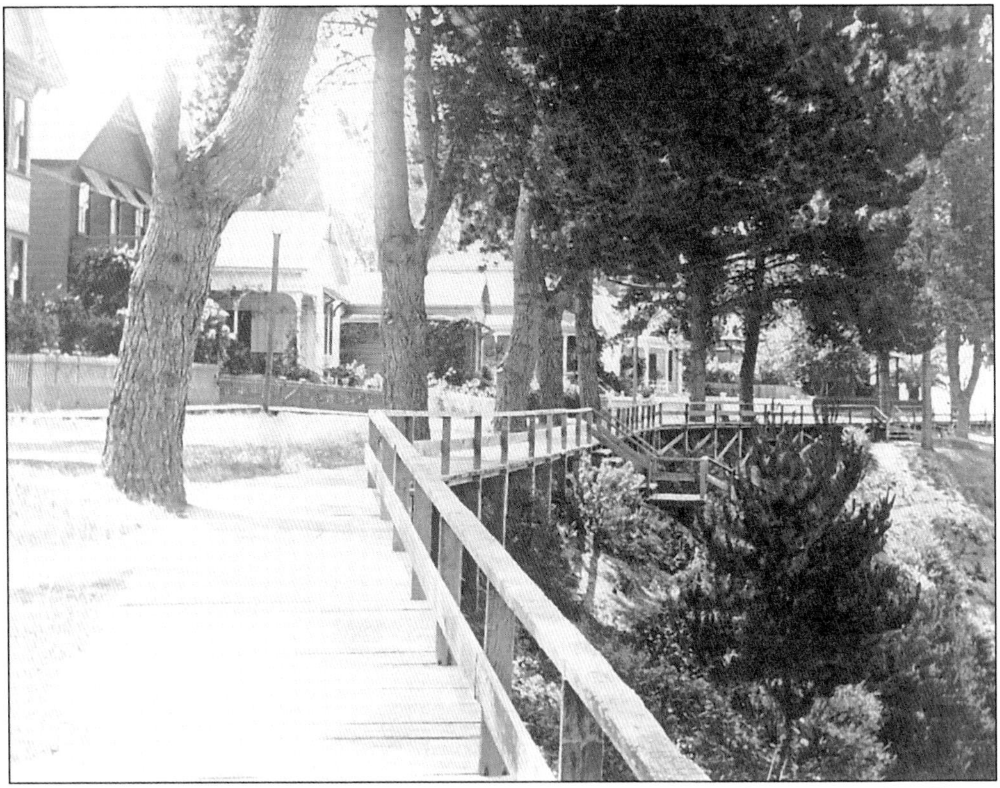

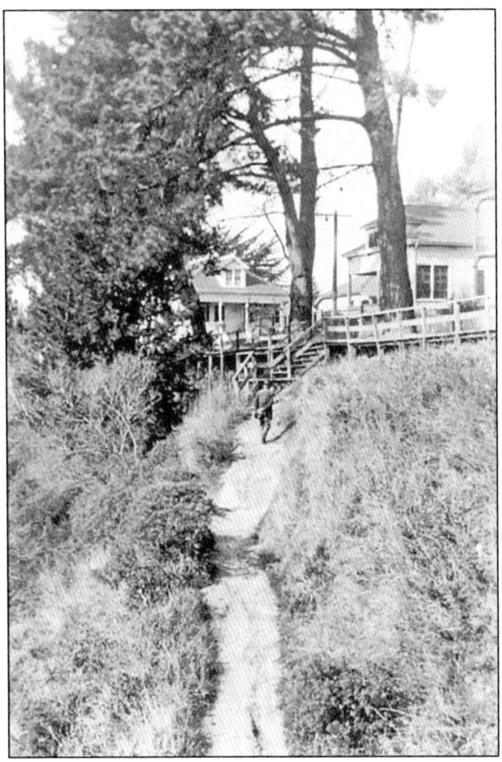

Depot Hill was also known as Nob Hill in the early years, although technically the name was given only to the ridge that is now El Camino Medio, above Monterey Avenue. Before the train station was built at the head of Railroad (Escalona) Avenue, the hilltop was a section of Capitola Park, dedicated in 1888. Although settled largely by members of the Turn Verein German American Club, Depot Hill was also the neighborhood of longtime residents who contributed to the resort as it moved towards city incorporation. Among them were Hotel Capitola owner Everard V. "Teddy" Woodhouse, often referred to as a "one-man Chamber of Commerce," and Frank Reanier, who had been superintendent for the F.A. Hihn Company.

Depot Hill's best-known resident was Harry Bartholomew Hooper (1887–1974), who broke into major-league baseball with the Boston Red Sox in 1909. On October 15, 1915, Hooper became the first to hit two home runs in a single World Series game, and he is the only one to play on four Red Sox World Series championship teams: 1912, 1915, 1916, and 1918. He was elected to the National Baseball Hall of Fame in 1971.

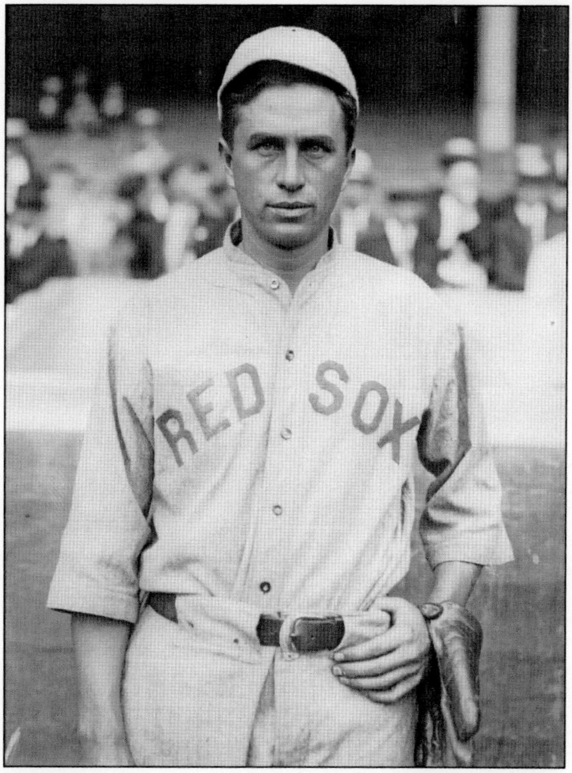

A commemorative plaque at the entrance to the Capitola Wharf honors Harry Hooper. He had joined his family in Capitola when he left his career in baseball. Hooper opened a real estate office and was then appointed postmaster, a job he kept from 1933 until his retirement in 1957. Hooper is standing at left with John Nicol, who delivered mail from Soquel by wagon with his horse Fanny in the 1930s. (Courtesy of John Nicol.)

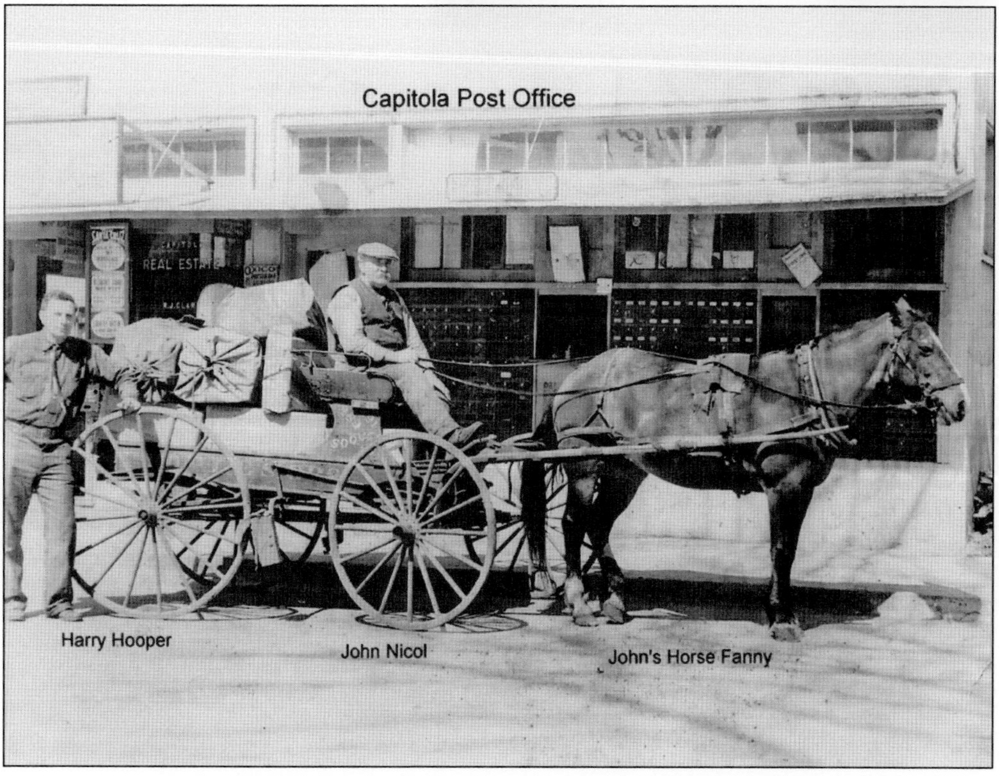

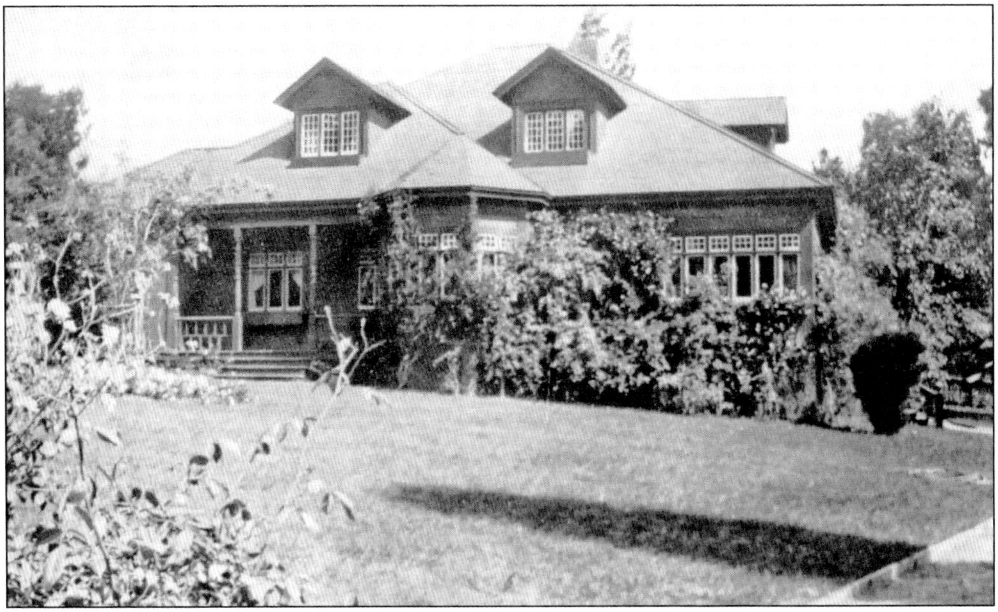

Four Victorian cottages were built in 1895 as the English Cottages at the east end of Grand Avenue on today's Depot Hill. Two families from England, the Robinsons and Rawlins, had migrated to Hanford, near Fresno, and bought the Capitola property as a summer refuge from the heat. Their haven grew with added spaces for guests and cabins for servants and a caretaker for the extensive garden. The summer residents joined neighbor Patty Reed Lewis in her work to establish Capitola's first chapel, St. John the Baptist Episcopal Church, below. It was completed nearby on Oakland Avenue lots donated by Frederick Hihn in 1898. The English Cottages were sold about 1911 to capitalist Lewis E. Hanchett, who changed the name to El Salto and enlarged it as a family estate.

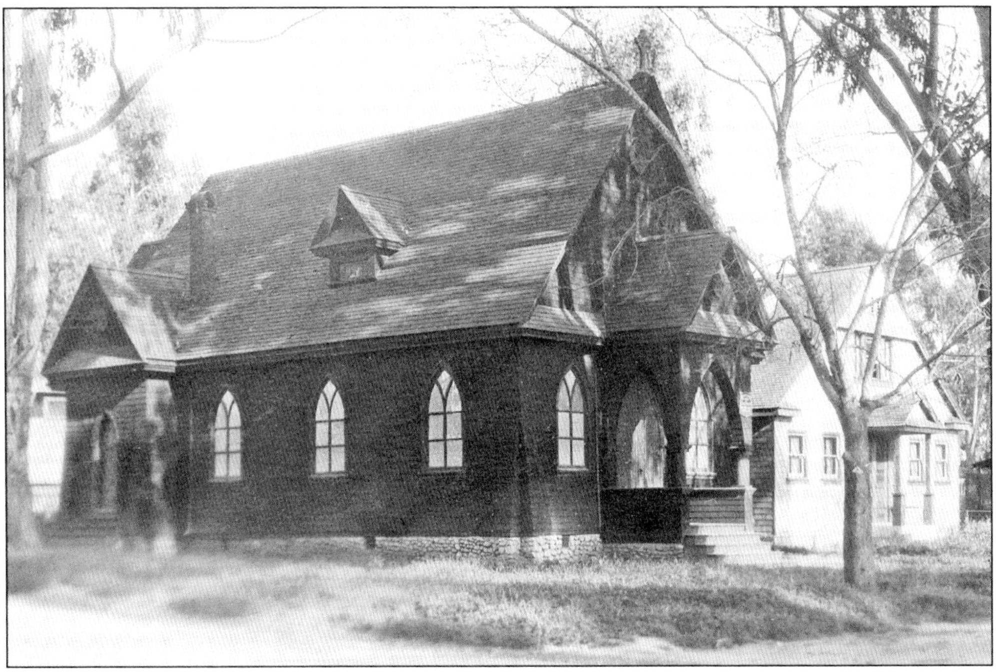

Five

Rispin, Rum-Running, and Religion

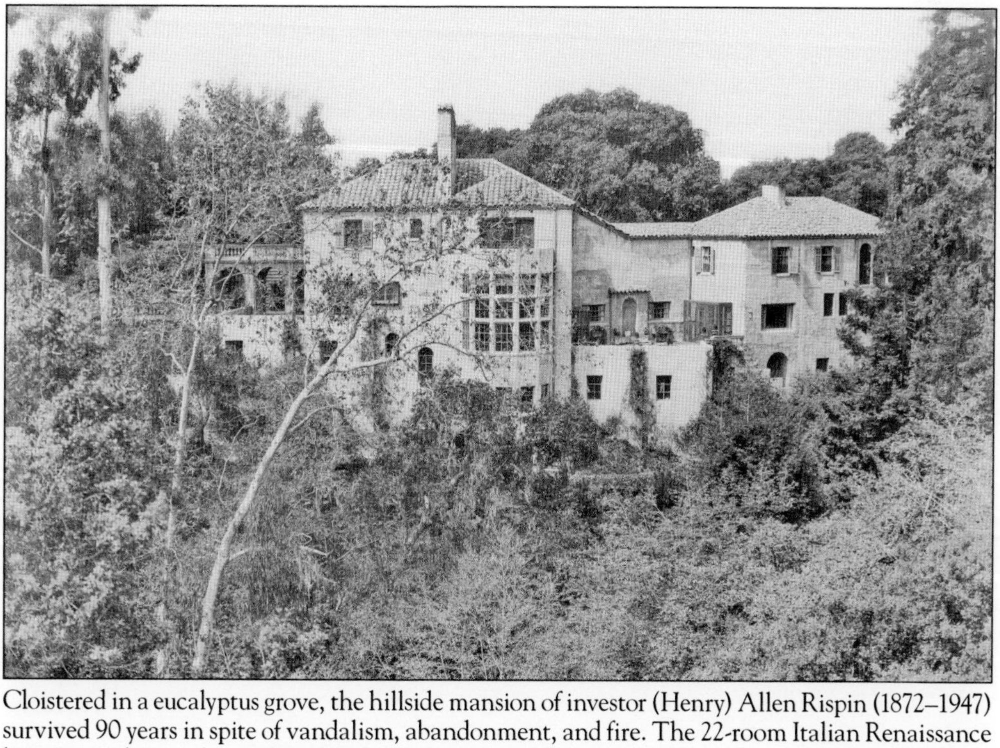

Cloistered in a eucalyptus grove, the hillside mansion of investor (Henry) Allen Rispin (1872–1947) survived 90 years in spite of vandalism, abandonment, and fire. The 22-room Italian Renaissance house was designed in 1920–1921 by architect George McCrea. Introduced to the community in 1918 as a San Francisco capitalist and oil tycoon, Rispin had set up a syndicate to invest in California coastal properties. He negotiated with the heirs of Frederick Hihn to buy the Capitola resort in 1919.

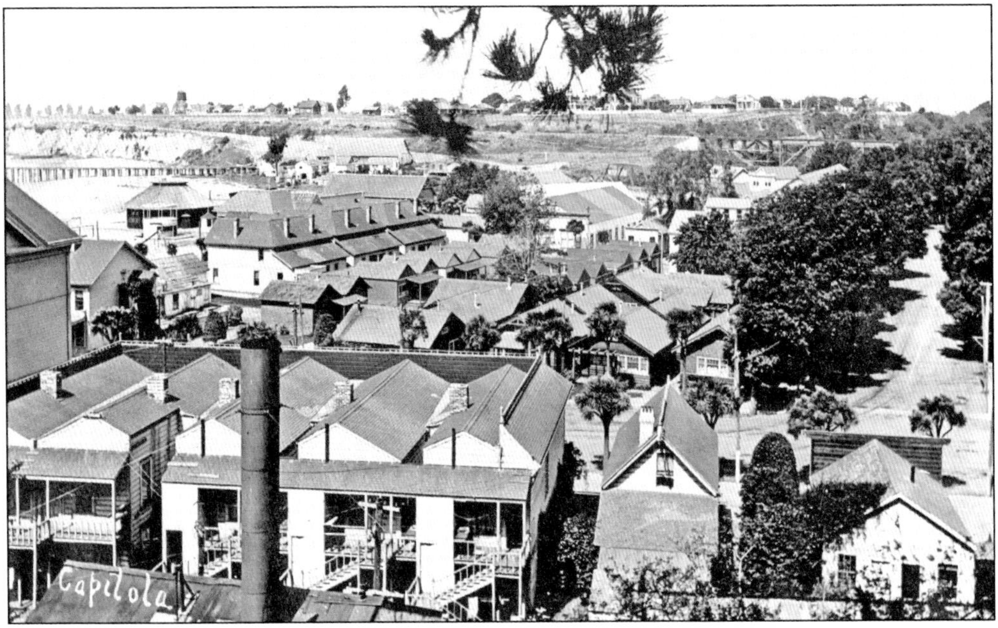

Capitola still had its Victorian character in 1913, when Katherine Hihn Cope Henderson (1857–1921) inherited the resort from her father, Frederick Hihn. She and her husband, Harry O. Henderson, moved to the village and took charge, continuing the business style of the F.A. Hihn Company. Taken from Depot Hill looking west, the 1913 view above shows the rear of the 1890s Bay View Apartments. The resort's firehouse, at far right, faces a tree-shaded Capitola Avenue. The circular, dark building on the beach is a steam calliope, also visible in the Fourth of July celebration photograph below, taken about the same time.

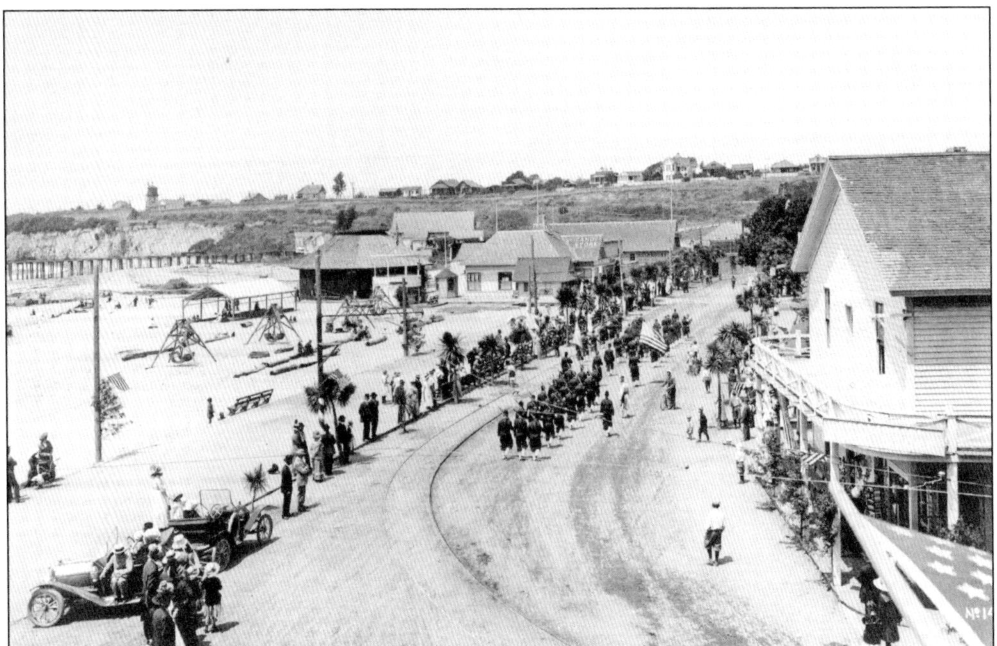

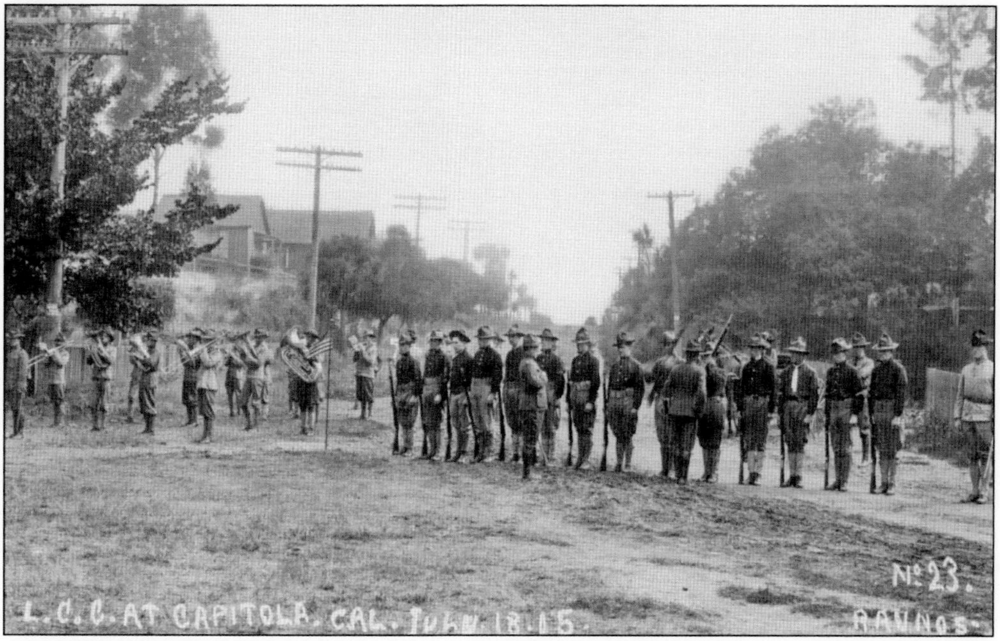

Capitola continued to be an ideal spot for old-fashioned encampments during World War I. League of the Cross Cadets, a Catholic temperance and anti-profanity league, gave young men the feel of military life. Above, cadets stood near their campsite on Capitola Avenue for a portrait as the camp drew to a close in July 1915. To the right, below, is the present site of Capitola City Hall. Situated just north of the trestle, this tract had previously been considered the outskirts of the resort. (Above, courtesy of Gordon van Zuiden.)

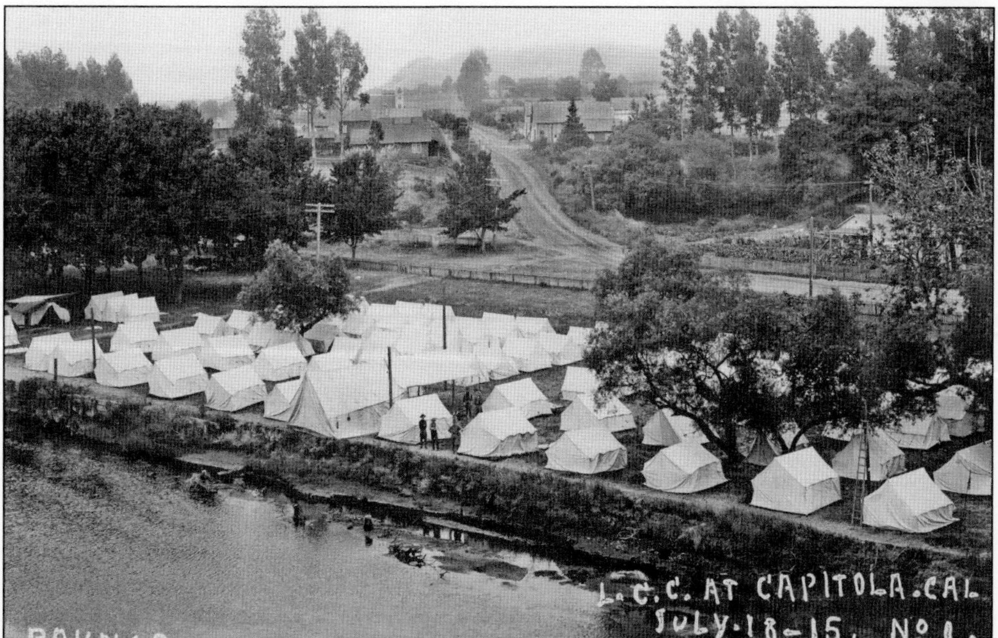

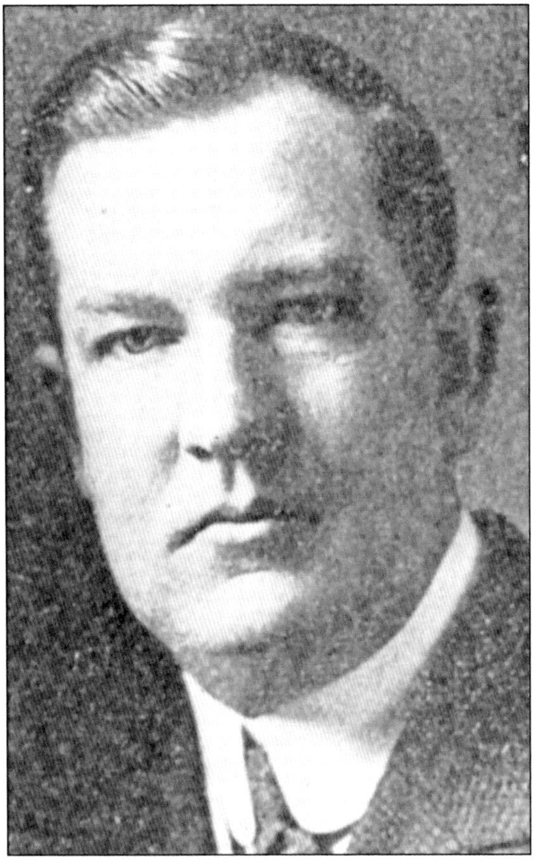

Allen Rispin came to Capitola as an oil millionaire, but his work experience was in sales. He wanted to quickly subdivide and market real estate, particularly along the eastern bank of the creek, where he could turn a fast profit for Capitola Company shareholders. Capitola's bathhouse and card room fronting the lagoon, shown below about 1909, were among the first buildings razed soon after Rispin's arrival. The salvaged wood was used to frame the mansion. Forty tubs for saltwater baths were saved from the bathhouse and relocated in the former bowling alley behind the hotel.

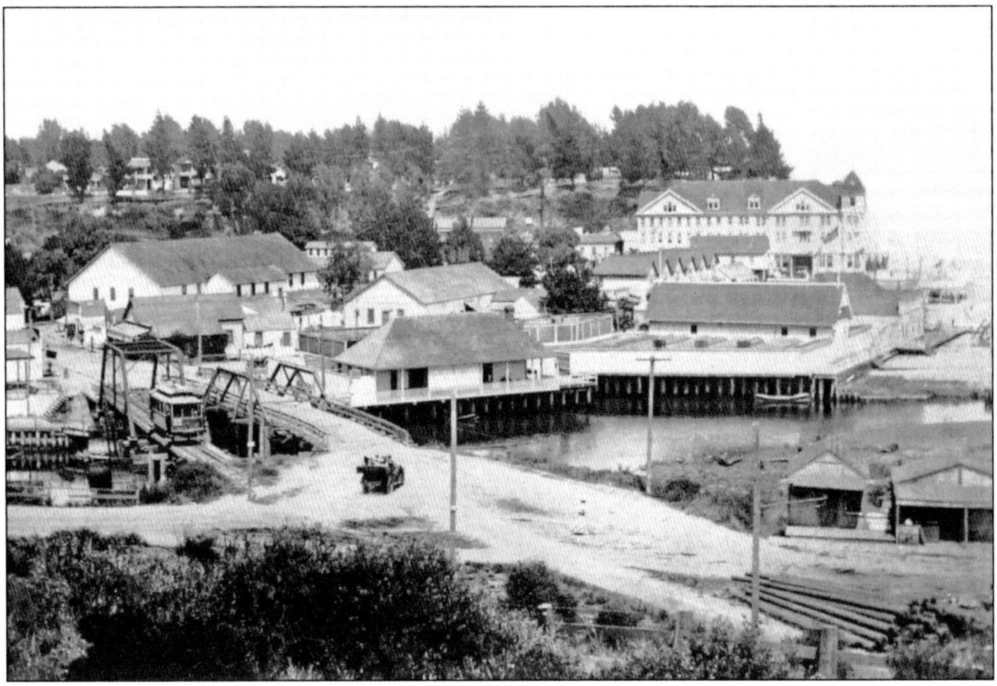

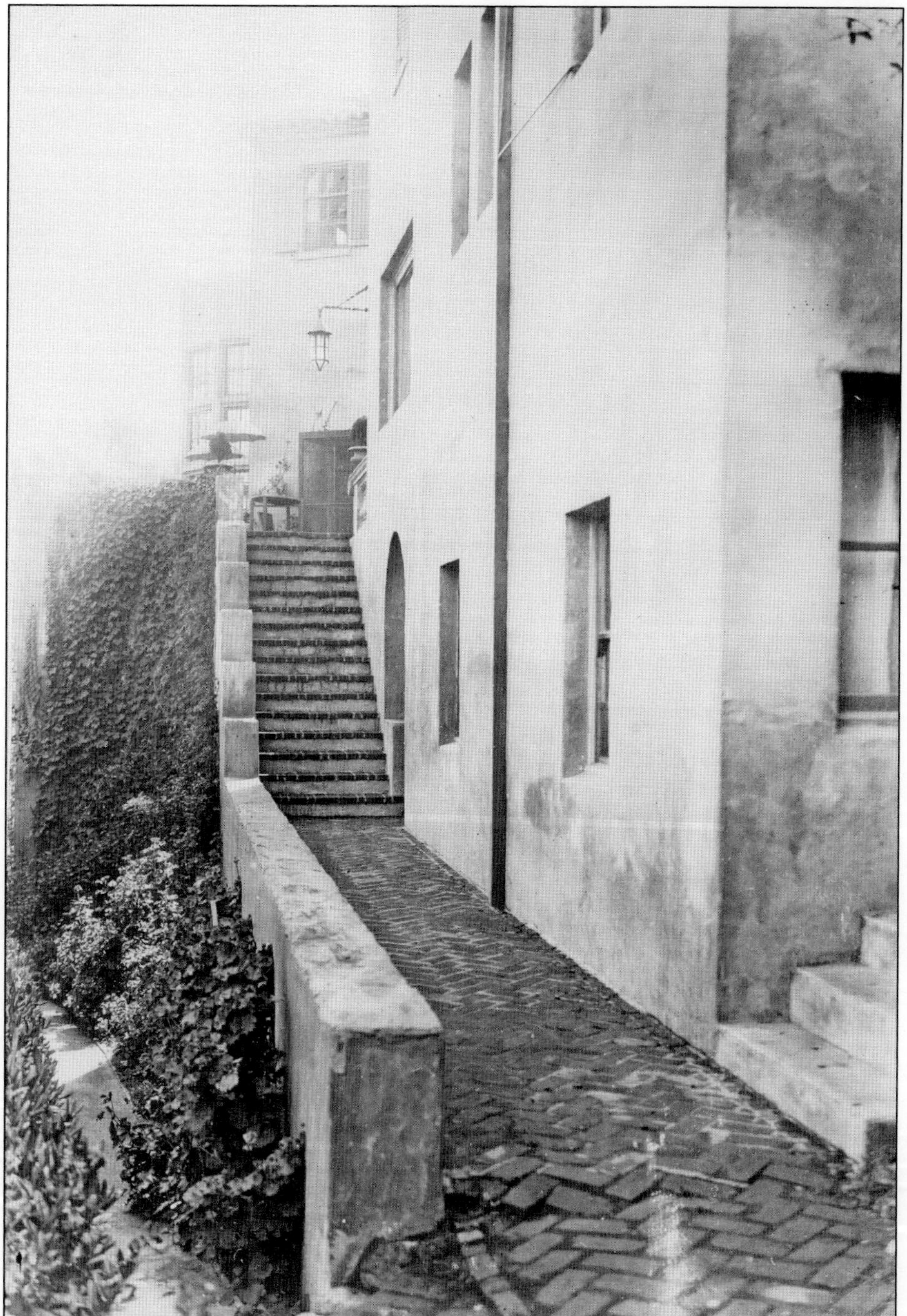

Allen Rispin's wife, Annette, was the daughter of Isaac E. Blake, the founder of Conoco Oil. The couple, with son Alan, kept their principal residence in San Francisco when they bought Capitola. For the new house, they chose a site on a sloping hillside to the west of Soquel Creek. Specializing in church buildings and Spanish Colonial Revival–style architecture, George McCrea was hired to design the 9,000-square-foot, $200,000 mansion. It was created as a showpiece to attract prospective wealthy vacation-home buyers. This photograph of the house and walkway was taken about 1935.

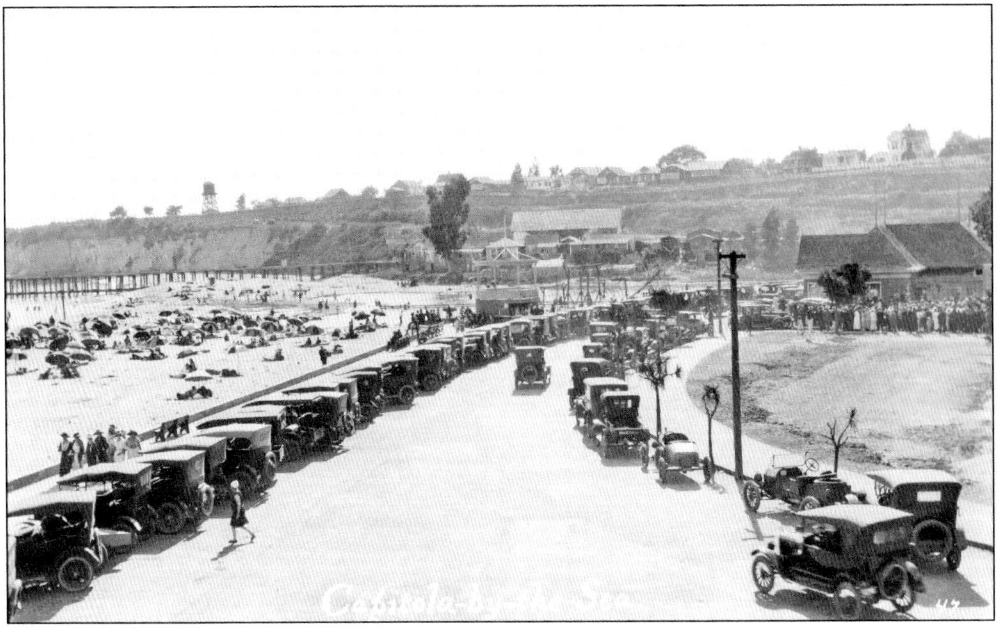

Allen Rispin leased apartments in 1920 for architect George McCrea and his assistant, Helen Benbow. The work crew was signed into village boardinghouses, where they lived for the next two years. The first task was to reshape the Esplanade, shown above just after it was paved and curved out onto the beach. As quickly as the concrete dried, all the parking spaces were filled. (Both, courtesy of Gordon van Zuiden.)

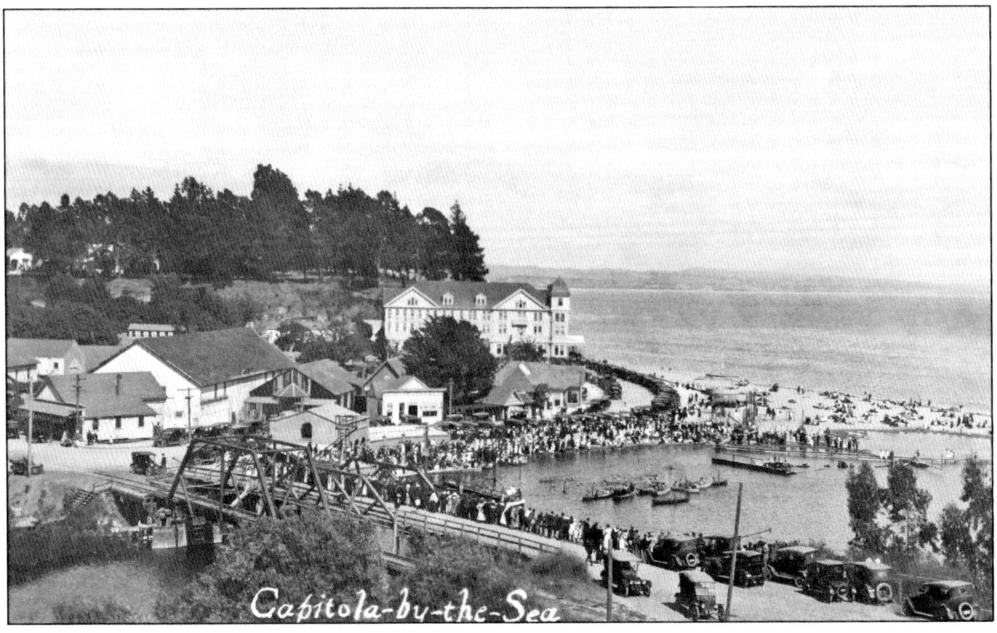

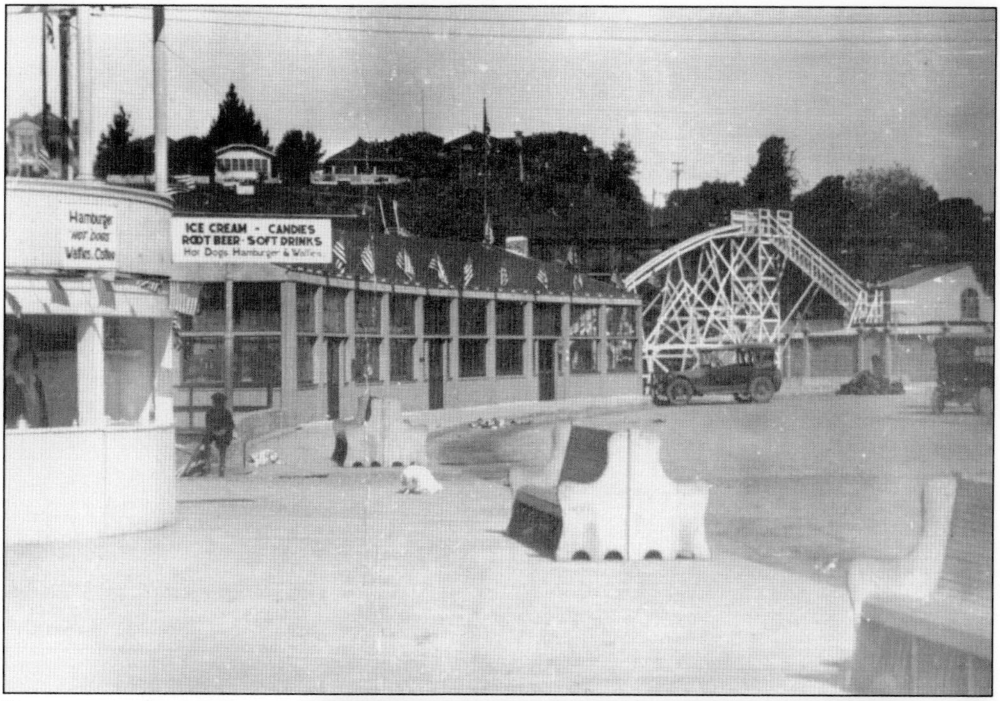

Rispin wanted to tear down the Hotel Capitola so he could construct a new one of reinforced concrete. By chance, Everard V. "Teddy" Woodhouse (1875–1947), a previous manager, inherited enough money to buy both the hotel and a section of beachfront property. He made improvements and invested in the casino amusement building, shown with flags above. Woodhouse, a native of Australia, was a popular community figure. He sits at his Cliff Avenue home, at right, with neighborhood children and his dog, Me Too, after hosting an Easter egg hunt. (Right, courtesy of Dick and Dave Lynn and Janis French.)

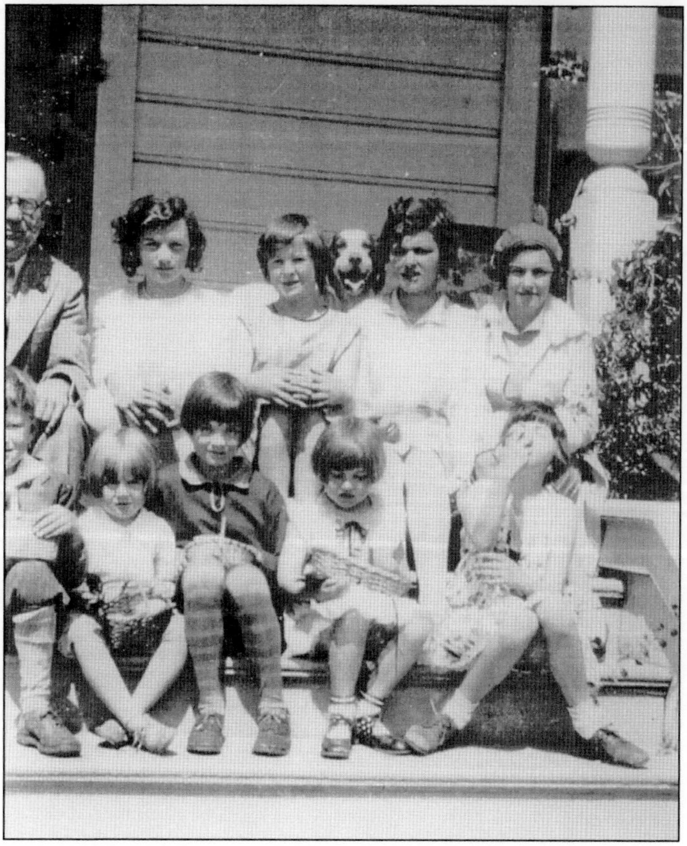

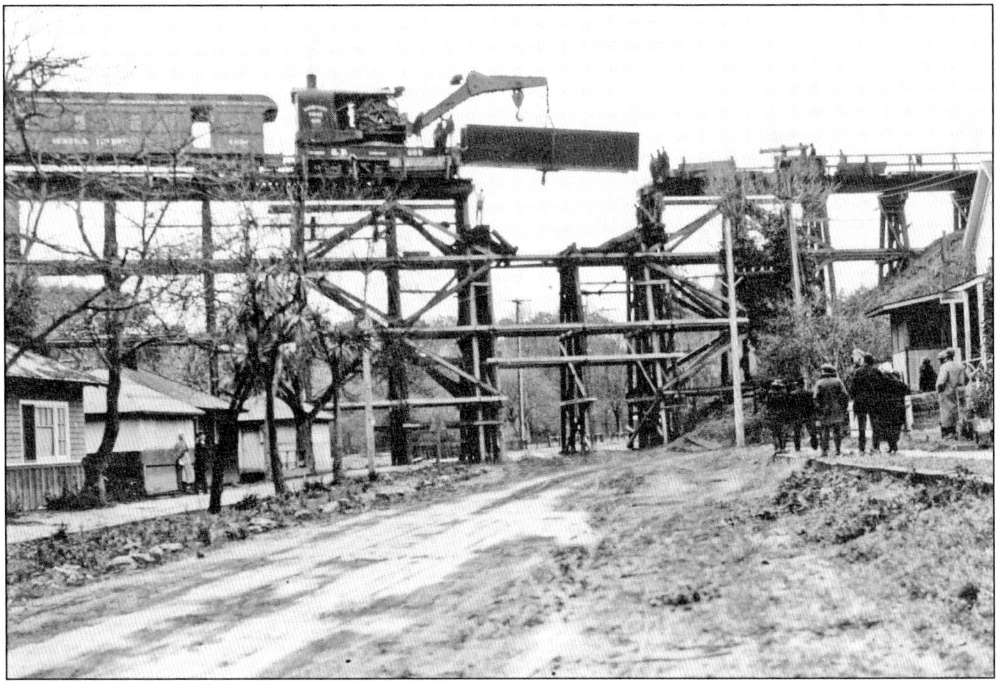

While the Capitola Company spent money to modernize the oceanfront, the older subdivisions just a few blocks away showed signs of neglect. The trestle was finally modified in the early 1920s so automobiles could drive under and through without dings and scratches, although getting stuck in the mud remained a possibility. (Courtesy of the Macdonald family.)

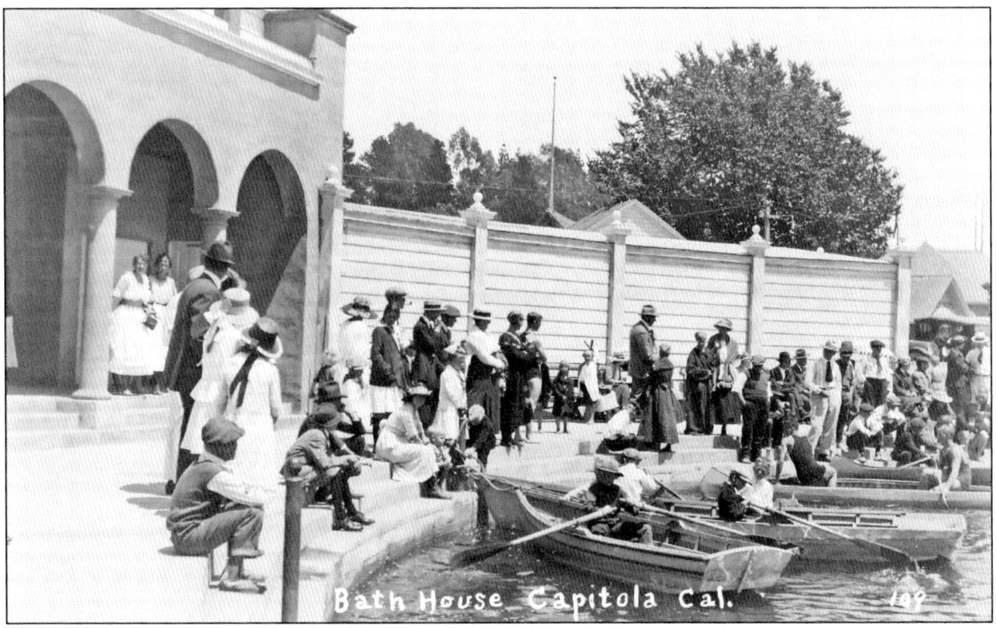

Capitola's up-to-the-minute look was finished in stucco. The stylish 1921 bathhouse and boat rental framed a concrete pool that still defines the lagoon today. Graduated steps into the water provided handy audience seating during boat and swim lessons, pictured here about 1922. (Courtesy of Gordon van Zuiden.)

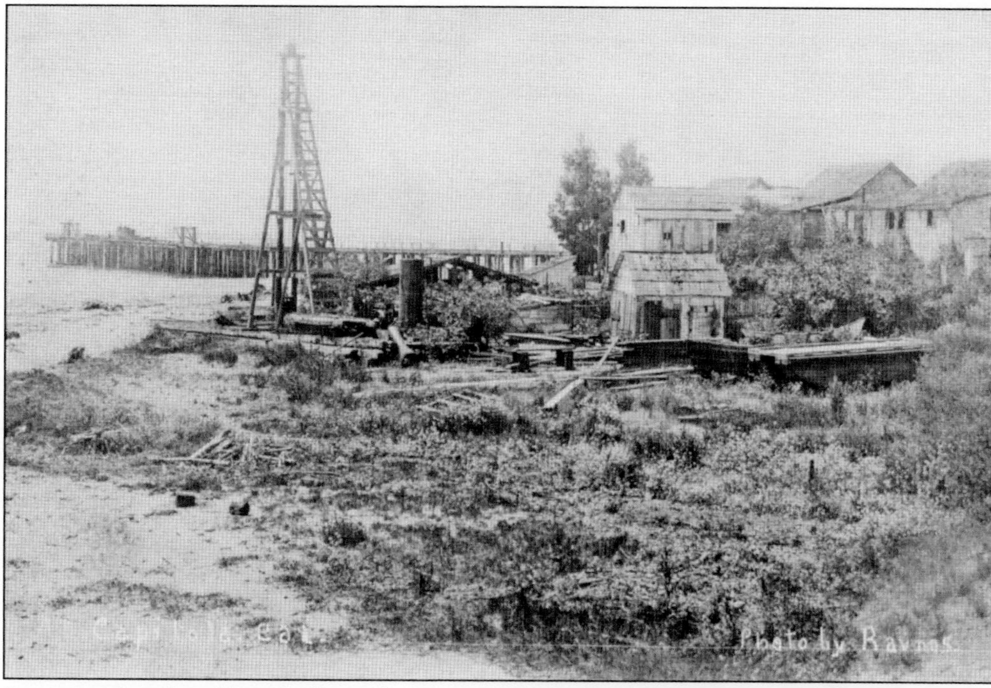

Surviving four decades at the base of the wharf, Capitola's fishing village slowly emptied as its population shifted toward Santa Cruz after 1912. Shortly before its 1920 demolition, the settlement, above, was used as a set for the silent film *Testing Block*. This was the last movie filmed in Santa Cruz County to feature cowboy star William S. "Two-Gun Bill" Hart, who is posed at right with young Capitola resident Harry Hooper Jr. (Above, courtesy of Gordon van Zuiden; right, courtesy of the Hooper family.)

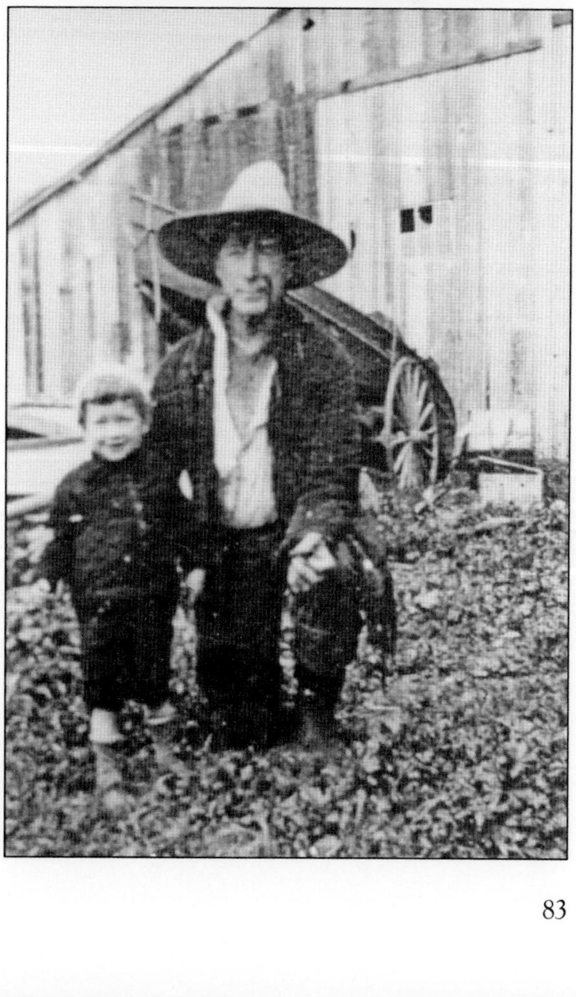

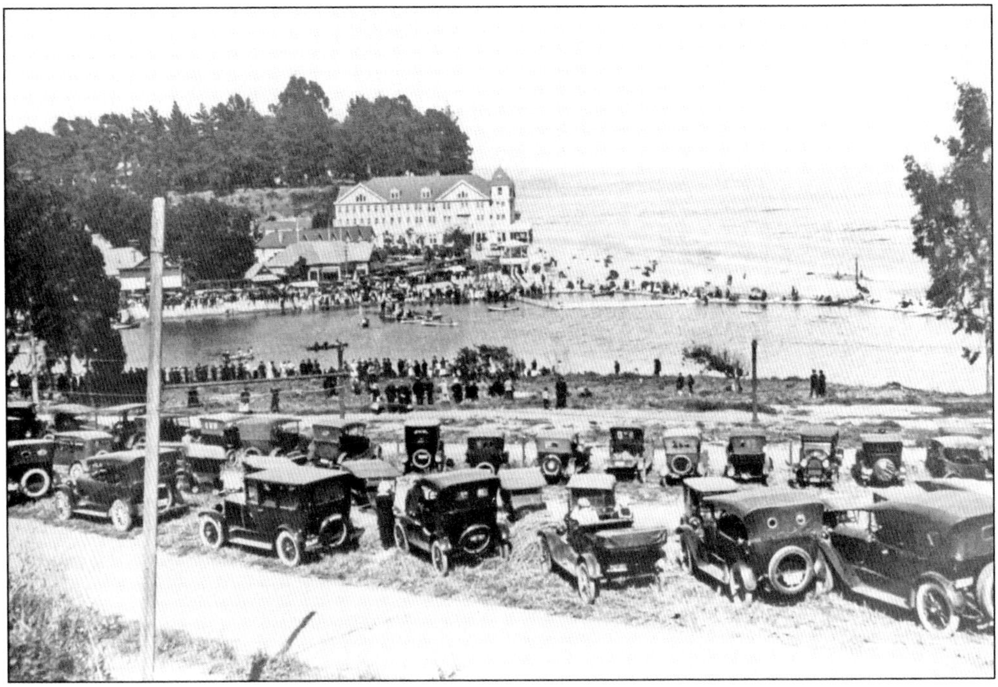

When the fishing village was demolished, workers discovered beneath it a burial ground for a Uypi tribal unit of Ohlone Indians, who had lived here hundreds of years before. Bones were taken away and the land used for parking until San Jose realtors Henry Roth and Homer Langdon secured it to build 46 bungalows. Architects Frank D. Wolfe and William E. Higgins designed the Spanish Colonial Revival–style Venetian Court, shown below under construction, in 1924. Contrary to local folklore, no evidence confirms that these units were the first condominiums in California. (Above, courtesy of Gordon van Zuiden; below, courtesy of the Macdonald family.)

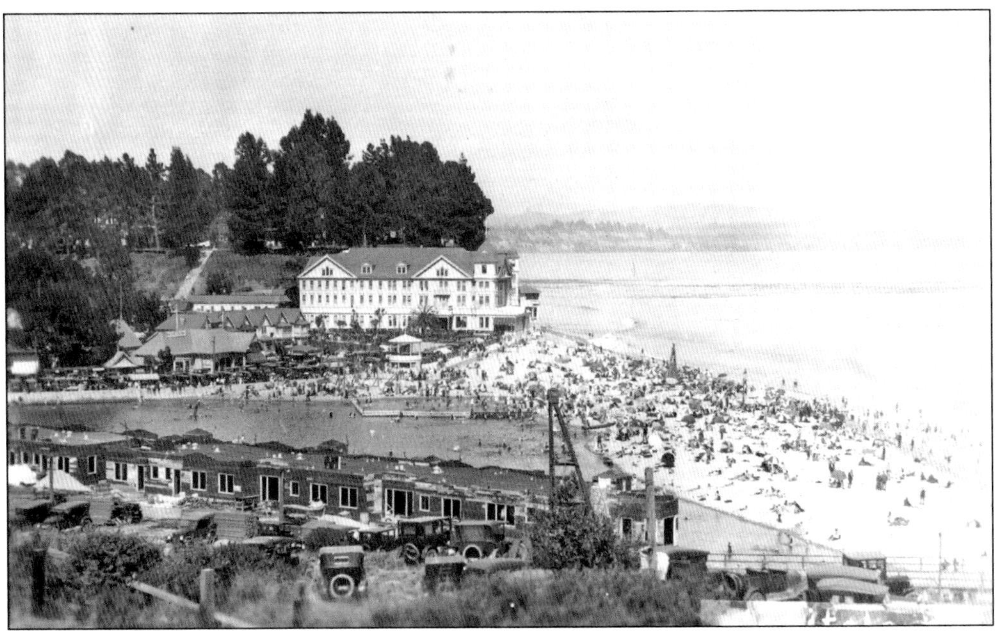

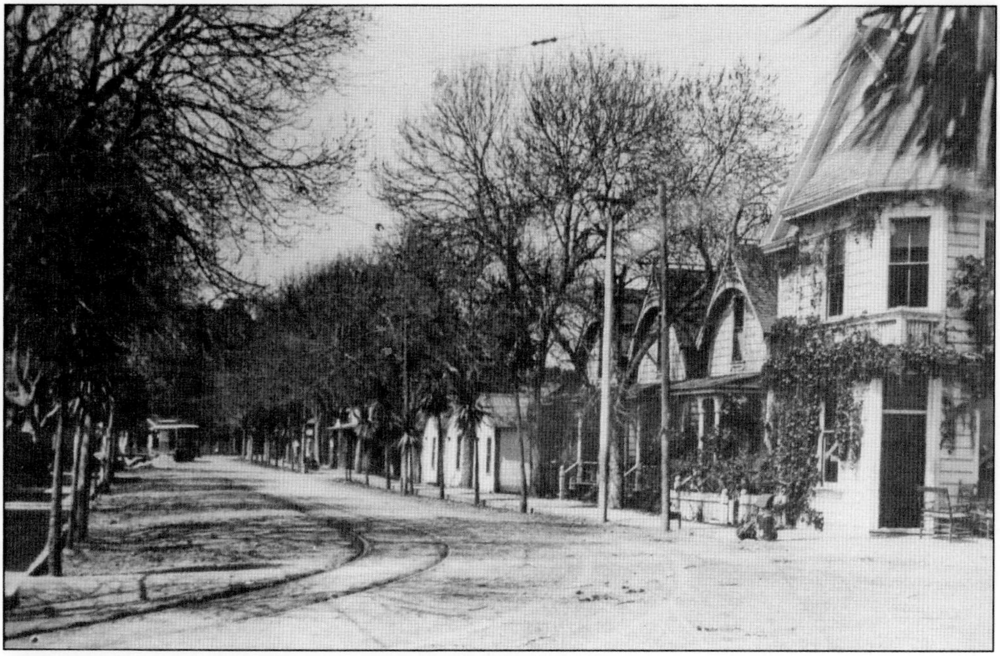

In the distance above, a streetcar on the Union Traction Company line rounds the corner from Capitola Avenue to Stockton Avenue as it begins the westbound return trip to Santa Cruz. The passenger station was moved to the east end of the avenue, below the stairway on Depot Hill, when the loop was rerouted in 1920.

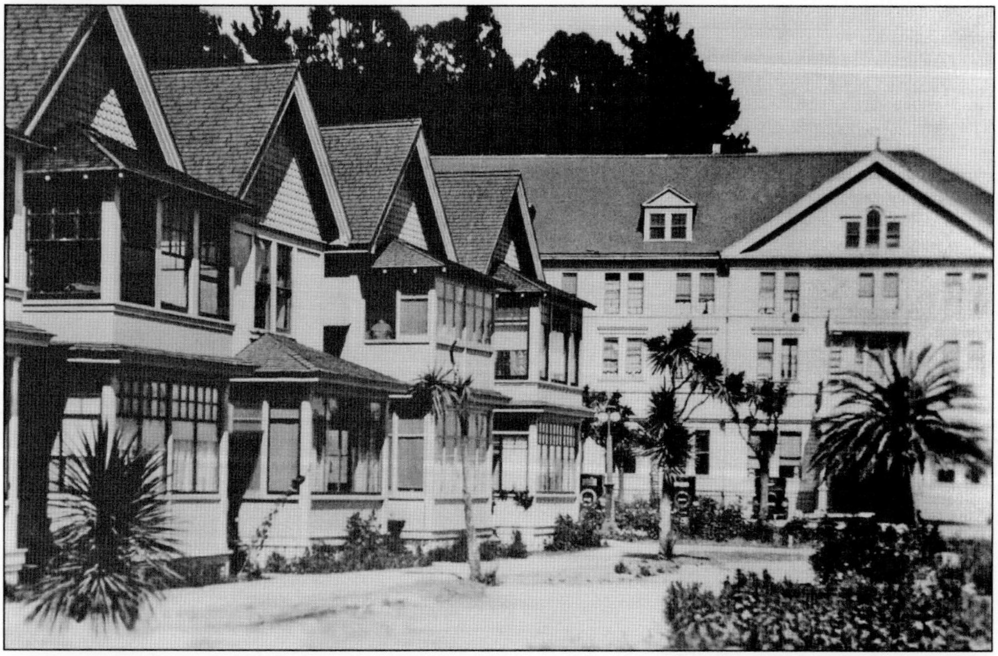

On the Esplanade, the former path of the electric car line was in need of landscaping once the tracks were taken out and the road realigned. Owners of the Six Sisters duplexes quickly and wisely chose to buy the new lots that were created beyond their front doors, where added construction would block the ocean view.

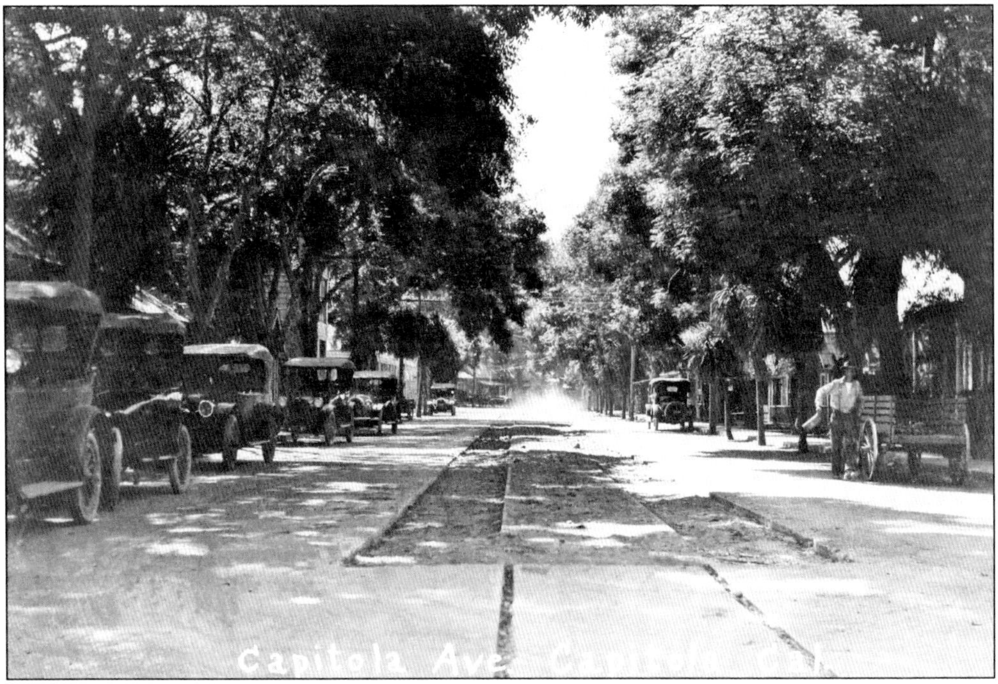

Union Traction Company buses replaced the electric cars in just a few years. The tracks were already being ripped out by 1925. In a later view of the streetscape, a banner invites visitors to "Talk with Fay" about buying a lot from the Capitola Company. Vacationers who had traditionally stayed a month or more now stopped by for an afternoon, and the tourist market was changing. Motor courts and an auto campground appeared on the resort periphery. (Both, courtesy of Gordon van Zuiden.)

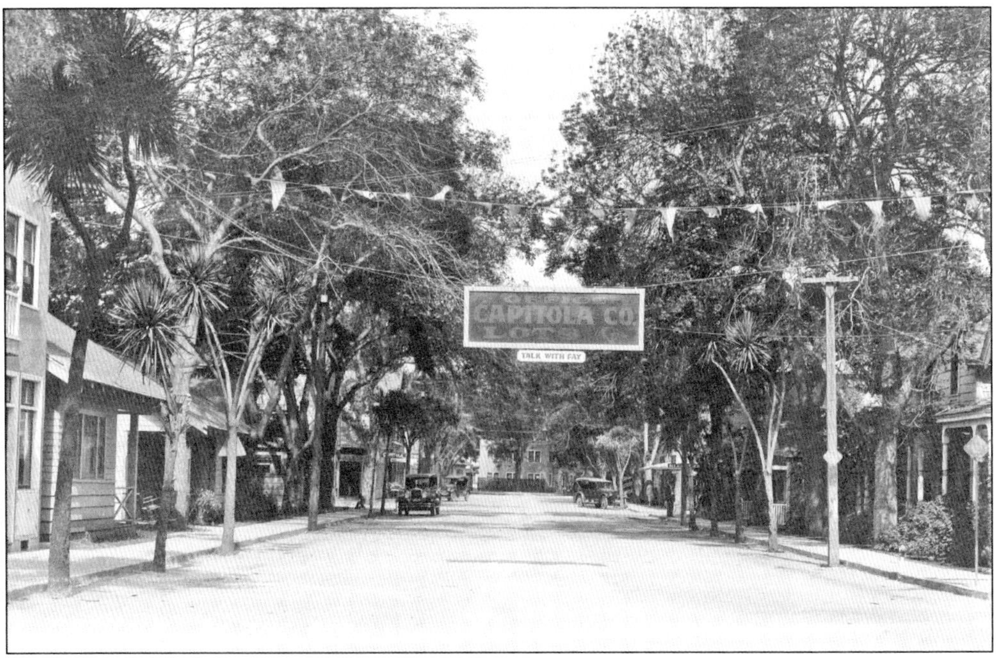

Vacation rentals and lot sales were transacted in the superintendent's building at the corner of Capitola and Bay (Monterey) Avenues. One of Allen Rispin's real estate agents in 1924 was a vaudeville actor and World War I veteran named Walter Brennan (1894–1974). Brennan worked at Capitola a short time before leaving for Hollywood, where he eventually became a three-time Academy Award winner as best supporting actor.

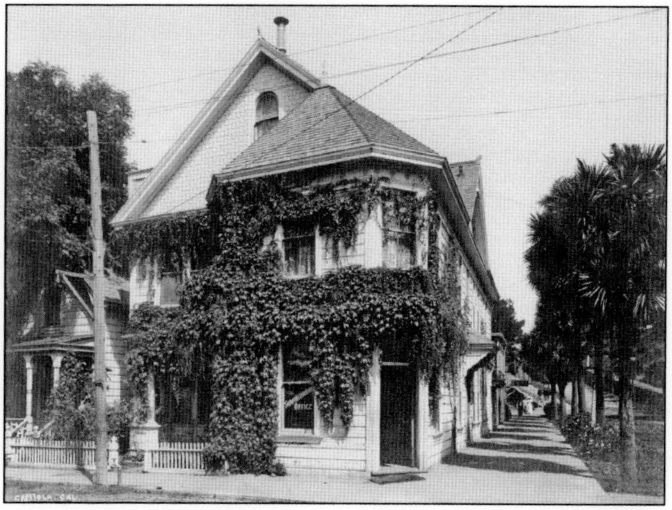

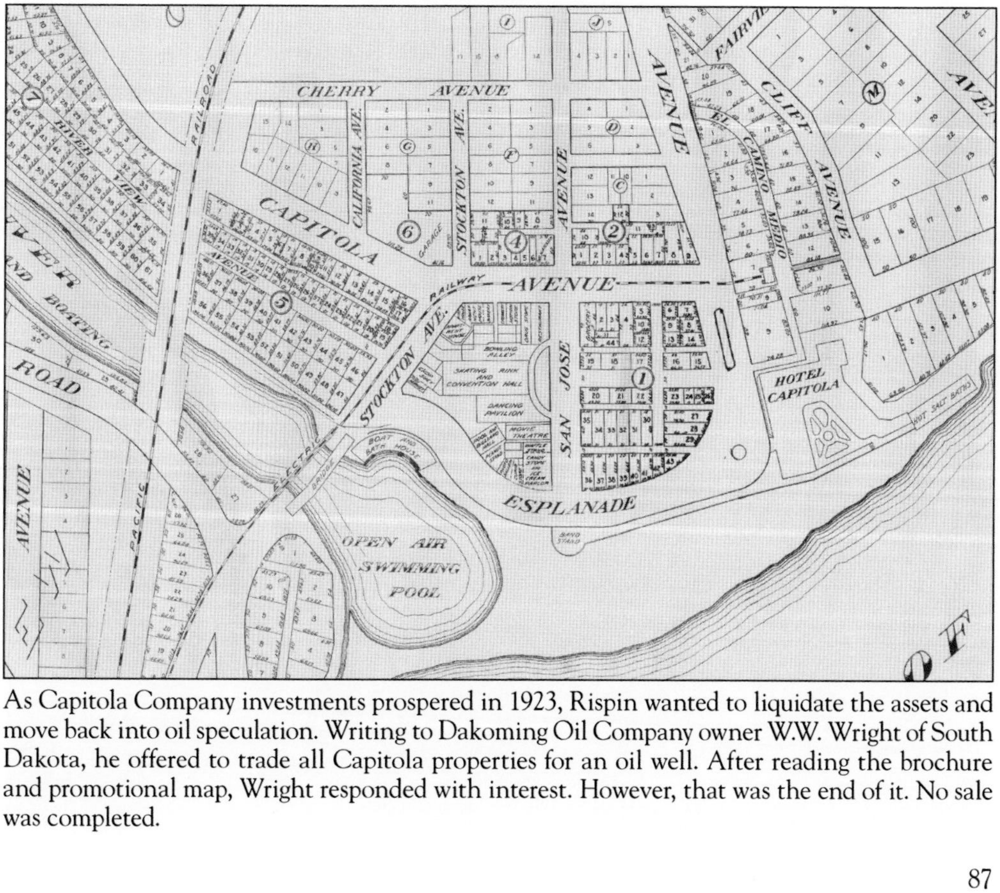

As Capitola Company investments prospered in 1923, Rispin wanted to liquidate the assets and move back into oil speculation. Writing to Dakoming Oil Company owner W.W. Wright of South Dakota, he offered to trade all Capitola properties for an oil well. After reading the brochure and promotional map, Wright responded with interest. However, that was the end of it. No sale was completed.

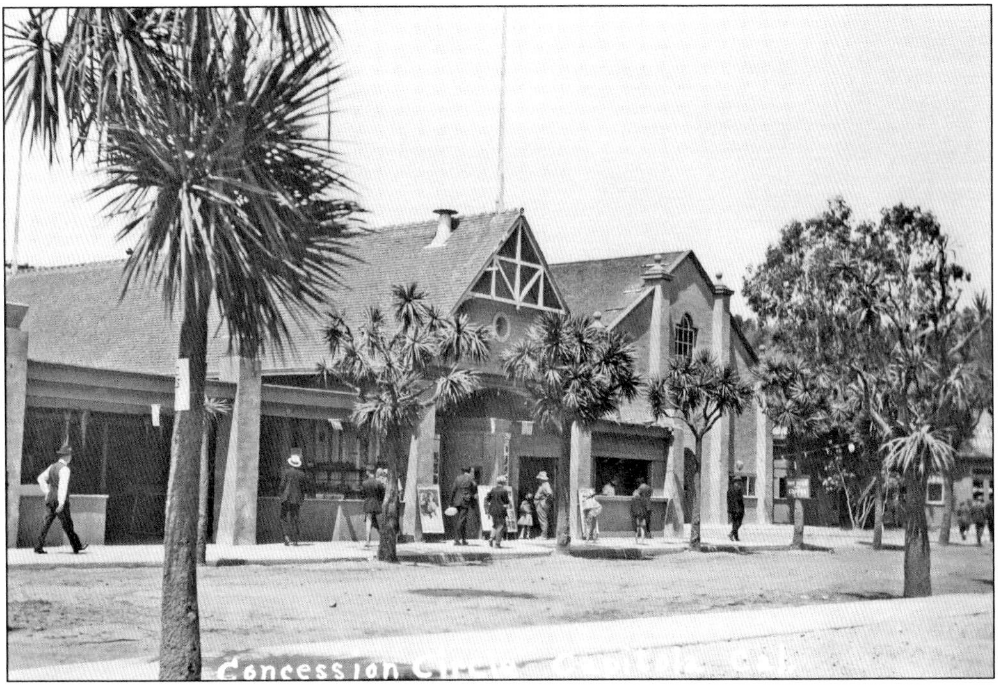

Camp Capitola's 1884 auditorium and roller rink—with its spring floor—was moved toward the beach in 1924 and remodeled in stucco. Welcoming patrons as the Hawaiian Garden nightclub, the dance spot set the rhythm for Capitola's economic success. Connected to an amusement pavilion with several cafés and a movie theater, the ballroom dominated the block between Stockton and San Jose Avenues. It had a Spanish Revival decor with a cobblestone fireplace, waterfall, and fountain. Fifty hammered copper lamps were shaped by Santa Cruz craftsman John Otar, famed as "Otar the Lampmaker."

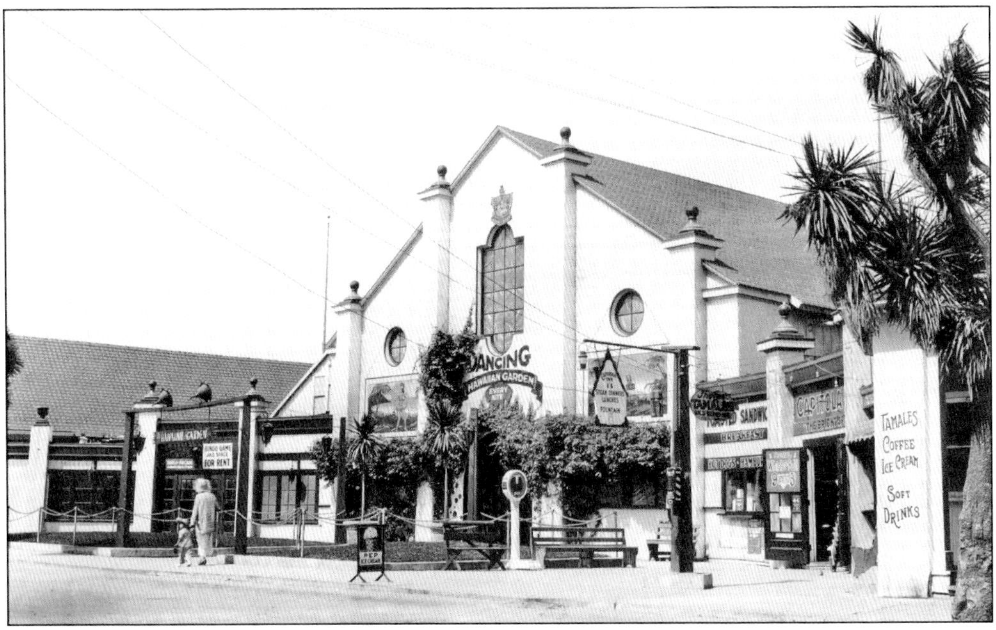

San Francisco Bay Area orchestras played all night long in rotation. Drawing an estimated 9,000 visitors on weekends, the Hawaiian Garden was a prized summer attraction. Predictably, it was also known for good times, as empty hip flasks were usually fished out of the fountain every morning. Since Capitola had no police department and the beach was rarely patrolled by sheriff deputies, the night spot was a Prohibition-era favorite.

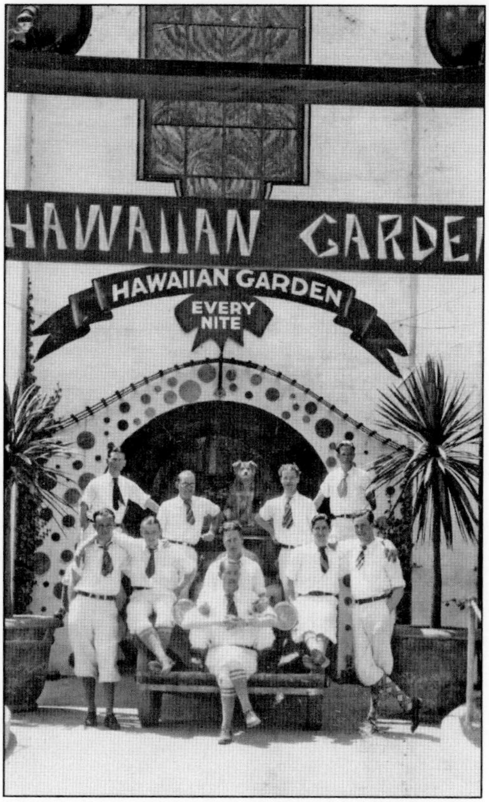

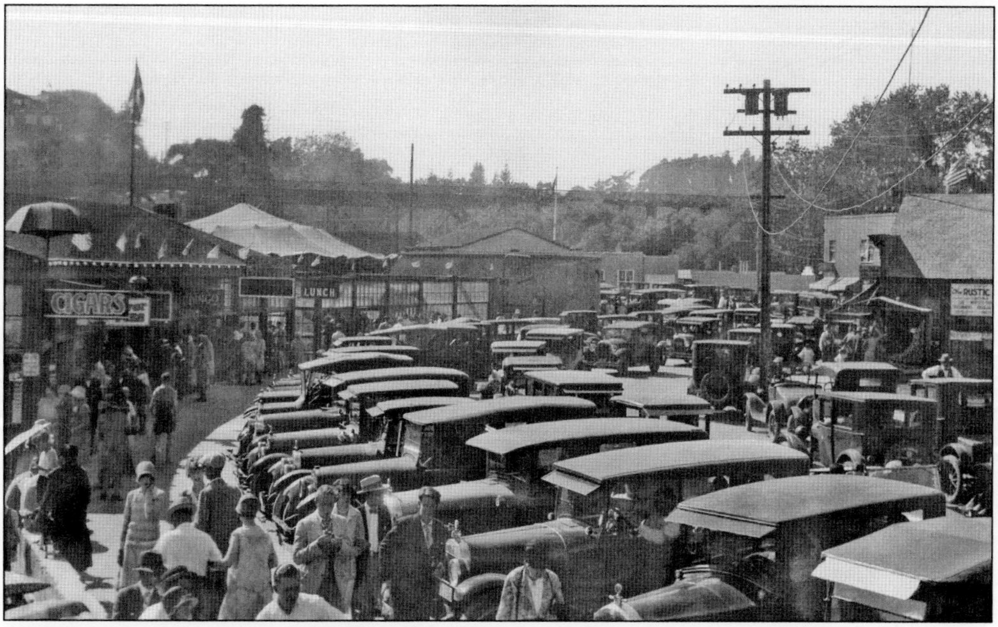

Completion of the Glenwood Highway from San Jose initiated the automobile era in 1923. Only a three-hour ride from San Francisco, Capitola packed in hundreds of vehicles on summer days. The needs of motorists were tended at three village gas stations and at least two garage repair shops by 1928. (Courtesy of Gordon van Zuiden.)

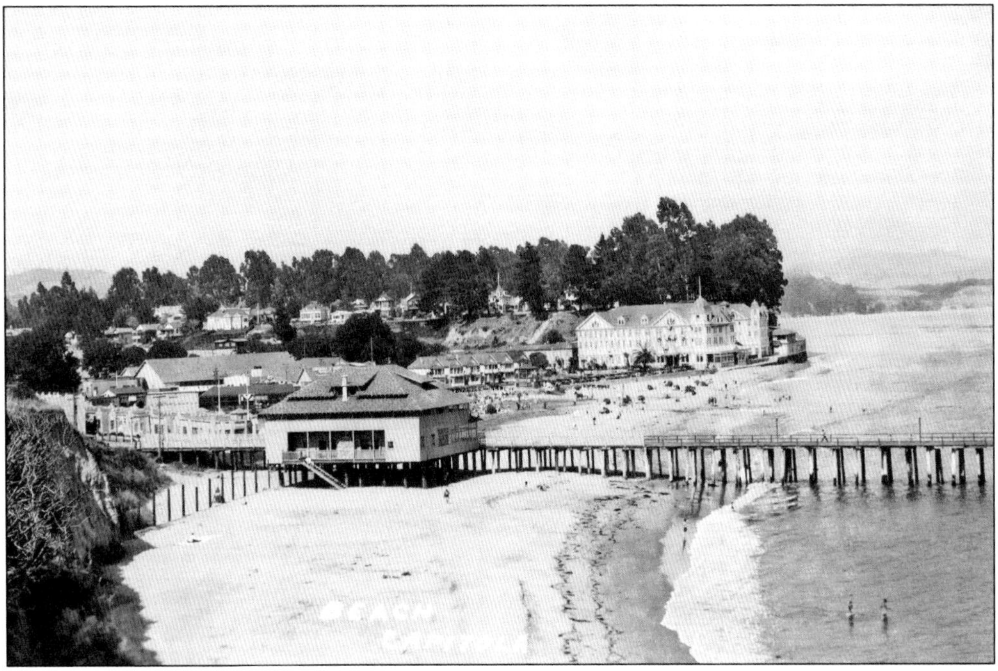

As soon as Frank Reanier, the former Capitola superintendent under F.A. Hihn, was appointed as a Santa Cruz County supervisor in 1928, he called for an end to late-night carousing. Meanwhile, Allen Rispin himself had become the target of rumors about bootlegging and rum-running. Gossip started with his growing financial troubles. That summer, 48 acres of Capitola Company properties—including the Rispin mansion—were transferred to developer C.E. Blanchard of San Francisco. Rispin insisted everything was fine. He diverted the public's attention to his newest venture on the wharf, the Capitola Light Tackle Club, which opened with fanfare as a comfortably designed mecca for sportsmen.

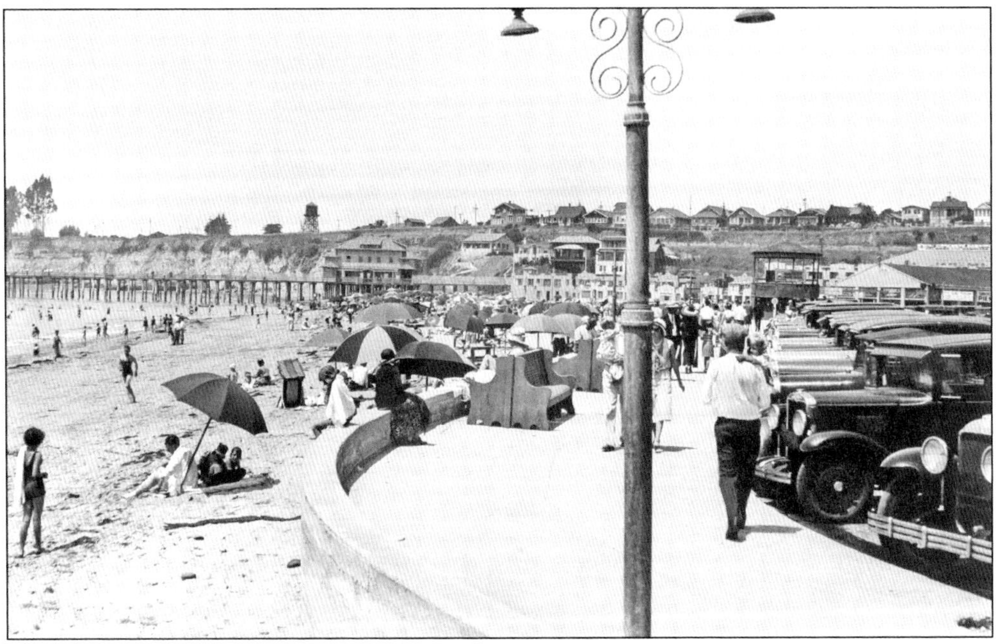

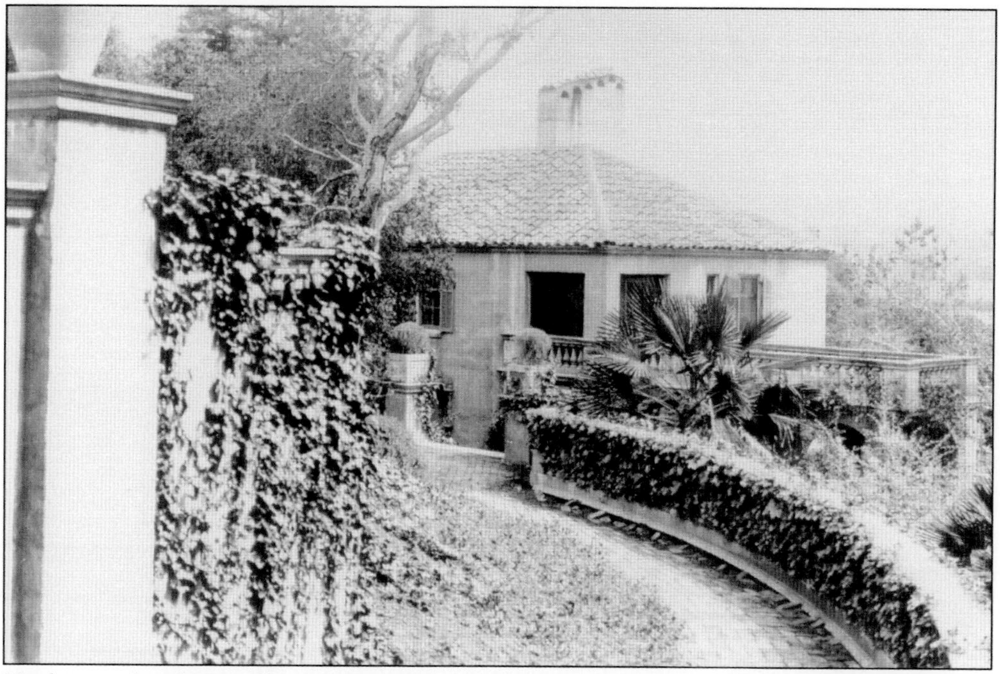

His fortune shrinking, Allen Rispin sank his last hopes for success on a golf course. Through real estate agent Harlan P. Kessler—a man later to become Capitola's first mayor—the resort's owner was able to recover his mansion in 1928. He then announced a plan to convert it into a 50-room clubhouse for golfers. Since no golf course existed nearby, however, the idea landed in the rough.

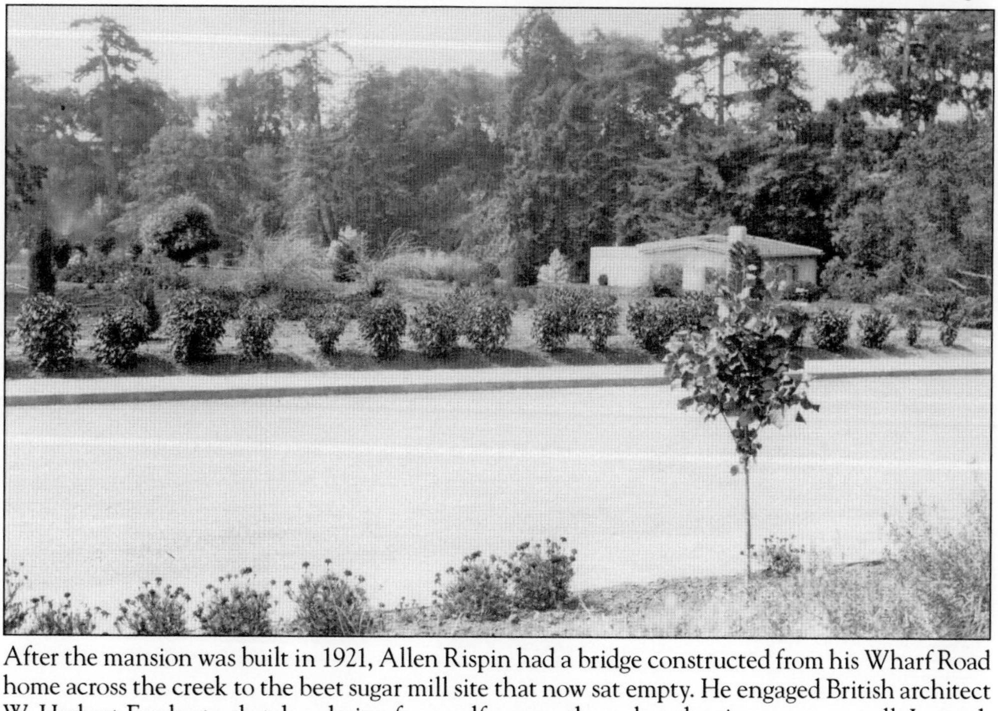

After the mansion was built in 1921, Allen Rispin had a bridge constructed from his Wharf Road home across the creek to the beet sugar mill site that now sat empty. He engaged British architect W. Herbert Fowler to sketch a design for a golf course there, but the site was too small. Instead, the tract was subdivided in 1929 as Riverview Terrace.

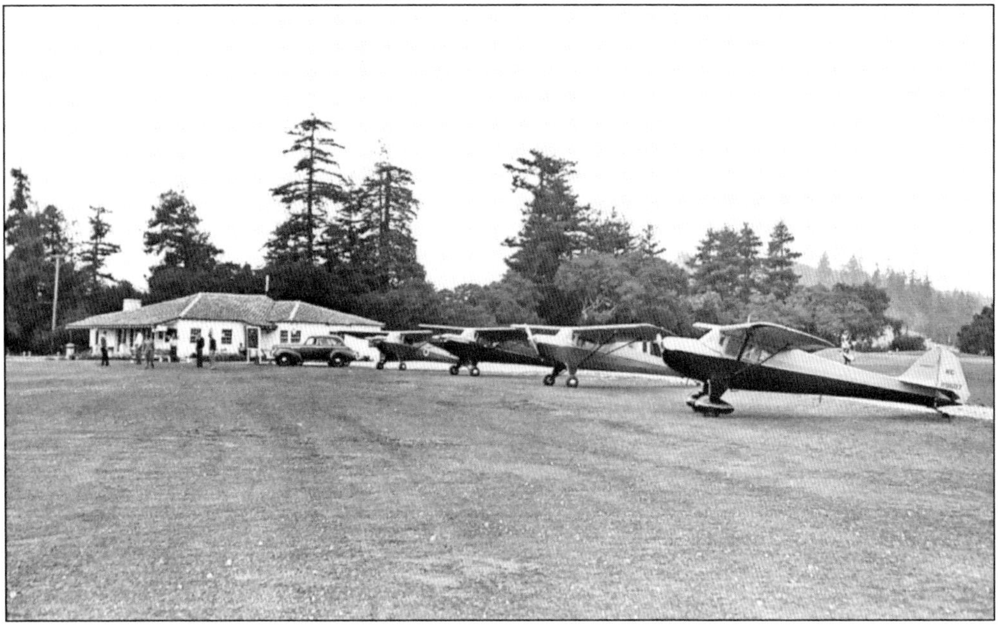

In 1928–1929, about the time Cypress Point golf course in Monterey was created, Allen Rispin developed his 300-acre Soquel property about a mile from Capitola. The 18-hole Monterey Golf and Country Club was set along Soquel Drive, shown after an airplane landing in the 1940s. Today, the property is the Monterey Heights housing subdivision, which retains such golf-themed names as Fairway and Putter Drives. (Courtesy of Gordon van Zuiden.)

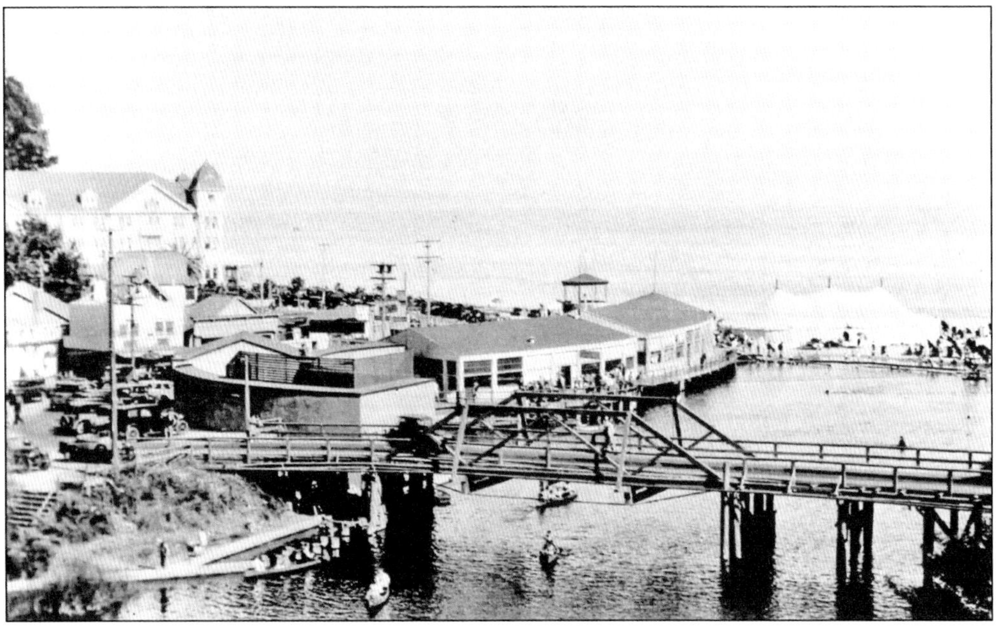

Preparations to sell off Capitola Company holdings were broadcast just after the golf course opened in July 1929. Auctioneers attempted the sale of 1,500 business and residential lots during a tent auction on the beach during the week of August 16. The wharf, esplanade concessions, and Rispin's estate were sold at the mansion. Bids for the Soquel property were taken on the golf course. (Courtesy of Norman Davis.)

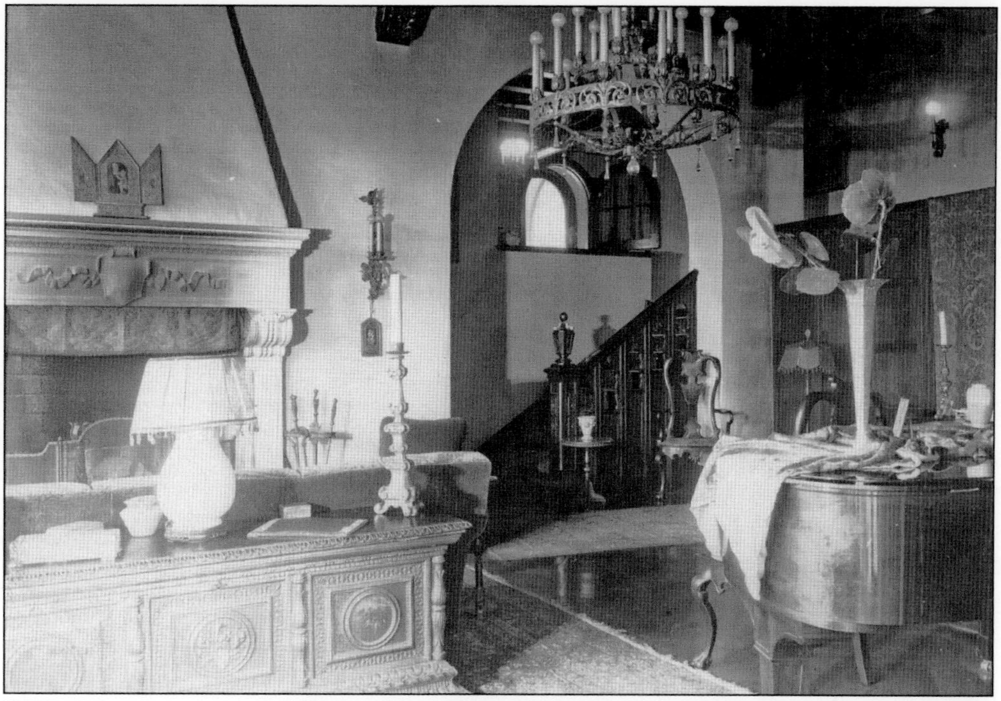

Rispin properties were tangled in court actions for years after the 1929 auction. Some were sold at sheriff's sales. Burlingame millionaire Robert Hays Smith, high bidder for the mansion and golf course, was actually one of Capitola Company's original investors and paid less than $20,000 for the mansion. Covertly, Rispin went to work for Smith in the San Francisco Bay Area, dropping from sight so thoroughly that Capitola residents never knew what happened to him. Smith's son, Nicol, stayed at the mansion occasionally in the early 1930s, checking on his father's investments.

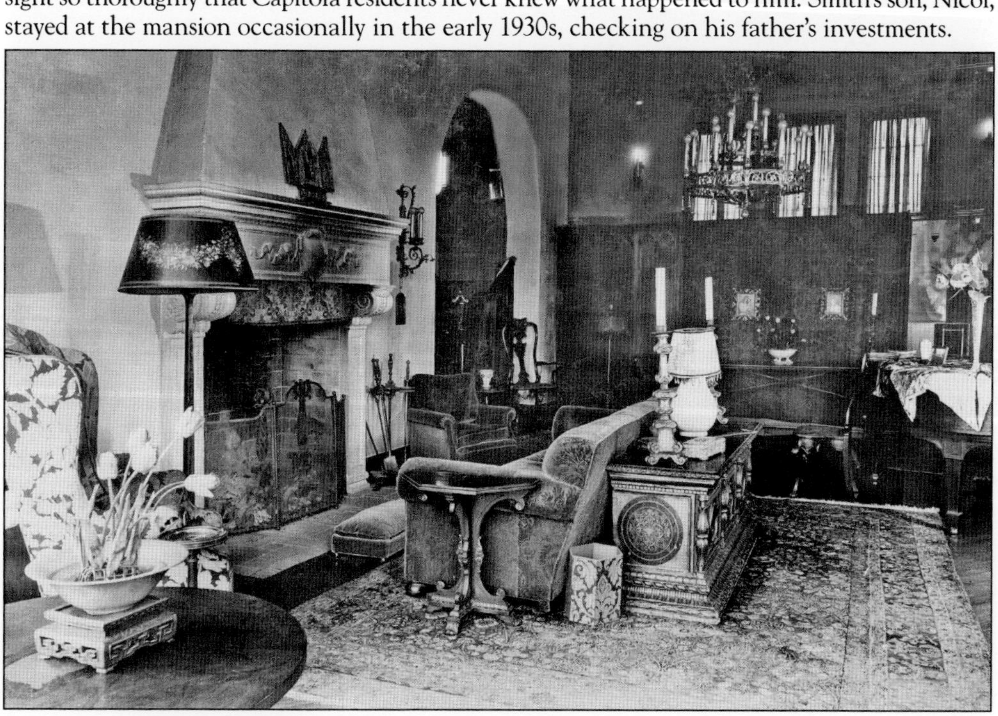

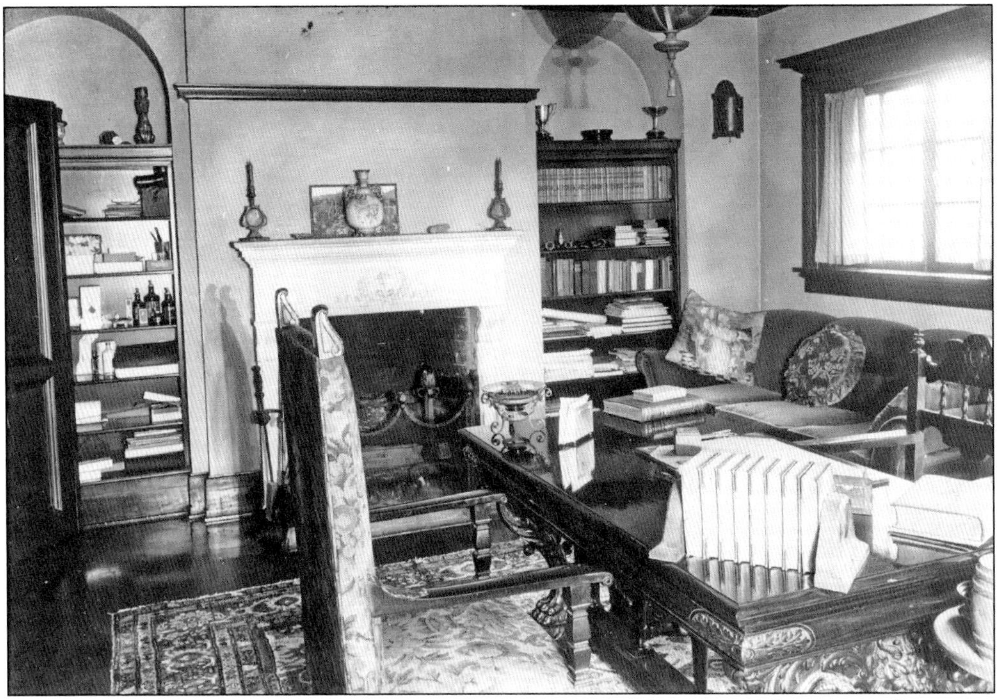

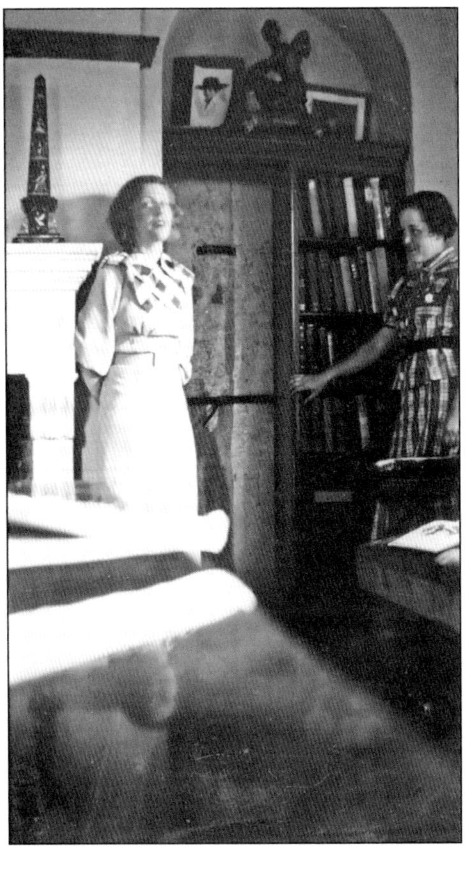

When Rispin disappeared from Capitola in 1930, he left behind unfinished business. It took years, for example, to determine legal ownership of Capitola's wharf and streets. Rumors about Rispin's Prohibition-era lifestyle magnified as the public gained access to the mansion. The bookcase nearest the library window, above, conceals a secret compartment and passageway. Another curious feature of the house was a hidden passage leading to a wine cellar that still contained its wine racks 20 years later.

Among the first visitors to discover the bookcase's hidden sliding door were a group of students and teachers from the San Francisco Bay Area who were visiting as the guests of Nicol Smith in May 1935. Jeanico Hill, left, and Charlotte Williams were thrilled with their find.

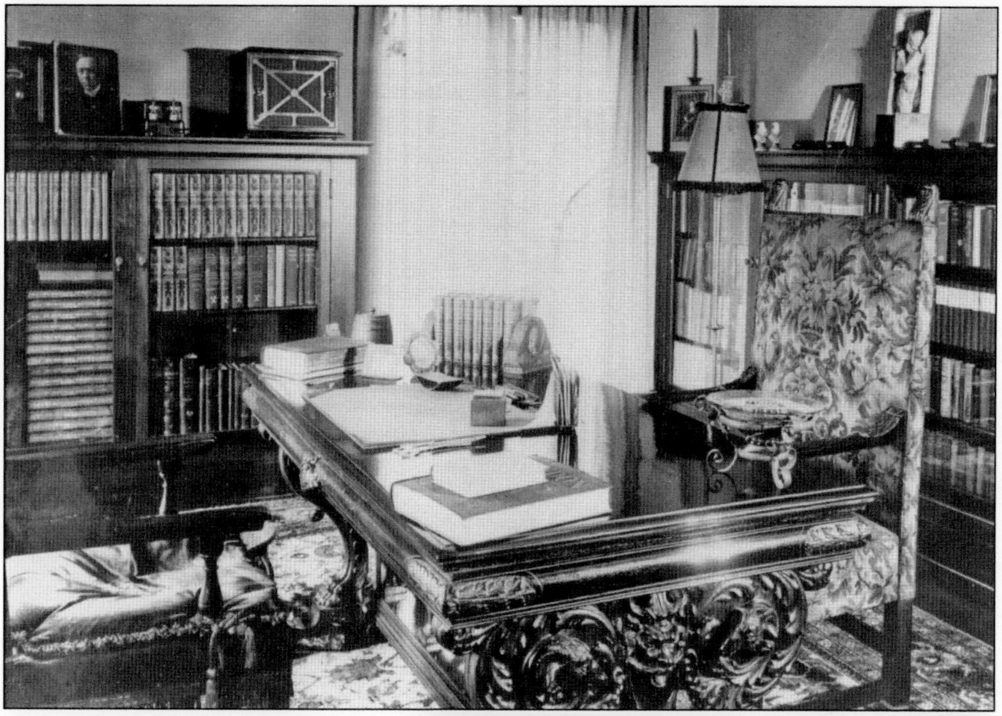

Oil industrialist Robert Smith was worth about $3 million in 1920, but he suffered financially during the Depression and was barely able to hold onto his investment within five years of his Capitola purchase. Elaborate furniture for the house, shown above, had been acquired by Smith from the James L. Flood estate in San Francisco.

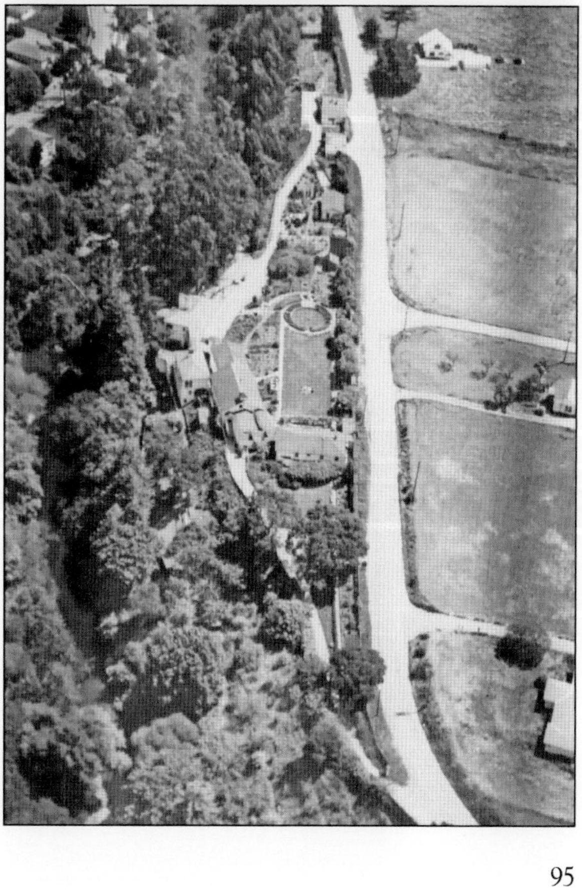

Robert Smith lost the mansion through foreclosure in 1936. The house stood empty until 1941, when it was secured for use by the Poor Clares, a cloistered order of nuns. Visible toward the bottom of this 1957 aerial photograph are the convent's chapel and novitiate. These additional buildings were removed after the mansion was listed in 1991 in the National Register of Historic Places. (Courtesy of Covello and Covello Photography.)

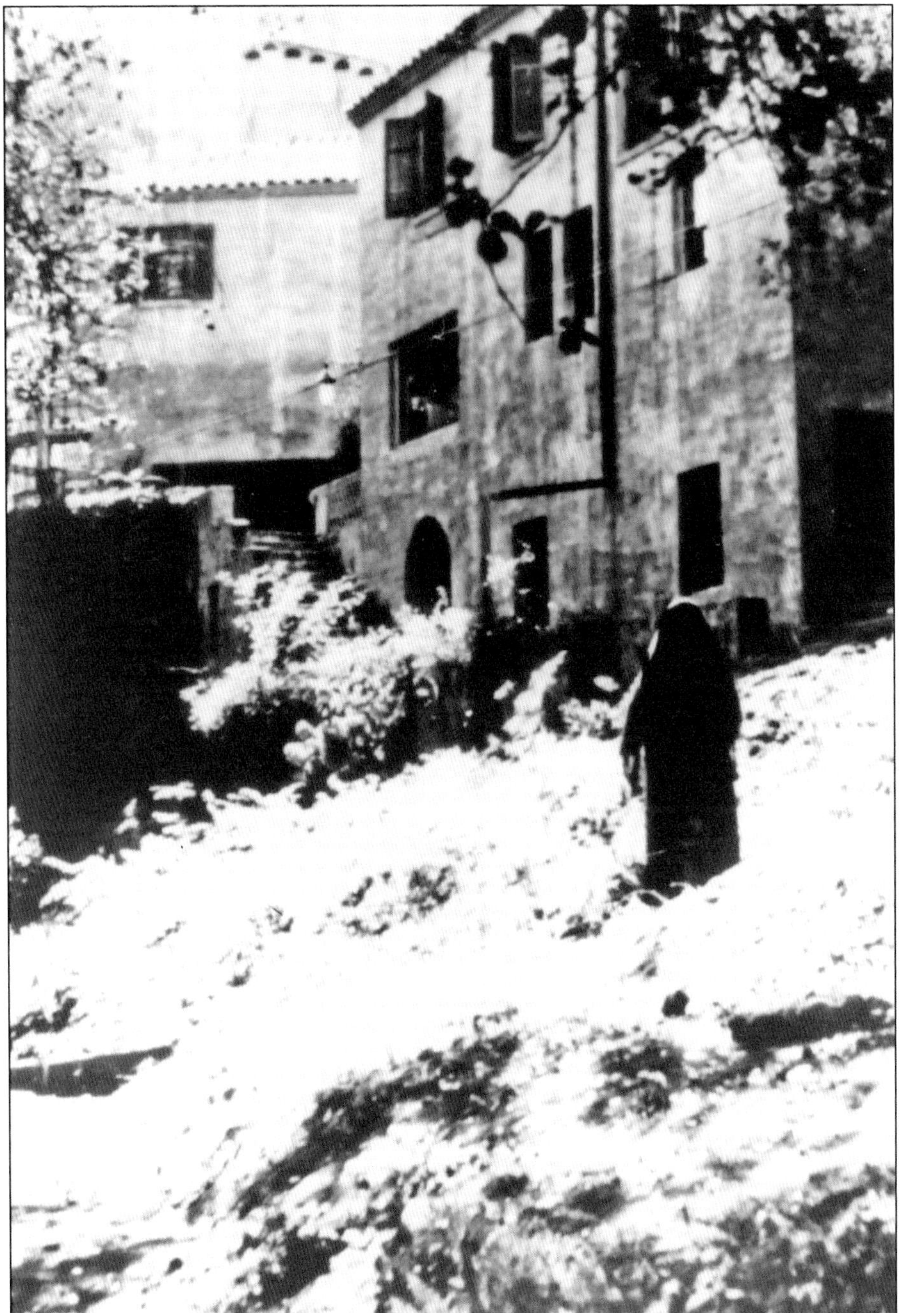

Years after the Poor Clares lived at the mansion, one of the sisters told how the nuns were surprised to find a labyrinth of pipes in the old wine cellar and a fireplace with six flues, including one blocked off with tile. Their sleeping quarters were in cubicles cut from larger rooms. Water was a problem. The heating was bad, the interior cold, and a number of the older sisters had arthritis. Another difficulty was uninvited guests. As a cloistered order, the nuns were taken aback when snoops wandered up the creek to peek in their windows. Finally, in 1959, the Poor Clares moved to comfortable, more spacious quarters in Aptos. (Courtesy of Sonny Futche.)

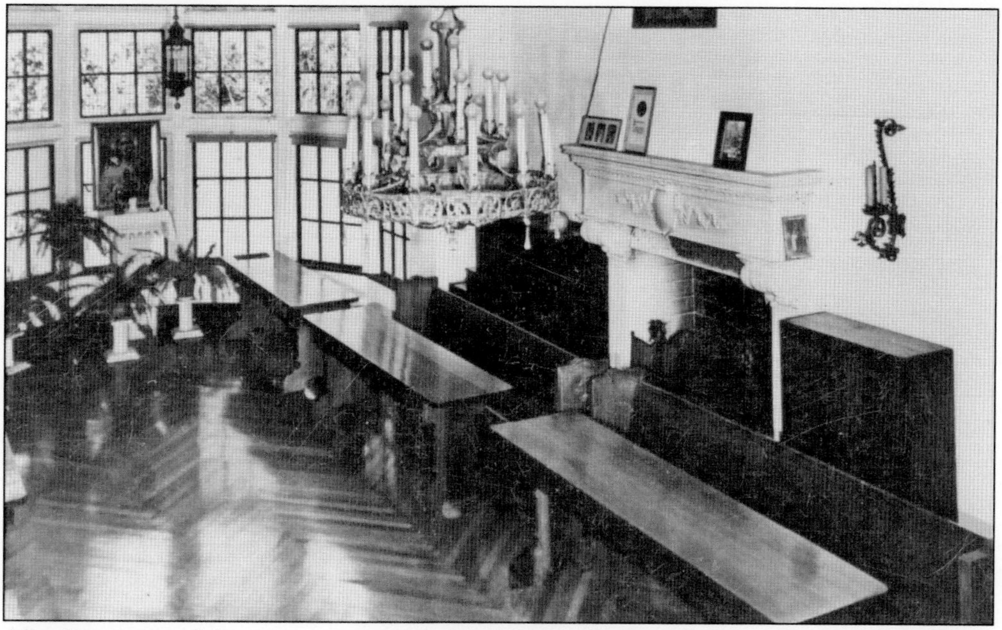

Allen Rispin visited the convent only once. A widower, he had returned to Santa Cruz County with his son Alan and lived in Boulder Creek in 1944. They moved later to the Watsonville YMCA. Alan suffered seizures there that ended his life in 1946. Soon afterward, Capitola's former owner had a stroke. He died in San Francisco and is buried in an unmarked grave at Olivet Memorial Park in Colma.

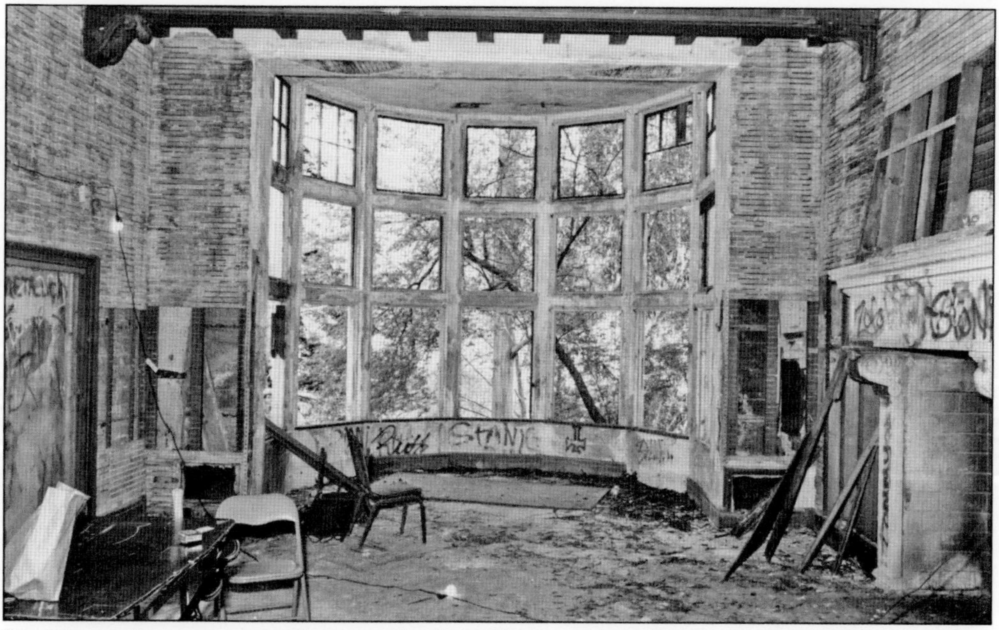

Rispin's mansion was technically vacant for about 50 years, although it was a home to scores of youthful vagabonds in the 1960s. Gradually, thrill-seekers destroyed the interior. Numerous development projects were debated until Capitola bought the property in 1985. After extensive study by citizen committees, city officials, and investors, a contract was finally signed in 2009 for a $14-million, 25-room hotel project. (Courtesy of Eric Fingal of Covello and Covello Photography.)

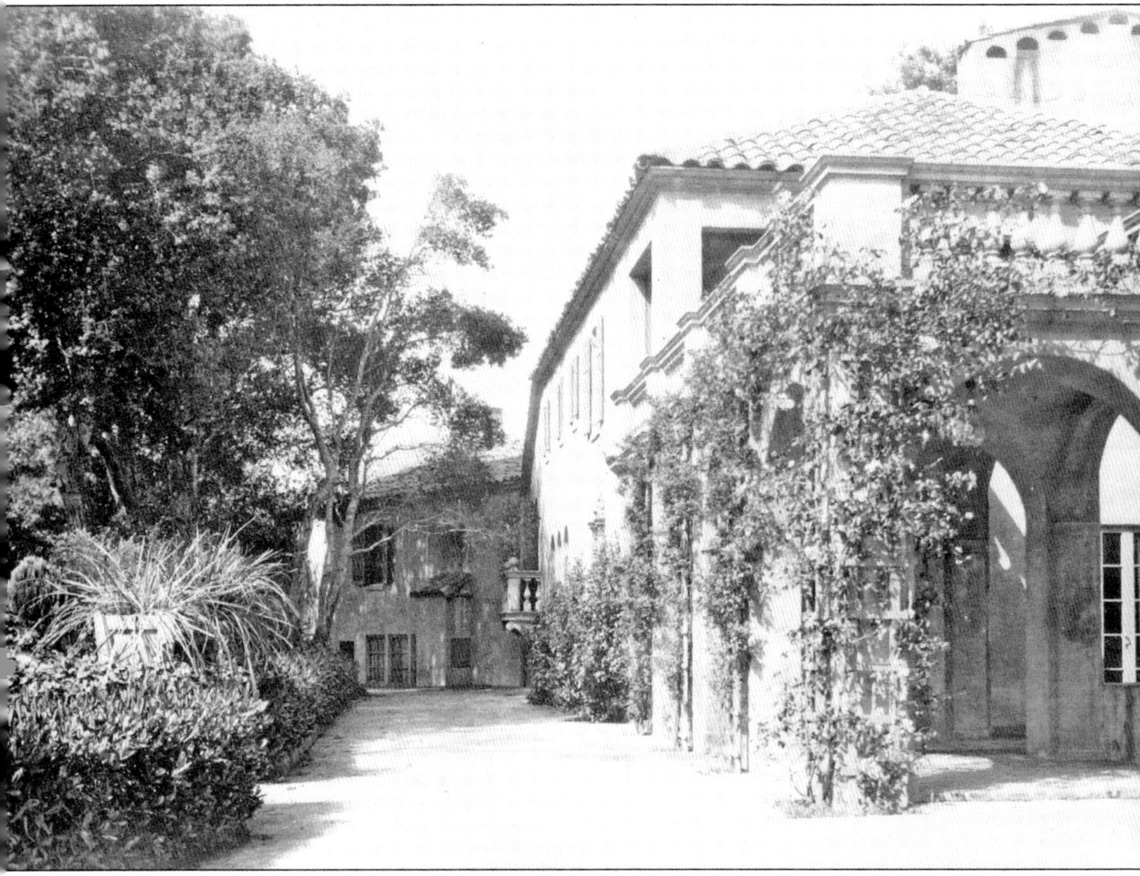

Shortly after 4:00 a.m., on May 28, 2009, fire destroyed nearly 75 percent of the four-story mansion. The blaze might have been set deliberately. The roof came down, and all the floors were in flames. Early in 2012, the city of Capitola hired crews to mothball and preserve the exterior. Inside debris was removed, windows sealed, the roof replaced, fencing and security doors installed, and a new coat of paint applied. City options now include the creation of a public park around the historic building. Meanwhile, attempts to climb the fence around the structure, along with legends and ghost sightings, continue. This photograph was taken by Al Lent about 1935.

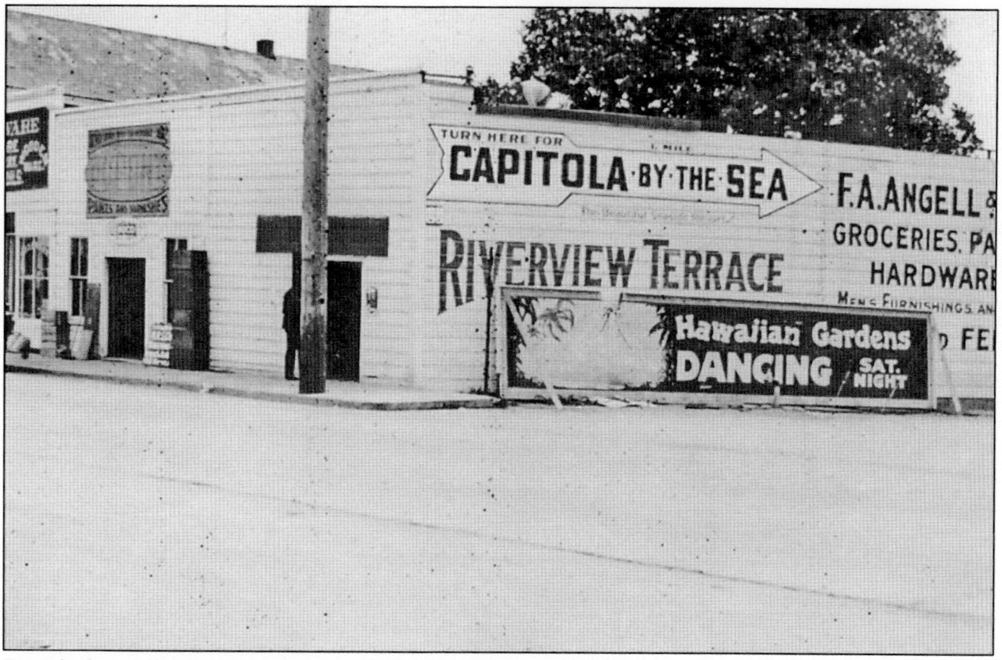

Even before Allen Rispin left town, Capitola and Soquel residents were increasingly vexed over the lack of services such as water and fire protection that Capitola Company was obliged to provide. An improvement club was organized in 1928, and although it never happened, discussions pondered a merger as the city of Sotola. Cooperation between the two villages continues, although each has chosen to retain its separate identity. Pictured above is Angell's Store at the corner of Soquel Drive and Porter Street in Soquel. Painted signs direct motorists toward Capitola entertainments, seen below in 1928. (Above, courtesy of Ted Maddock; below, courtesy of Gordon van Zuiden.)

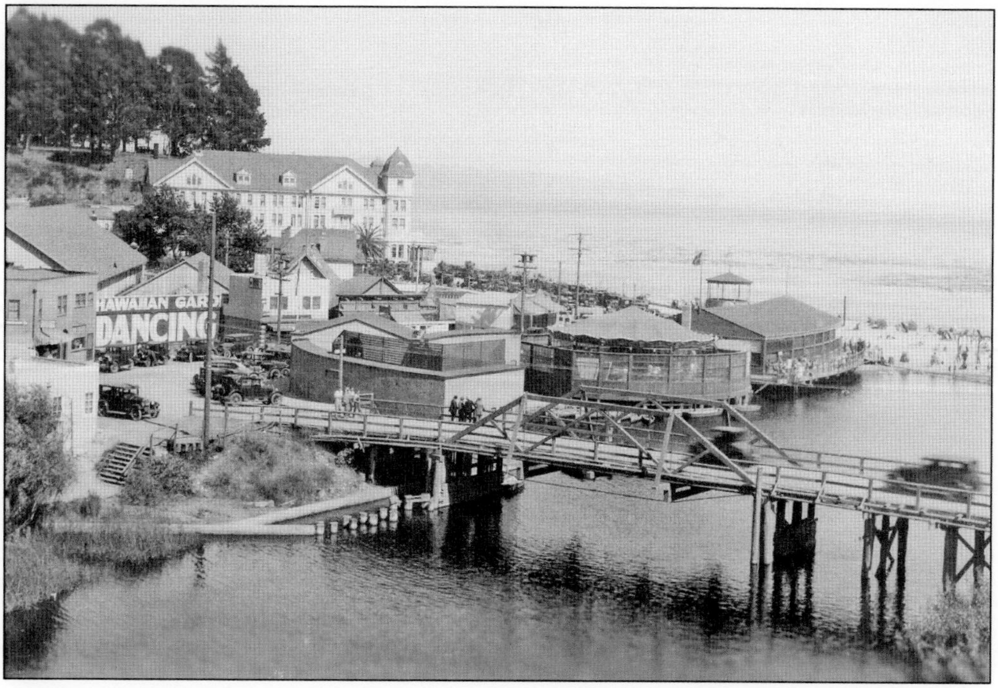

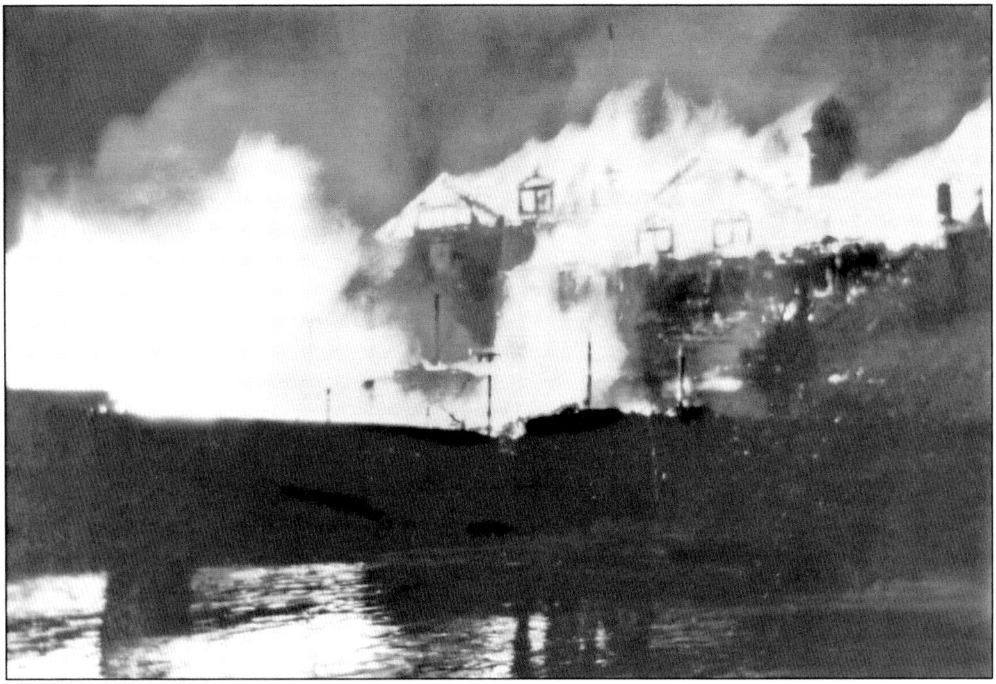

Teddy Woodhouse was at the Hotel Capitola on December 16, 1929, planning for a New Year's Eve party. As twilight approached, he walked the path up to his Cliff Avenue home. A while later, he heard the honking of car horns. Stepping onto his porch, Woodhouse saw flames shooting through the hotel roof. By morning, Capitola's celebrated landmark was gone. The fire was blamed on faulty electrical wiring.

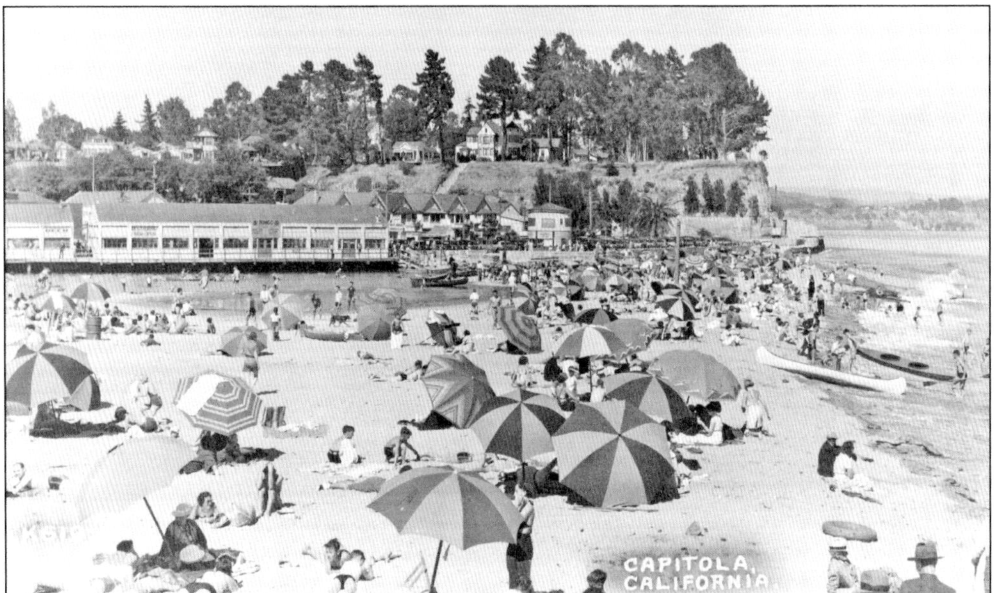

As the Great Depression began, Capitola faced a worrisome future without the advantages of private ownership. Fortunately, vacationers still arrived in droves every summer and filled the beach, seemingly oblivious to any changes in their surroundings. (Courtesy of Gordon van Zuiden.)

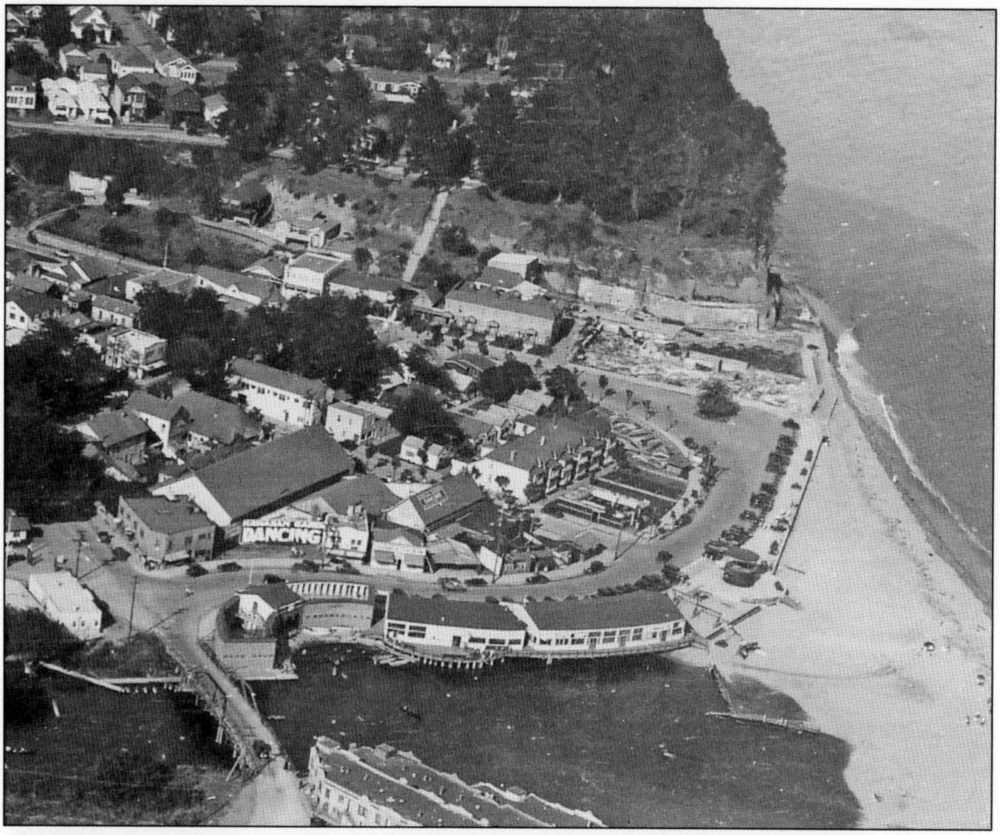

The 1930 aerial photograph above shows the aftermath of the Hotel Capitola fire and the debris under the bluff. The Hawaiian Garden nightclub is the long building at left nested in the block bordered by Capitola Avenue, the Esplanade, and San Jose and Stockton Avenues. In February 1933, all of these buildings were destroyed in an early morning fire. The blaze started at the theater and spread quickly. Firefighters struggled to get water pressure, which had been minimal for years. The only survivor, the Canepa Fish Market on the corner of the Esplanade and Stockton Avenue, was saved because the family was able to pump water from Soquel Creek.

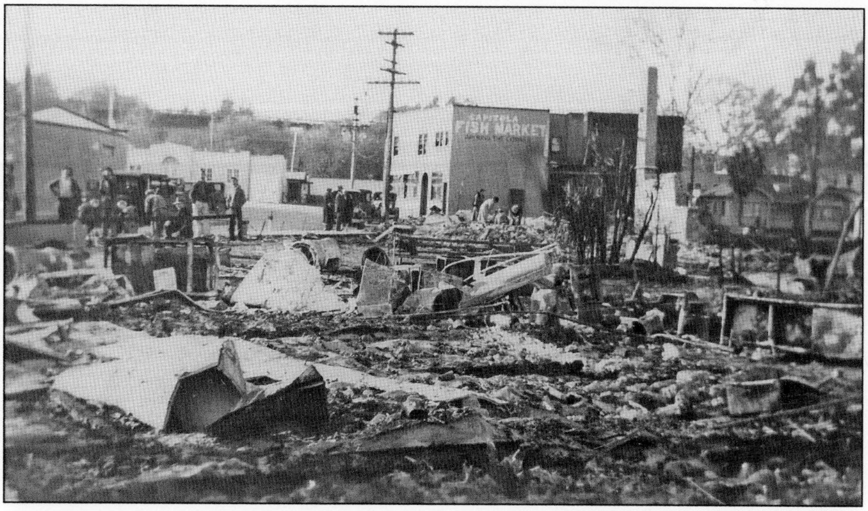

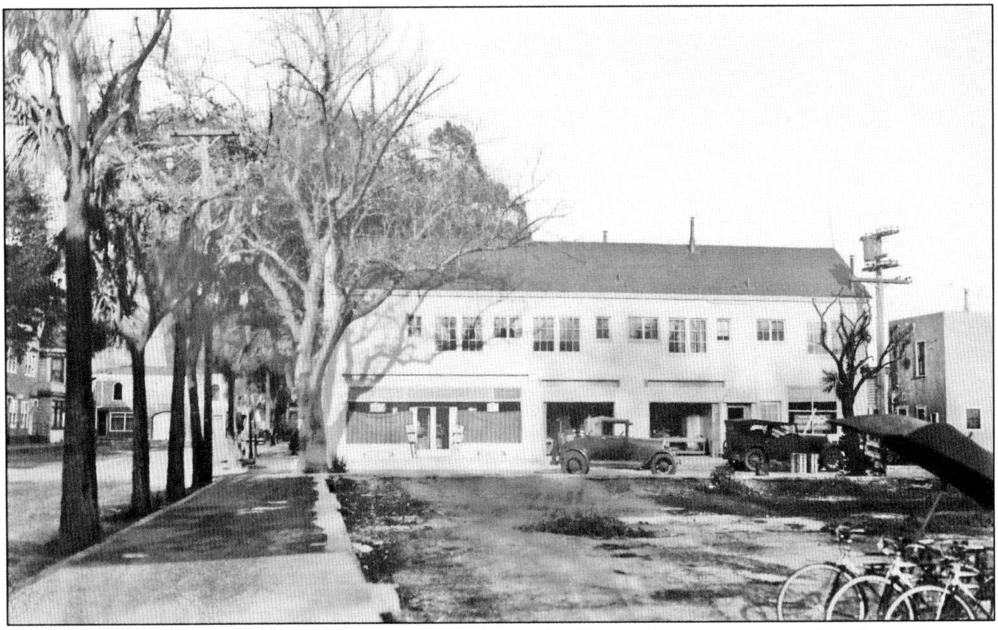

A rare photograph taken after the 1933 fire shows the Dunn Apartments on San Jose Avenue. Sleeping upstairs, postmistress Lulu Dunn was the first to see the blaze and sound the alarm. Six weeks later, a new and cheaply built pavilion opened on the site of the Hawaiian Garden. Named the Big Top, it was soon dubbed "the Big Flop," as it was a graceless stand-in for its predecessor. (Courtesy of Gordon van Zuiden.)

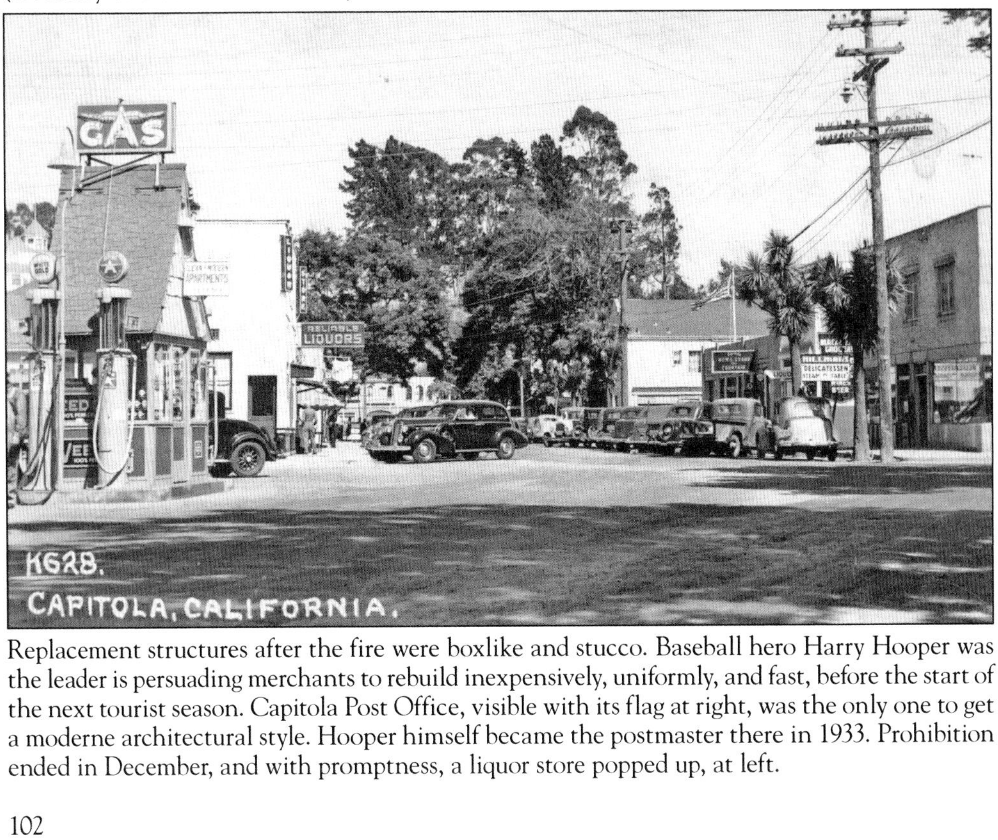

Replacement structures after the fire were boxlike and stucco. Baseball hero Harry Hooper was the leader is persuading merchants to rebuild inexpensively, uniformly, and fast, before the start of the next tourist season. Capitola Post Office, visible with its flag at right, was the only one to get a moderne architectural style. Hooper himself became the postmaster there in 1933. Prohibition ended in December, and with promptness, a liquor store popped up, at left.

Six

Guns, Gliders, and the National Guard

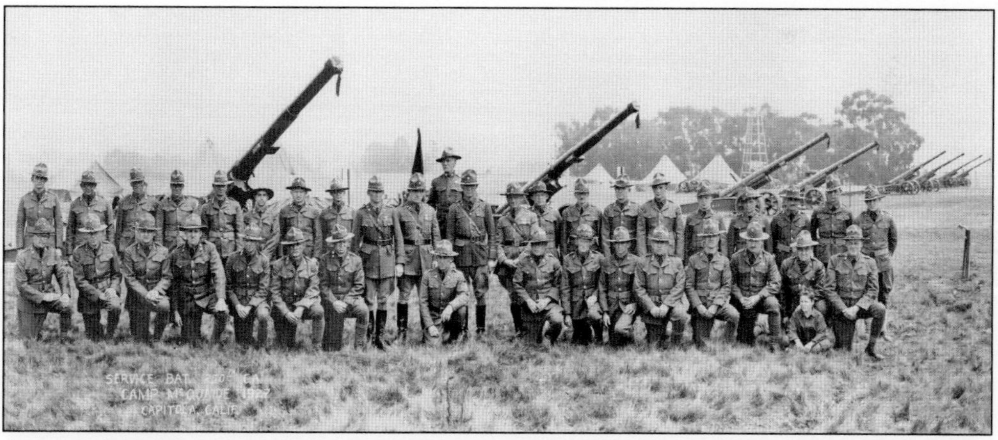

An anti-aircraft battalion training camp known as Camp McQuaide was initially set up in Santa Cruz for the 63rd Coast Artillery, but when that location proved inadequate, F.A. Hihn's eastern field at Capitola was chosen instead. The service battalion of the 250th Coast Artillery posed for this photograph in 1927. The camp was named for National Guard chaplain Joseph P. McQuaide, who died in 1924, shortly before the encampment was founded.

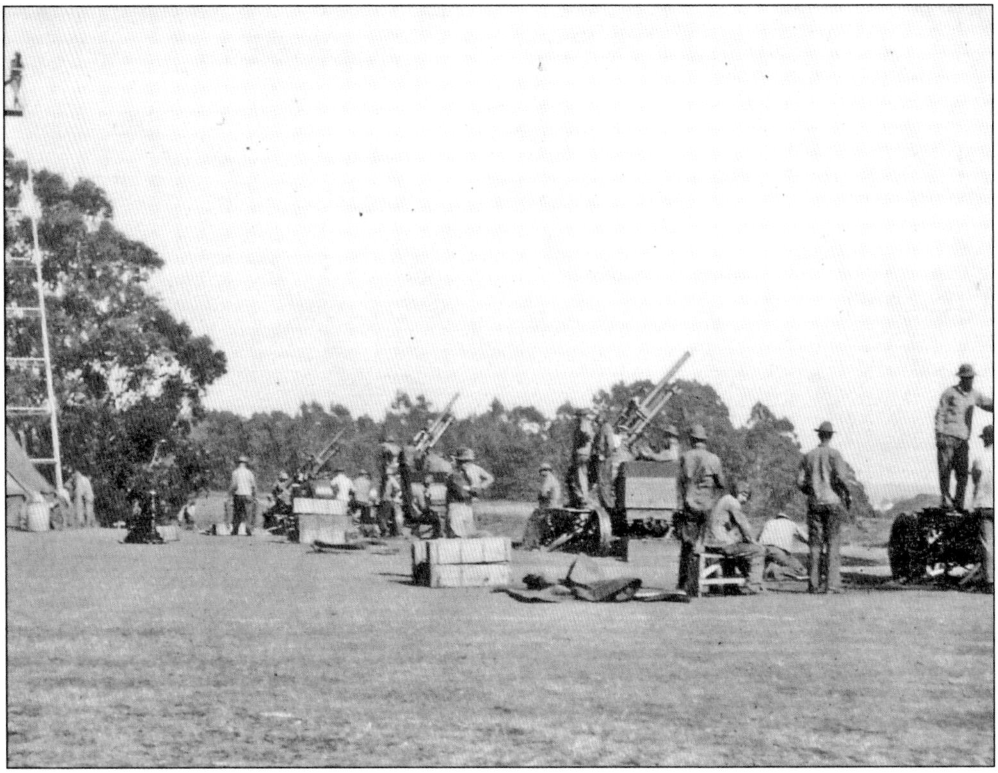

For several weeks every summer the compound of tents, barracks, guns, and airplanes stretched across the 27-acre tract. Camp quarters were set up near Capitola's eastern boundary. Every summer, a large shipment of munitions and weaponry was delivered, and the guns were discharged at targets towed either by airplane or by boat. Firings were heard in Santa Cruz, continuing daily until all the ammunition was spent. Shown are scenes from a firing practice in 1928. (Both, courtesy of Cecilia Riddell.)

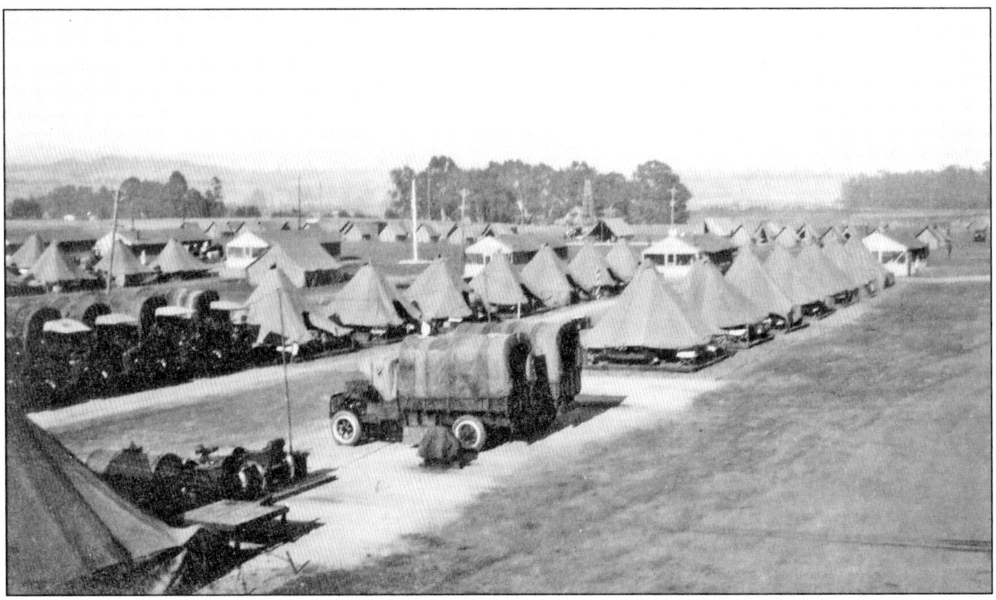

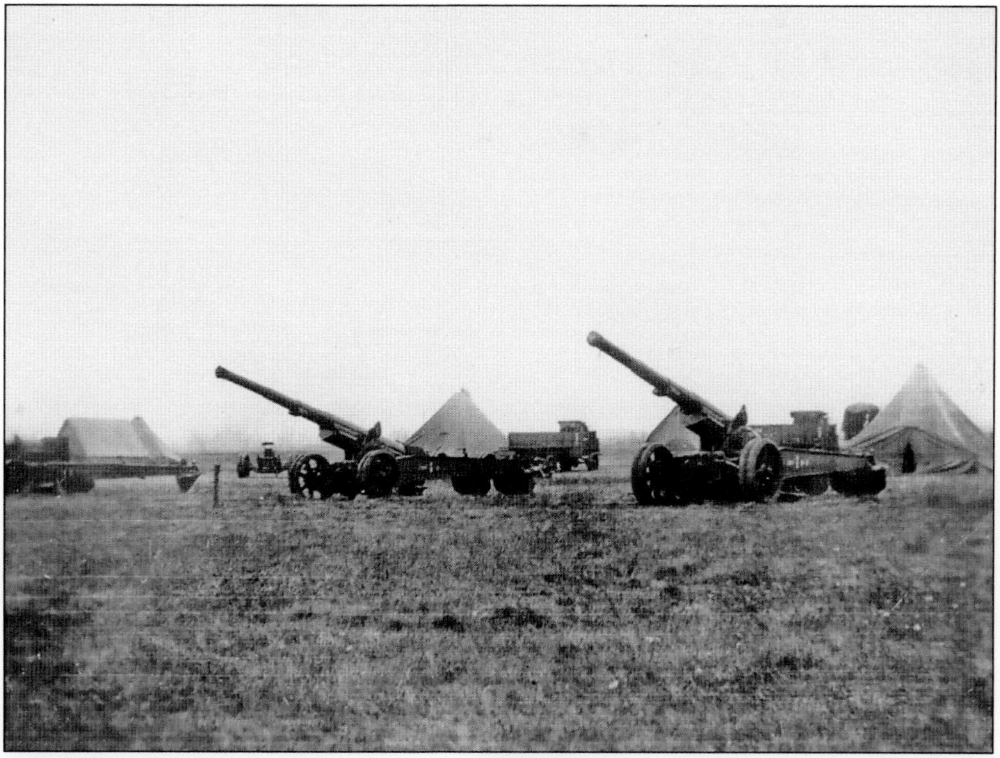

In 1928, Battery B of the 63rd Coast Artillery Unit pointed its guns offshore, toward China Beach (known today as New Brighton Beach State Park). The safety officer in an observation tower signaled to hold off when fishing boats or passenger trains were in the line of fire. Since Capitola fishermen routinely worked along the coastline, the warnings were imperative. (Courtesy of Cecilia Riddell.)

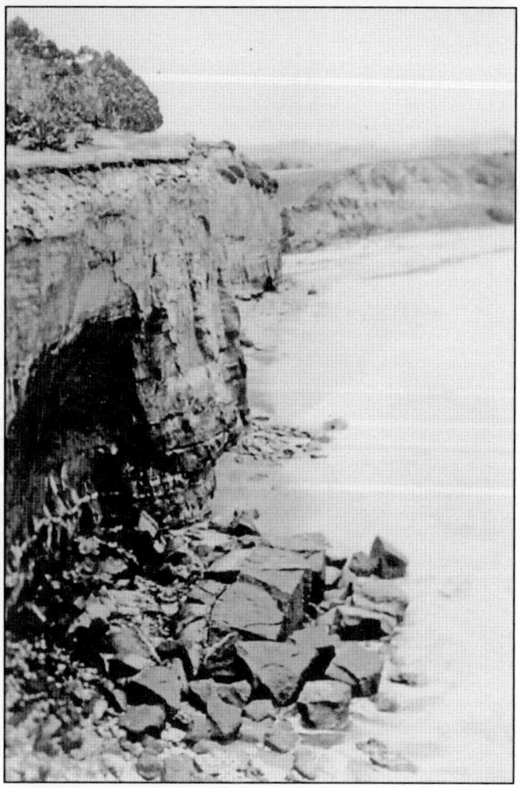

Bluff erosion was a concern by the early 1930s. Lewis Hanchett, owner of the El Salto family retreat on Depot Hill, argued that reverberations from the big guns weakened the cliff face. Neighboring ranchers were upset about the stress reactions of chickens and rabbits. Complaints eventually led to the 1938 relocation of Camp McQuaide to a site on San Andreas Road near Watsonville, occupied today by Monterey Bay Academy.

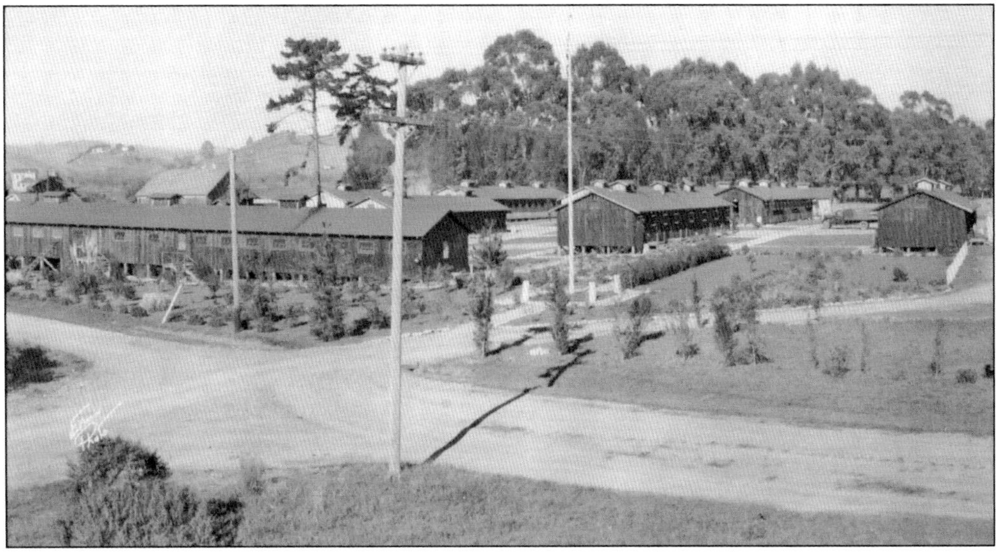

Camp McQuaide barracks housed the 5447th Company of the Civilian Conservation Corps beginning in 1937. Improvements to state park access at Seacliff and New Brighton supplied on-the-job training for 70 men. From 1942 to 1944, the base quartered soldiers of the 54th Coast Artillery Regiment, an all-black unit assigned to protect the California coastline from attack during World War II. Military camp structures were moved or demolished for the construction of Capitola Elementary School in 1952.

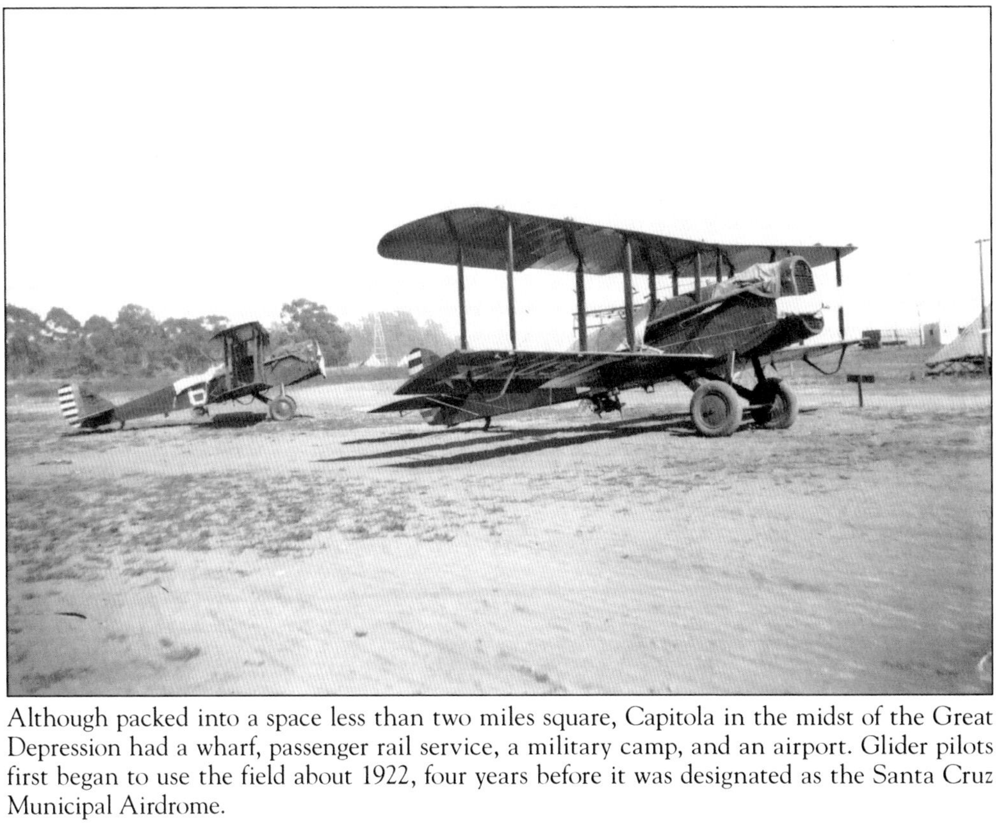

Although packed into a space less than two miles square, Capitola in the midst of the Great Depression had a wharf, passenger rail service, a military camp, and an airport. Glider pilots first began to use the field about 1922, four years before it was designated as the Santa Cruz Municipal Airdrome.

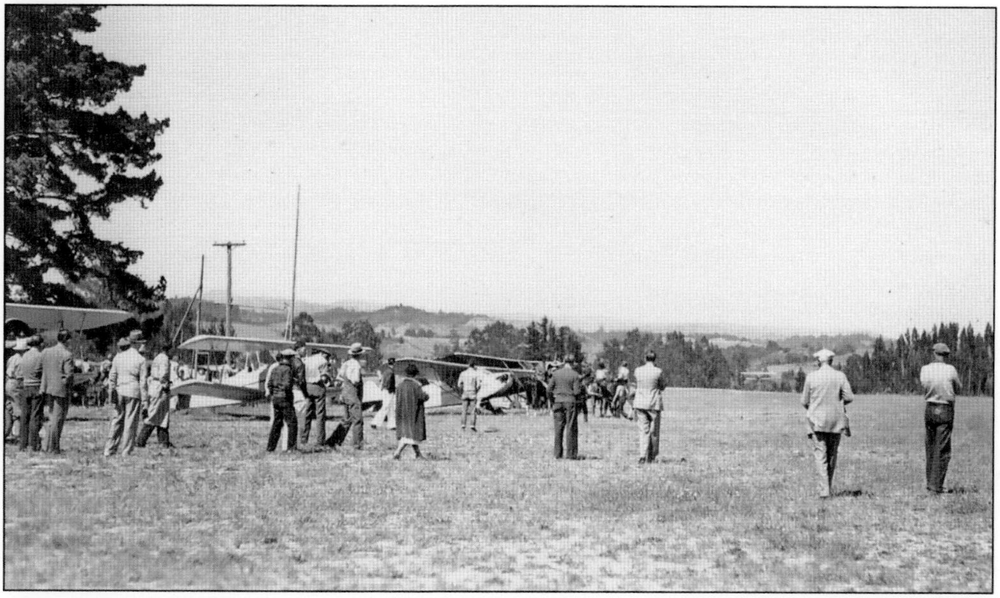

Once the airdrome was leased to the city of Santa Cruz, Works Progress Administration hands graded the field and laid two runways, while the American Legion and the Santa Cruz Exchange Club built the clubhouse. Santa Cruz–Capitola Airport was dedicated in November 1934. These photographs were taken about the time the airport was opened. (Above, courtesy of Richard Nutter.)

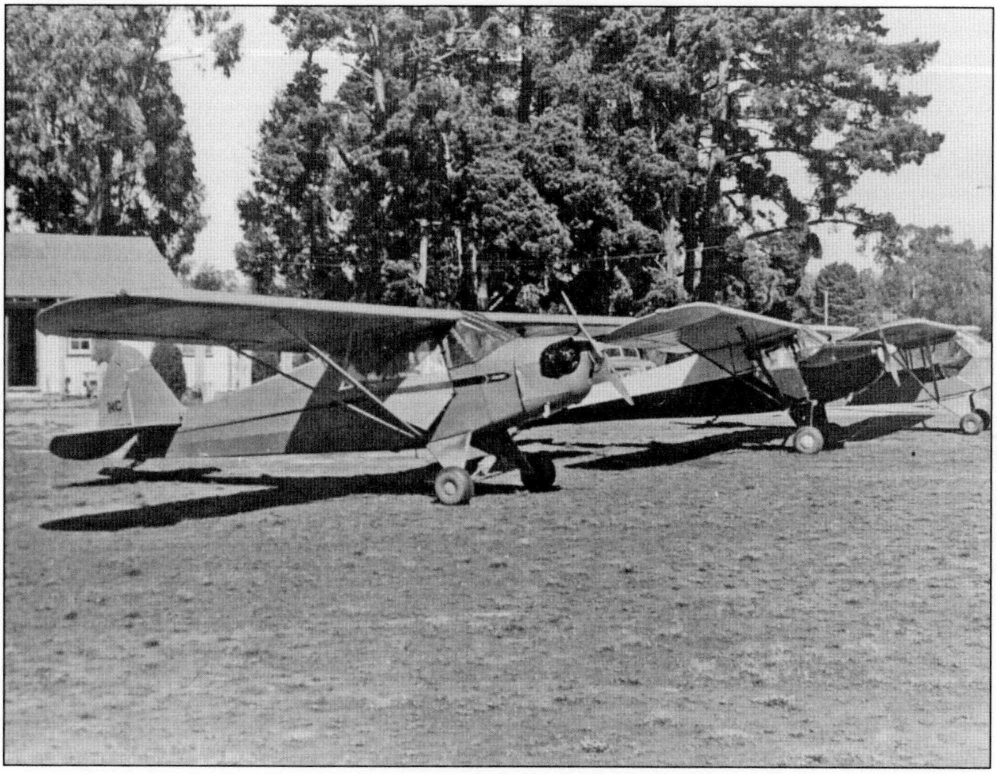

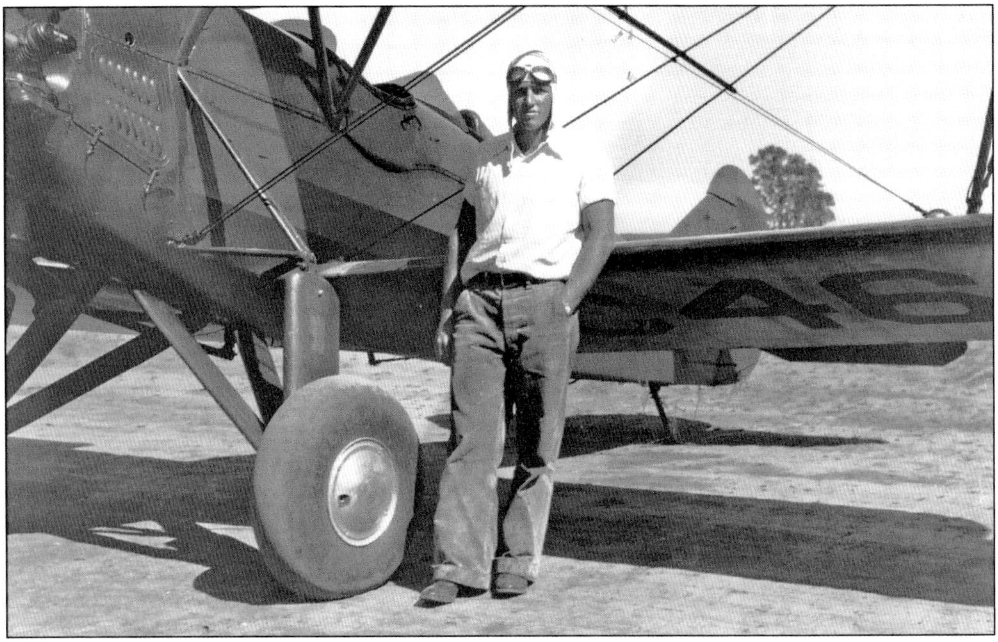

Exhibiting the flamboyance of the barnstormers from an earlier era, pilot Ray Gillen took off from the airfield at Capitola wearing his trademark leather cap and jacket. On a cloudless day in June 1930, his passenger in the Waco plane, shown above, was 23-year-old Gorman Woody of Twin Lakes. As the plane flew over Capitola, Woody leaned over the side of the open cockpit and captured both a clear shot of the village and a companion plane flying alongside. Riverview Terrace, seen at center right, had been subdivided by developer C.E. Blanchard, although only a few homes had yet been built. Woody remained in Santa Cruz throughout his lifetime and was a well-known artist.

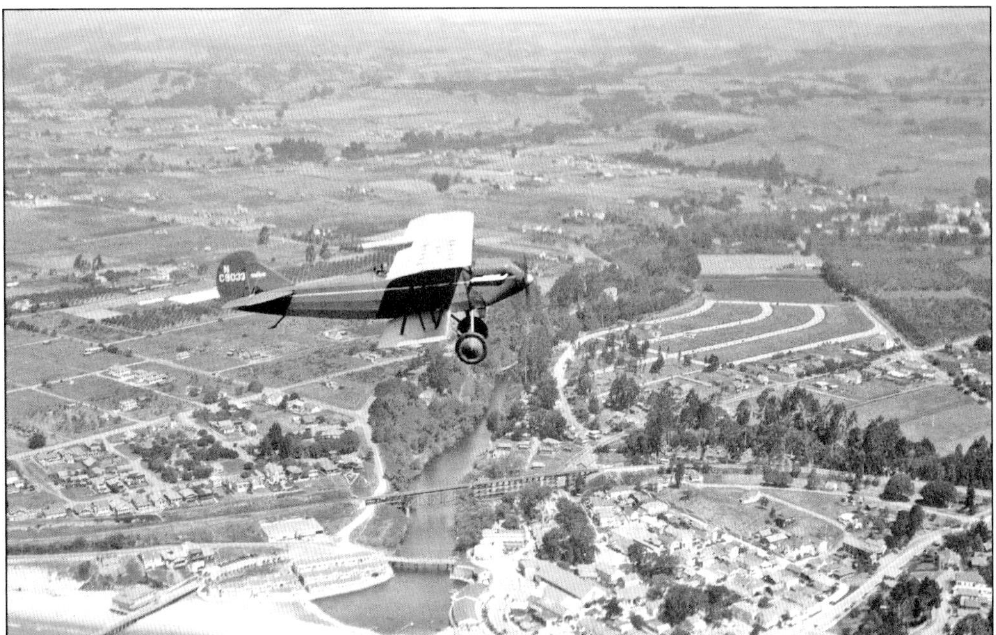

Managing the Santa Cruz–Capitola Airport for nine years after the end of World War II were two pilots, Russell and Esther Rice (right), a couple who grew up in the local community. After serving as a USO hostess at Camp McQuaide during the war, Esther welcomed incoming pilots with Hawaiian leis made of begonias. Writing for *In Flight Magazine*, she gave Capitola a new reputation as "The Waikiki of the West," a title Capitola kept from 1950 until the airport closed in 1954 and the Rices went on to manage the Sky Park Airport in Scotts Valley. (Right, courtesy of Covello and Covello Photography; below, courtesy of Esther Rice.)

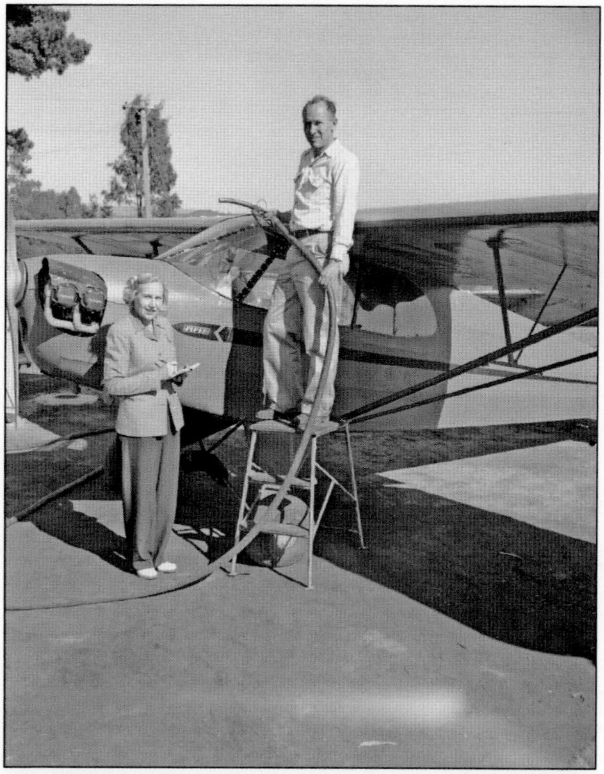

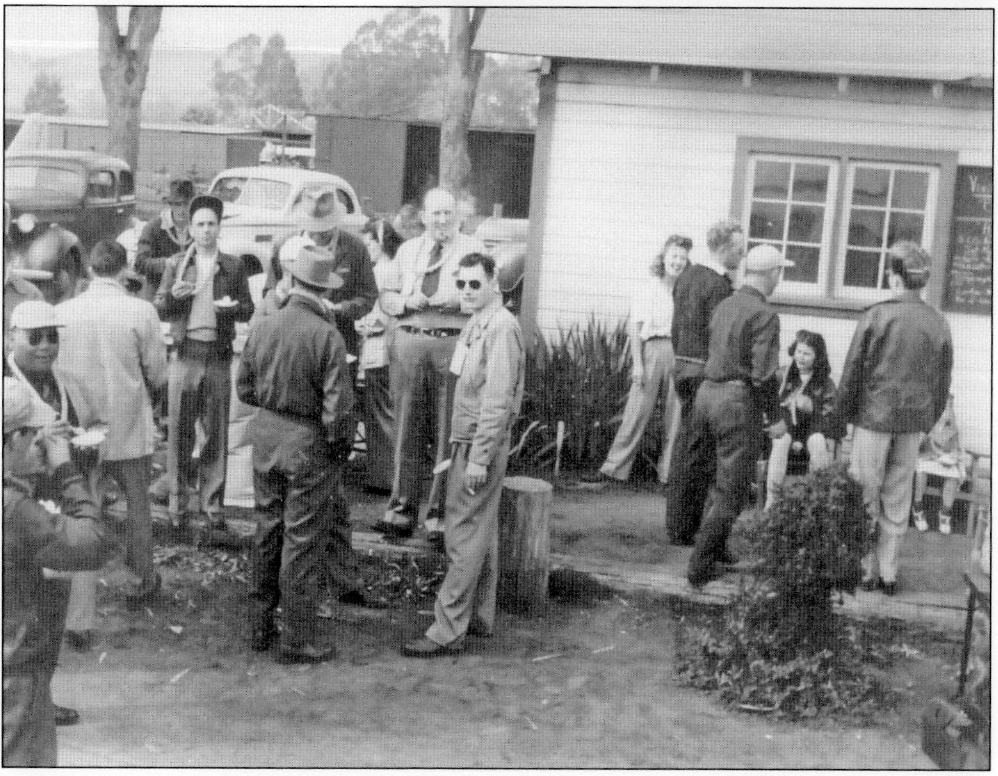

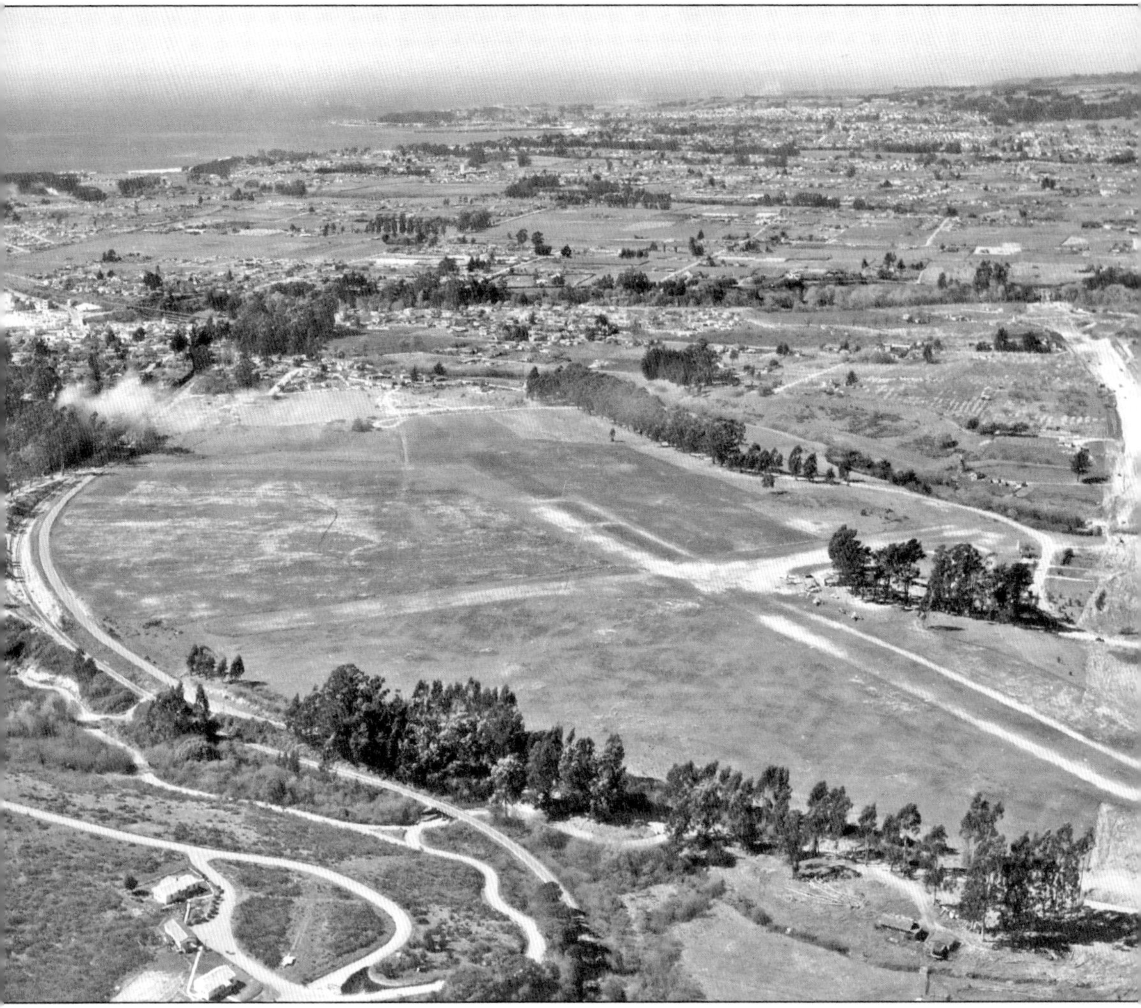

Almost a year after Capitola was incorporated as a city in January 1949, Highway 1 was paved from Watsonville to Santa Cruz. Begun through Capitola and Soquel in 1947, the artery sliced 200 feet off the airport runway, shown above at right. The landing strip and site previously used for the Camp McQuaide firing range are center left. At bottom left is the entrance to New Brighton Beach State Park. Today, the airport property is covered by the Cliffwood Heights subdivision. (Courtesy of Covello and Covello Photography.)

Seven

Capitola's Peril or Troubles in Paradise

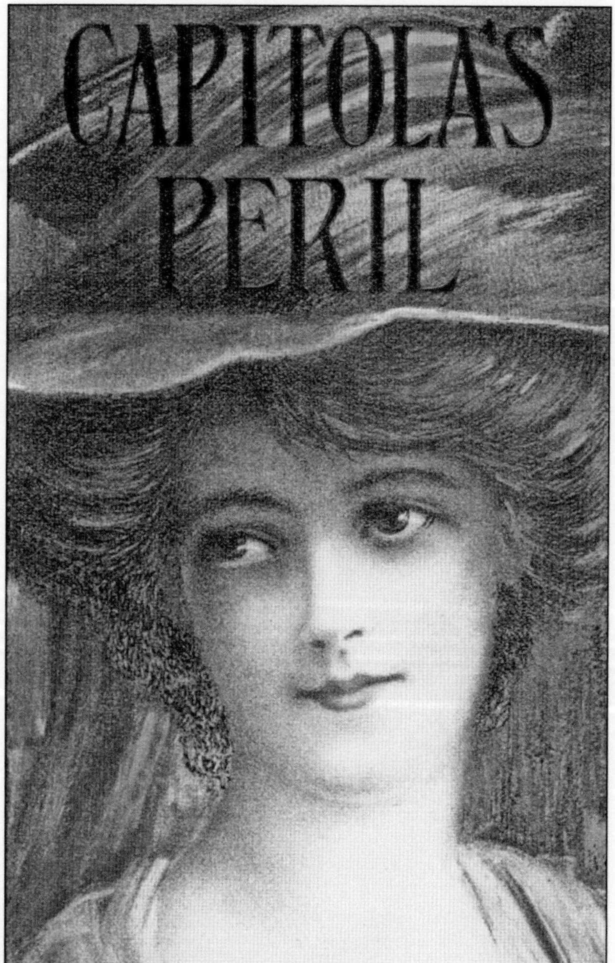

Capitola's Peril was E.D.E.N. Southworth's title for the sequel to her best-known work, *The Hidden Hand*, which first appeared in serial form in 1859. Capitola Le Noir was a tomboyish character who disregarded many of the conventional behaviors expected of young women. When the adventurer's name was given to California's rough-and-ready Camp Capitola in 1874, the title was a good fit. Like the fictional heroine, the resort has bravely stood its ground in the face of peril.

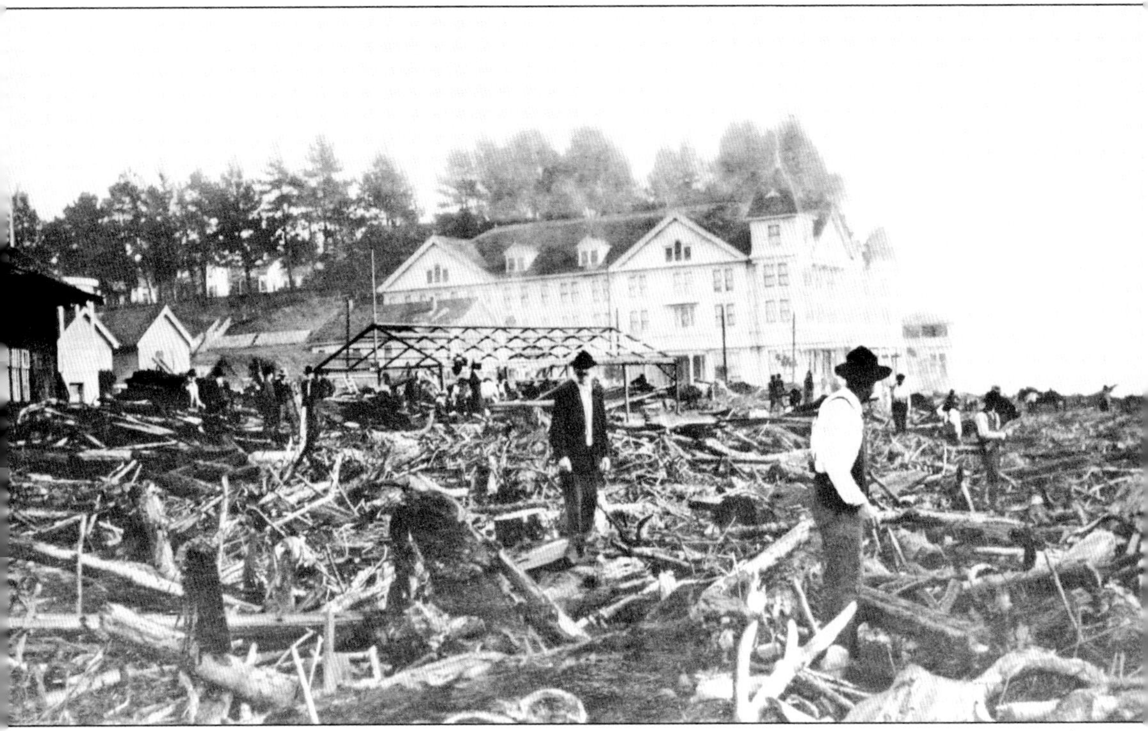

Scavengers combed the beach after a storm surge on the morning of November 26, 1913. The event was a recurring experience in the resort's history. The tide was so high that water swept up Capitola Avenue and over the tracks of the Union Traction Company streetcar line. "Monster waves" dashed against the wharf, taking out a 200-foot section that was broken up in the turbulent surf. Although efforts to clean the beach of pilings, logs, and other rubble took more than two months, the beach was spotless when the next season started in May.

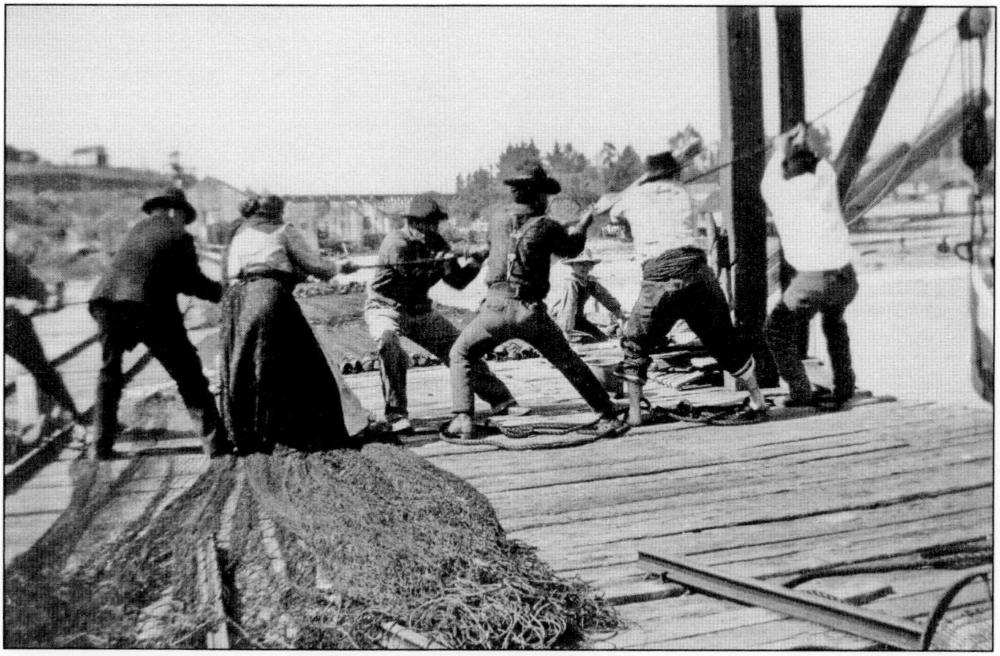

Living at the wharf's base, the fishing community was alert to perils of flood and high tide. All hands pulled to help lift the boats out of the bay on davits, hoisting the fleet out of the water to rest like lifeboats when rough weather threatened. Seen in this 1900 image are fishing nets and the rails used by a flatcar to transport cargo for shipment. (Courtesy of Karen Nevis.)

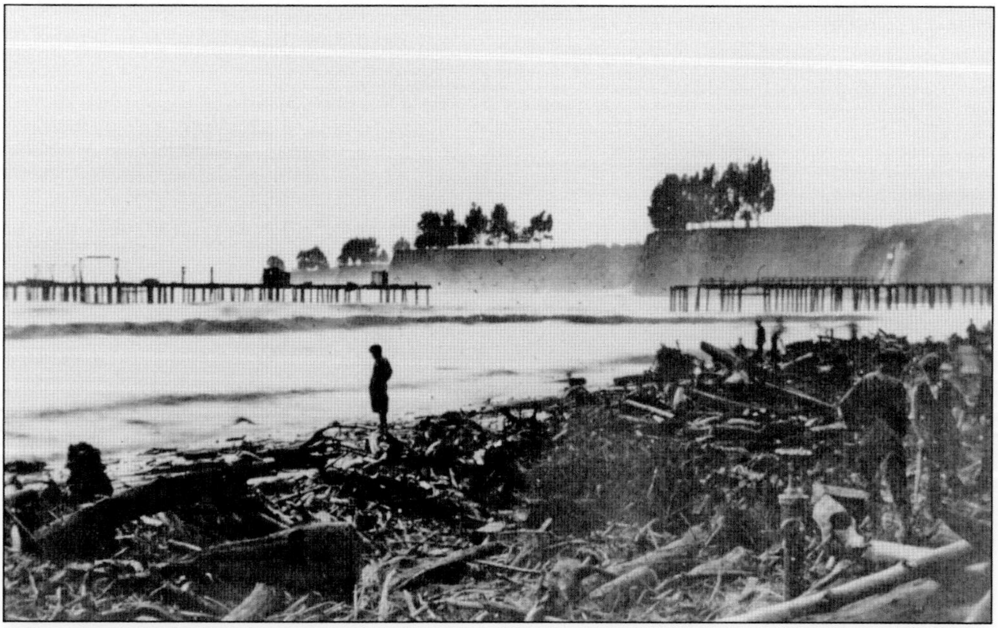

When the 1913 high tide appeared, fisherman Alberto Gibelli hurried to secure boats and gear on the wharf. Suddenly, the midsection slumped and collapsed, stranding Gibelli on the end. He waited for hours until a boat arrived and a line was tossed with a rope and life preserver. The fisherman tied the rope under his arms and leapt into the ocean. Pulled to safety, he resurfaced "as calm as a cucumber."

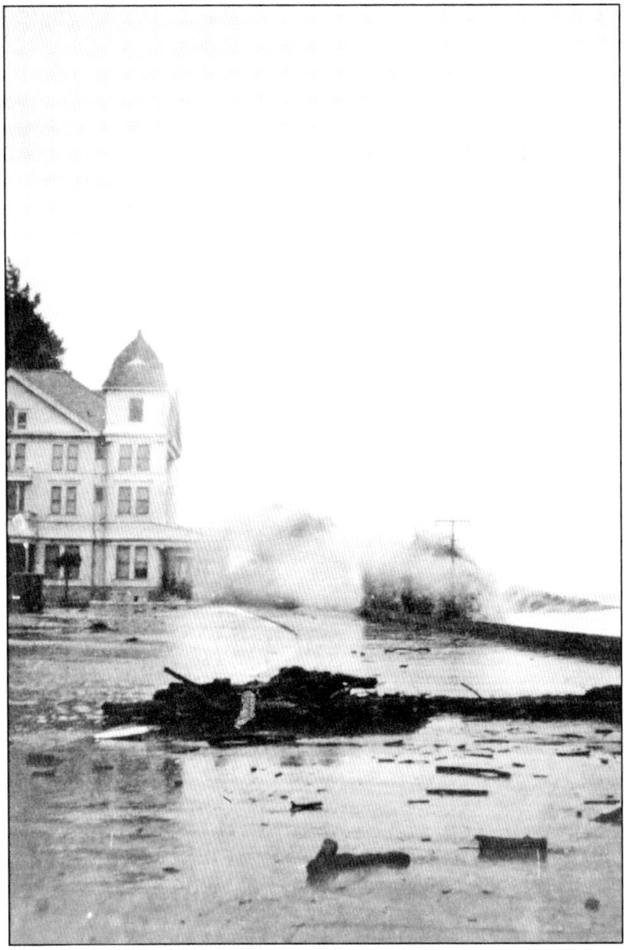

Monterey Bay communities are battered by storms on an average of once every three to five years and are becoming more vulnerable to flooding as the sea level rises. Traditionally, however, each calamity is met with both amazement and tolerance. On February 12 and 13, 1926, waves 20 feet high surged against the seawall and slammed the second floor of the Hotel Capitola facing the beach. Water more than a foot deep swamped vacation homes and the business district on Capitola Avenue. One resident, meanwhile, traded his automobile for a paddleboat and blithely navigated up San Jose Avenue, past the entrance to Lawn Way. (Both, courtesy of the Macdonald family.)

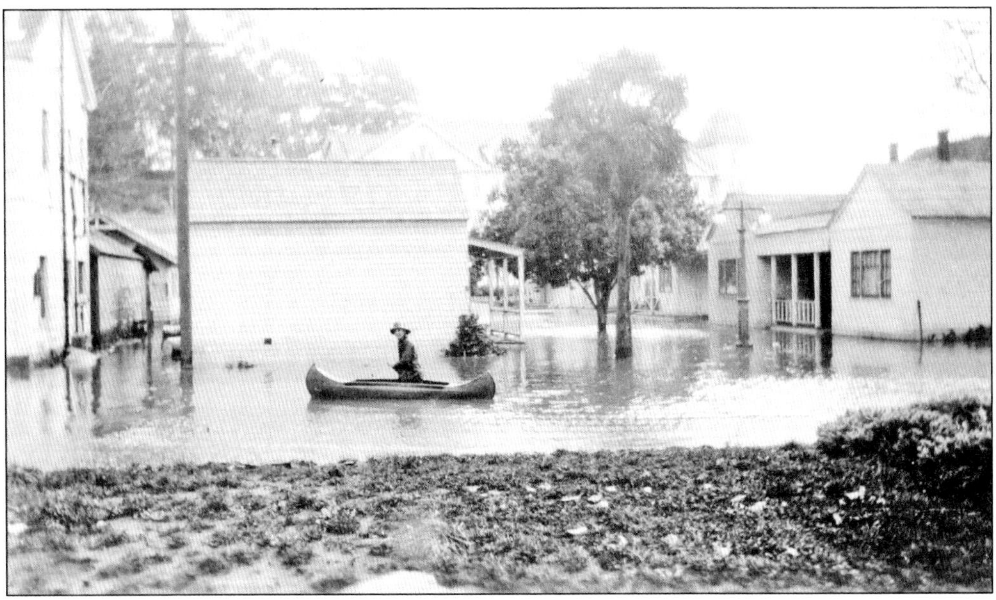

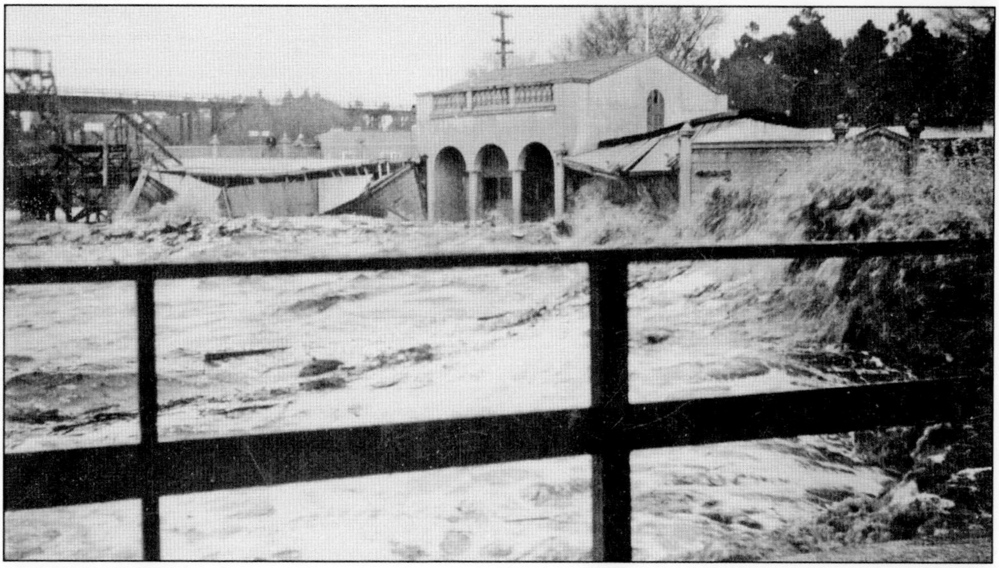

New concessions on the Esplanade crumpled just as easily as older ones under the force of the waves. The boat and bathhouse, above, was designed in the early 1920s with a distinctive archway that withstood the 1926 tide, while the wings for the dressing rooms were splintered into board piles. The damage is comparable in the photograph below. The triple arches, incorporated into the reconstructed building, again survived an equally brutal storm in January 1983.

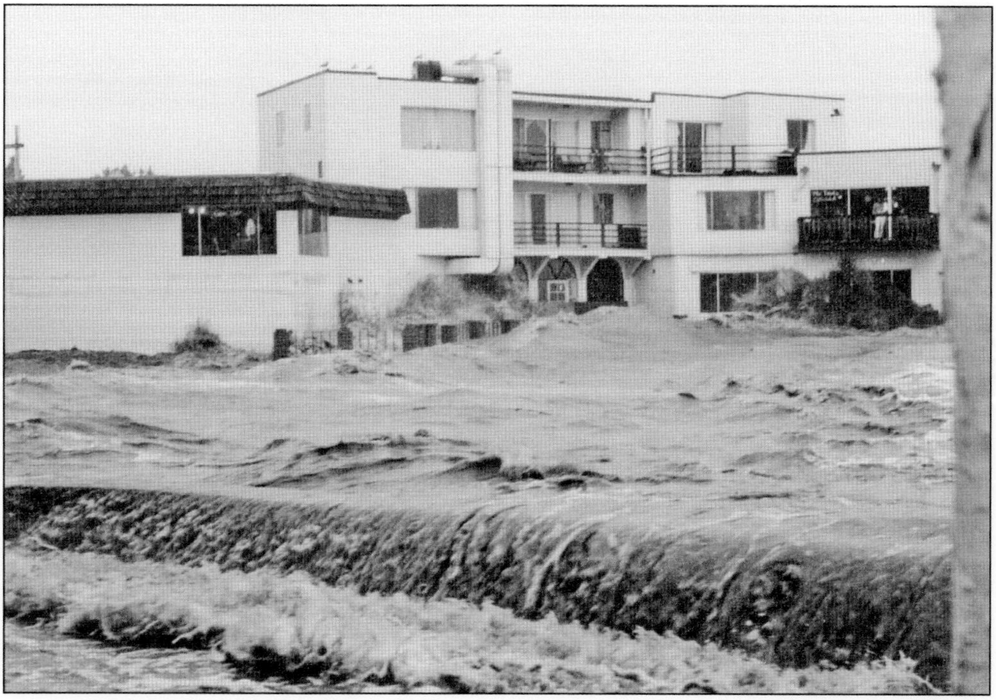

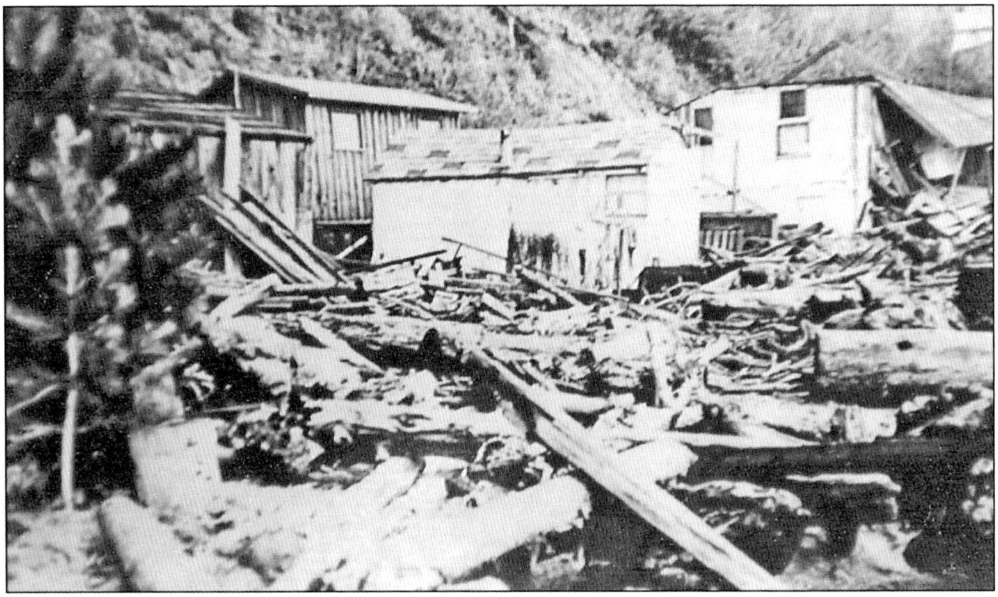

Debris from Soquel Creek swept onto the beach at China Cove (New Brighton Beach State Park) during a squall the day after Christmas in 1931. The miserable weather persisted, and two days later, on December 28, a high tide smashed vacation cabins and filled coastal roads with "the muck of the sea," as one news reporter observed. (Courtesy of Lee Lester.)

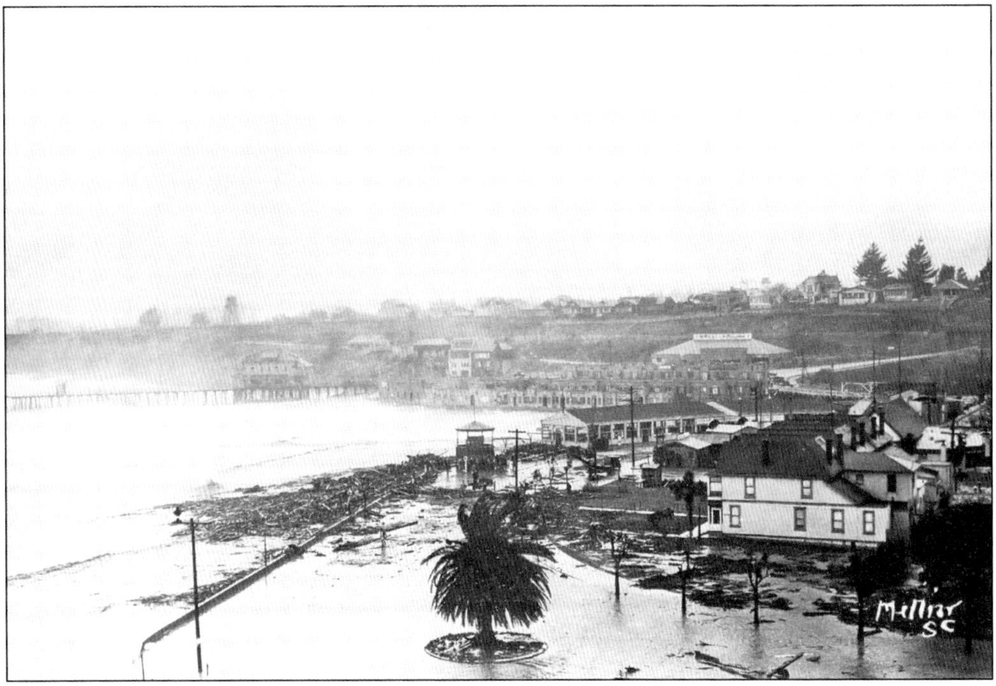

The 1931 storms widened Soquel Creek to 60 feet, nearly double its size, scarring the landscape from Soquel to the sea. Hundreds of people watched as waves smashed the Esplanade amusements. The resort's landmark palm, above center, weathered the action as one of many threats it has survived over the years. A casualty, however, was the short-lived miniature golf course, lower right, installed the previous summer. (Courtesy of Gordon van Zuiden.)

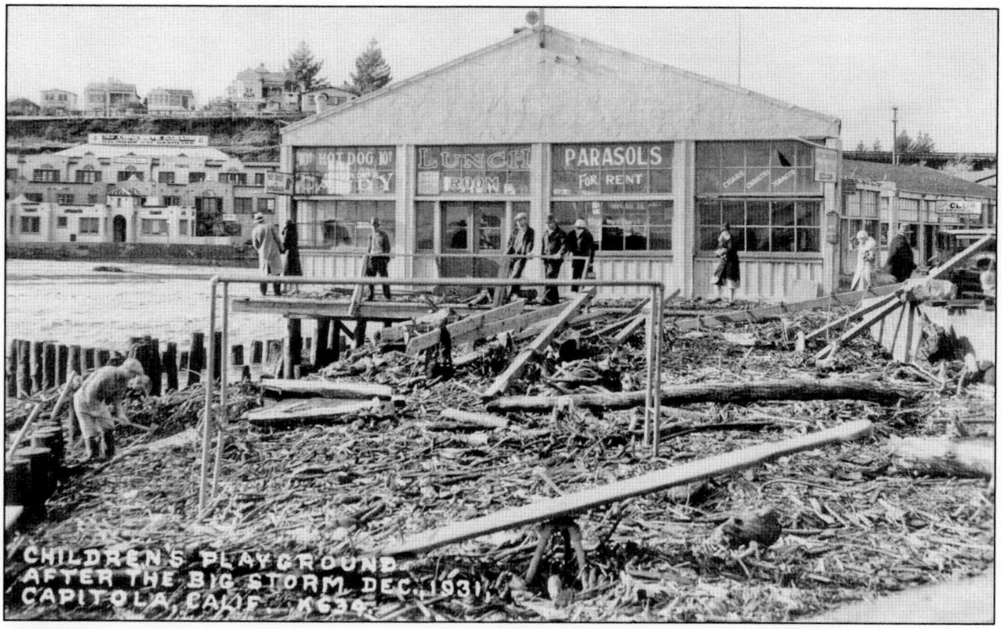

Capitola residents waded through a series of storms during the Great Depression. The 1931 devastation, above, was repeated as the playground washed out to sea again in 1935. Another surge in March 1937 damaged the Venetian Court Apartments and the seawall. As the decade drew to a close in 1939, the ocean swept over the Esplanade during the night, carrying sand and up to eight-inch rocks covering terraces and porches. The Capitola casino was nearly demolished on January 8, 1940. News reporters said it had capsized under the force of the waves, shown below. The year was one of the wettest recorded in county history.

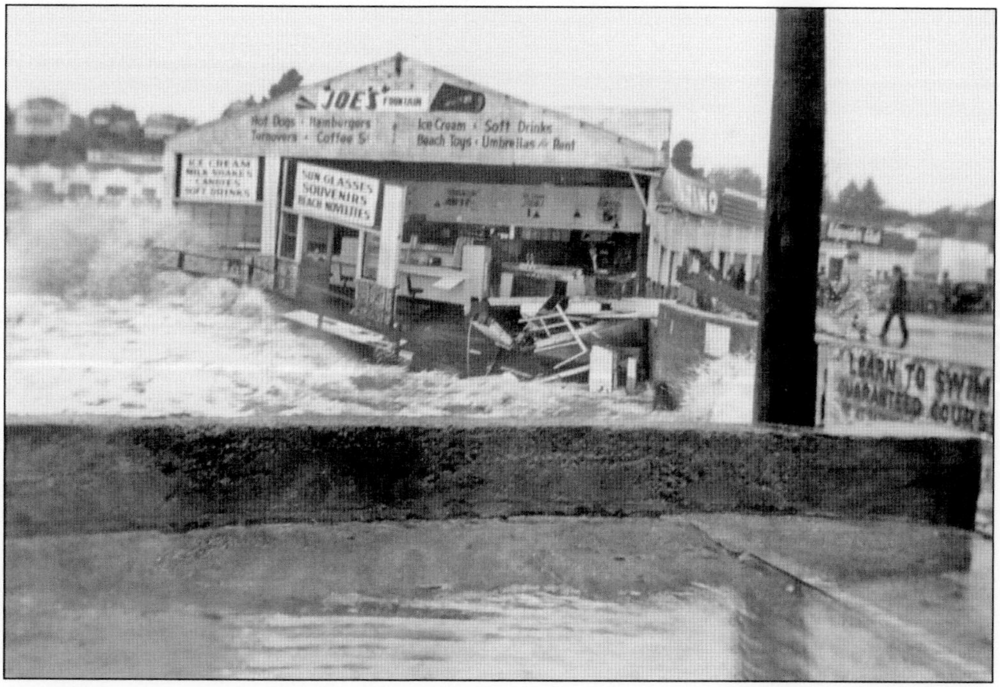

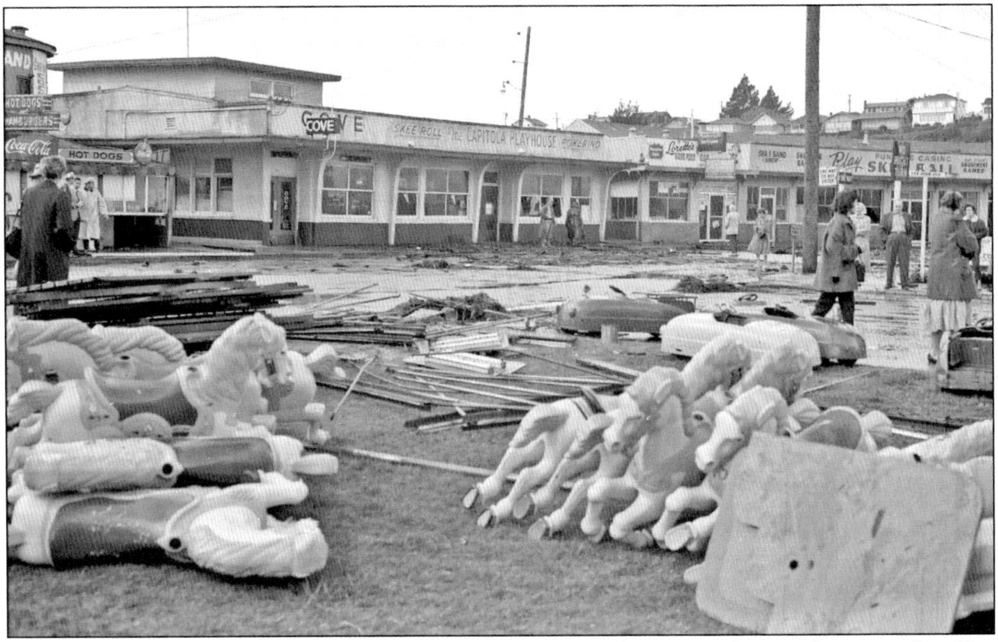

Although giant swells were less frequent in the 1950s, Capitola's pier and oceanfront were hard hit at least twice. The second time, on April 3, 1958, the Esplanade was bashed by a tide so forceful that it knocked the carousel horses from Andy Antonetti's merry-go-round. The wayward steeds were picked up by passersby, who stacked them up on the Esplanade. All were accounted for afterward. (Courtesy of Covello and Covello Photography.)

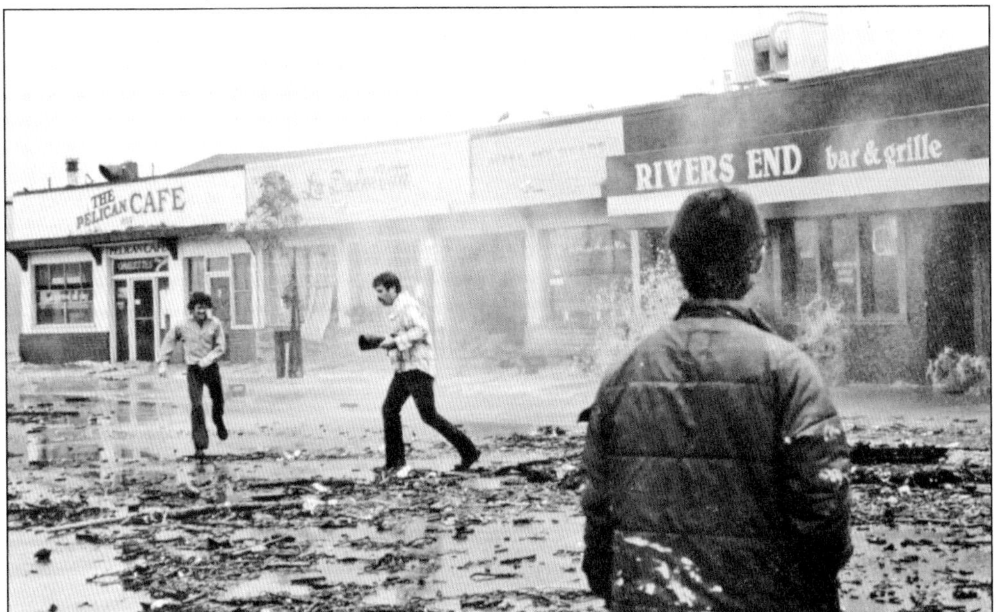

The 1983 tides were the most dramatic in recent history. The first one on January 27 flooded the wharf, Venetian Court, and structures all along the Esplanade. The giant surf destroyed a 30-foot section of the wharf that had just been renovated the previous year. Waves are seen crashing directly through the buildings in this photograph, spraying onlookers. (Courtesy of Minna Hertel.)

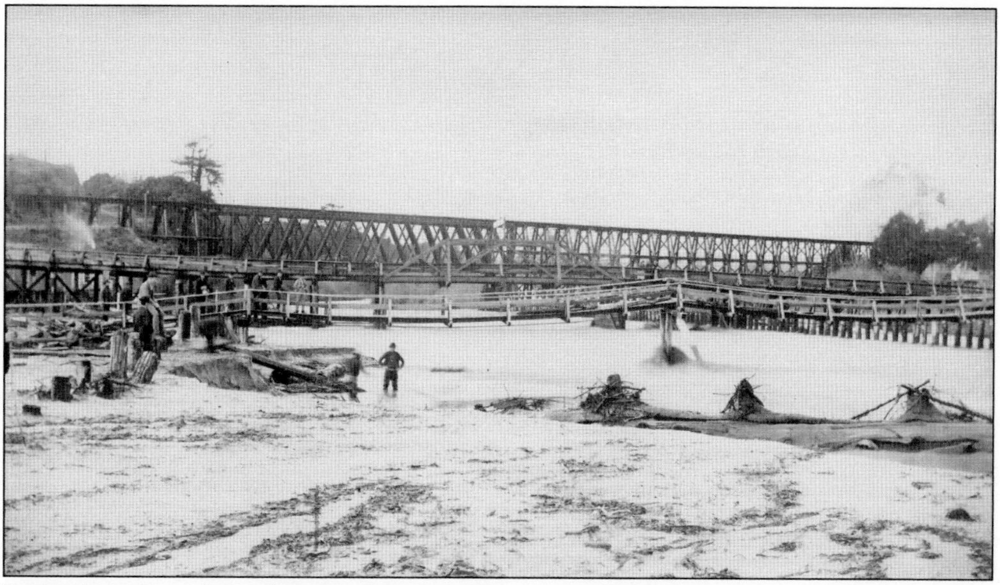

Built where Soquel Creek enters Monterey Bay, Camp Capitola rested in lowland that was swamped every so often, despite attempts to build it up with earth fill. The torrent above occurred about 1890, when the wagon and foot bridges were both damaged. Even though the village has remained in a floodplain, Capitola historically has suffered damage from creek flooding less often than neighboring Soquel.

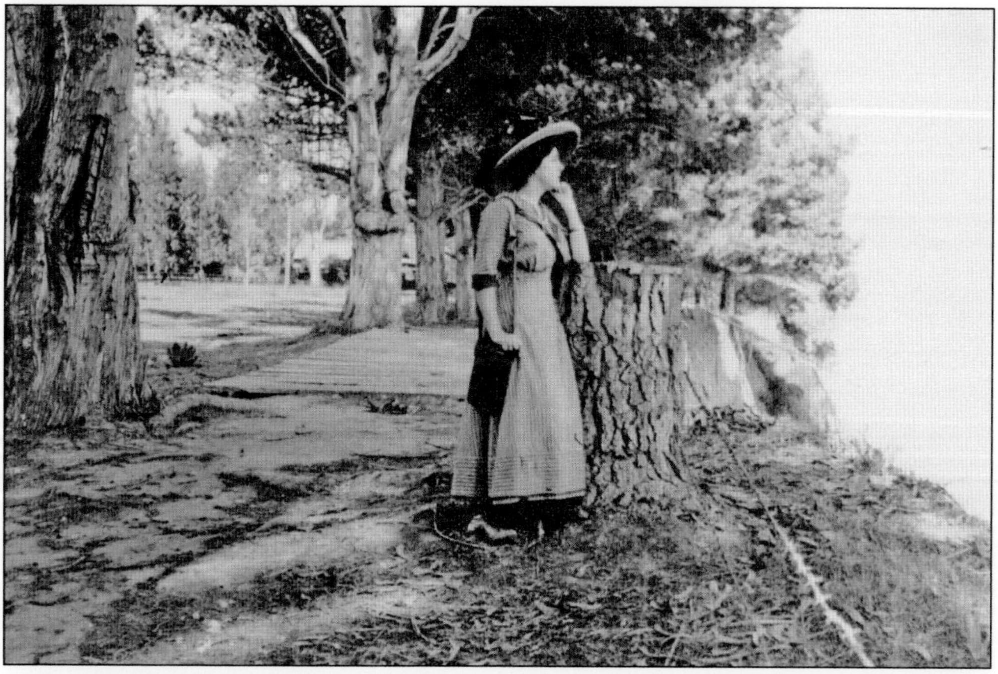

Capitola's eastern bluff is losing an average of one foot a year to erosion. When Frederick Hihn subdivided Depot Hill in 1884, he created Lover's Walk as a tree-shaded buffer between Grand Avenue and the cliff. By 1912, when this photograph was taken, the lane was disappearing. The spot where the woman is seen standing, and most of the roadway behind her, went over the bank decades ago. (Courtesy of the Alfred Sutton family.)

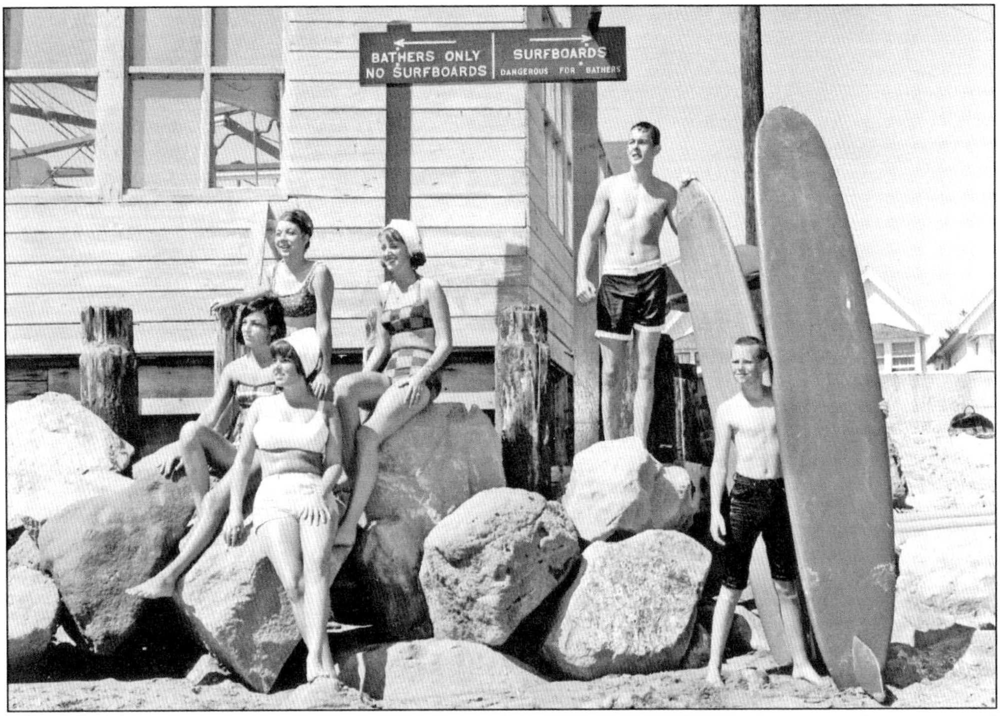

Completed in 1964, the Santa Cruz Small Craft Harbor at Woods Lagoon created unexpected troubles for Capitola. The harbor blocked the sand that previously drifted southward with the current and replenished the resort's coastline. To protect the Esplanade, boulders were piled against the seawall, further covering up the beach. Without the shore, sunbathers endured "rock bathing" by the sea. Competition grew fierce for space on the sand. (Courtesy of Covello and Covello Photography.)

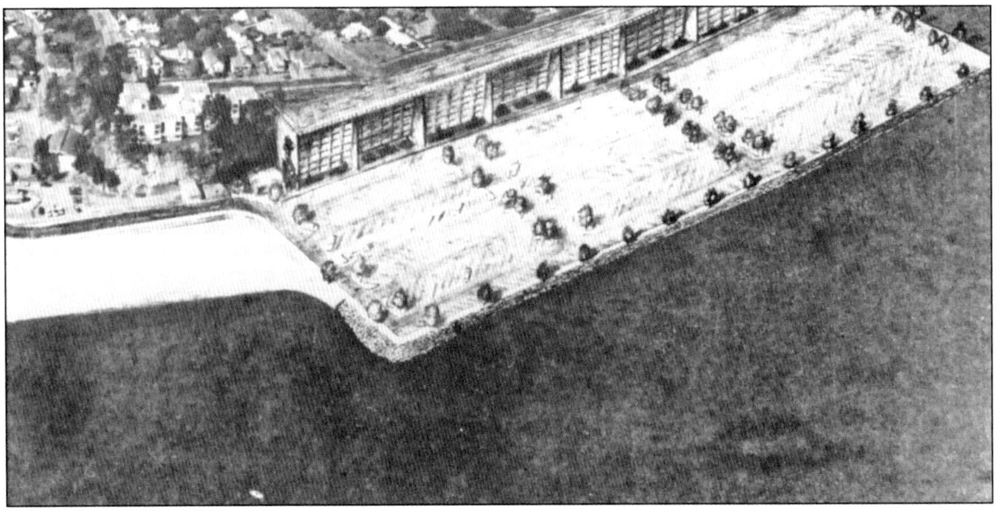

Although the project never happened, plans were approved in 1965 for a parking lot to stretch far out into the bay and along Grand Avenue. Superimposed on an aerial photograph, above, is a drawing for the parking lot and a proposed multiple-story hotel that was intended to stop bluff erosion. Capitola suffered without its beach until the end of the decade, when a 250-foot jetty was constructed and the sand was restored. (Courtesy of Covello and Covello Photography.)

Eight

Just Beachy

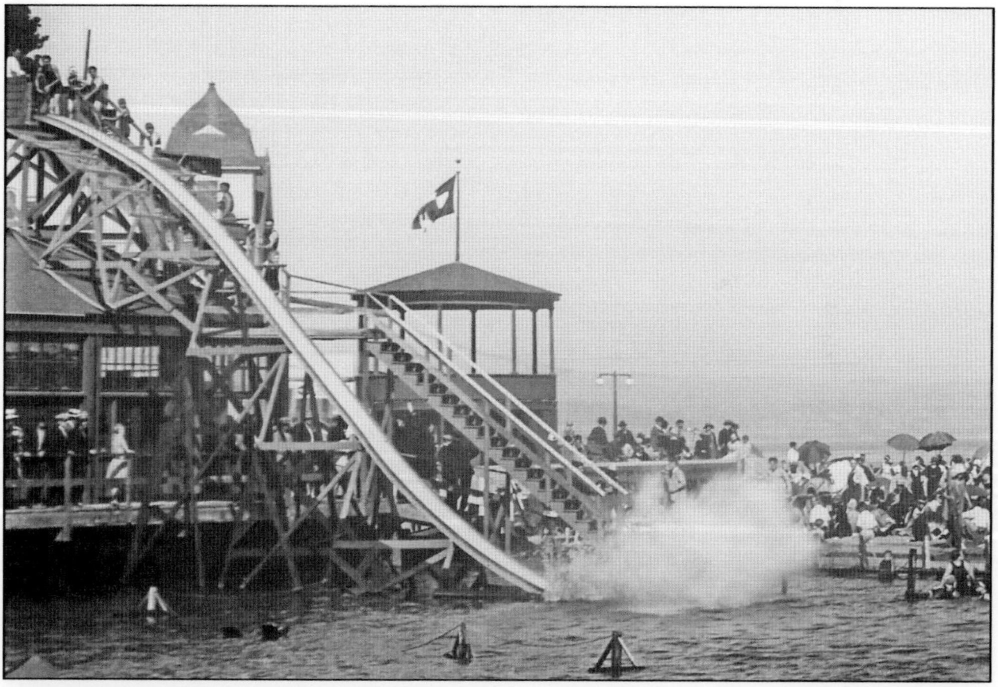

Although Pennsylvania musician Frank Hoyt Losey probably never heard of the resort, he gave the name Capitola to a piano march he composed in 1913. Losey's waltzes, marches, and ragtime compositions were among dozens performed every summer at the concert stand on the Esplanade. In 1927, the beach sounds were a mix of carousel tunes, laughter, and the shrieks of swimmers blasting into the lagoon on a slide called Chute-the-Chutes.

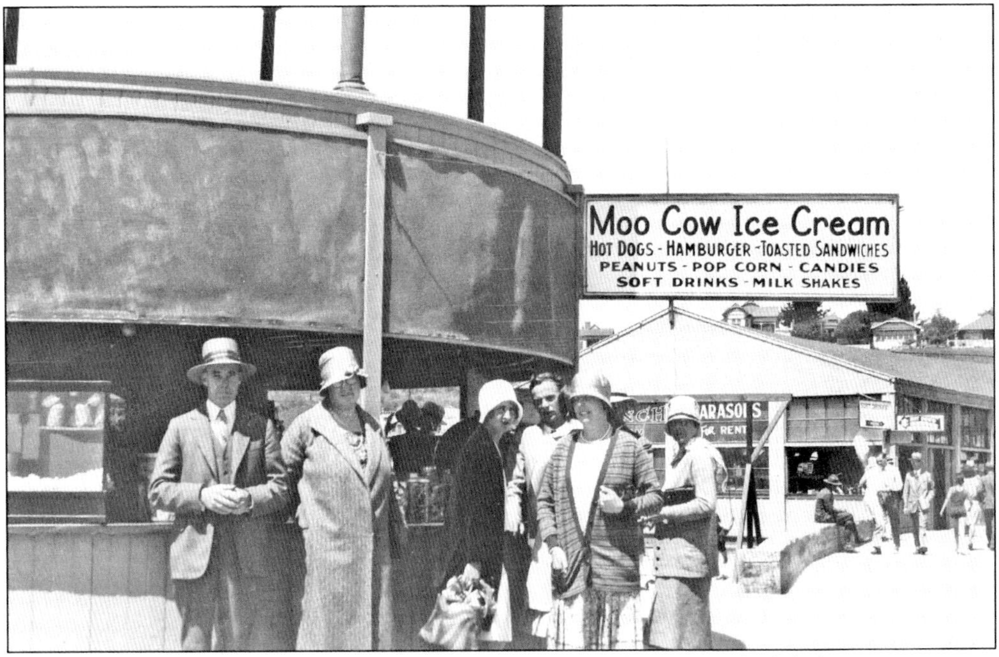

Frederick Hihn had boarded musicians at the hotel while they were scheduled to give concerts in the ballroom and outdoors at the concert stand. Later, when the music was replaced by a food concession, the round stand became a Moo Cow fountain, selling ice cream from the nearby Golden Guernsey Dairy. Gradually, the sides of the bandstand were filled in, until it became a diner, appropriately named the Bandstand. Aug "Babe" Yakobovich made the restaurant famous for its fries in the 1950s. His secret ingredient was lamb lard. Below is a view of the Esplanade about 1956. Andy Antonetti ran the merry-go-round and the casino concession next to the Cove tavern. (Above, courtesy of Gordon van Zuiden; below, courtesy of Covello and Covello Photography.)

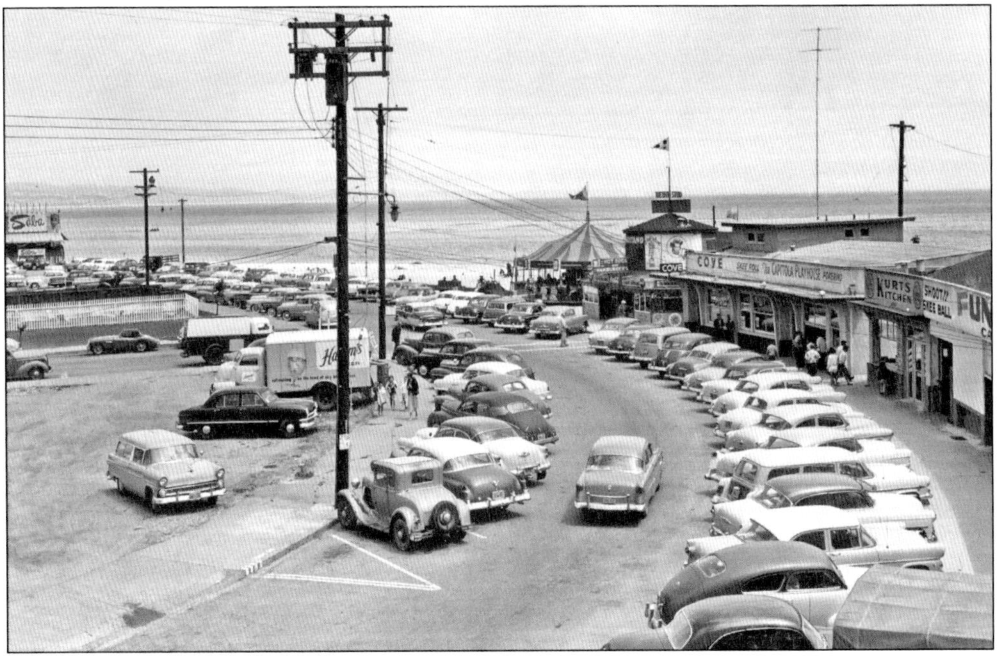

Generations of former children return to Capitola each year with tales of their youthful exploits on the beach. The luckiest among them were the ones free to play on their own for the entire summer. Horton Kooser came on the train to stay with his aunt, who placed him under the watchful eye of a canine companion named Ginger. The hound was faithful to duty except when asked to sing, which Ginger would do on command in both bass and tenor. As a young girl, June Burbick, below, loved the thrill of the carousel. The rides on the Esplanade came and went over the years. (Right, courtesy of the Kooser family; below, courtesy of June Burbick.)

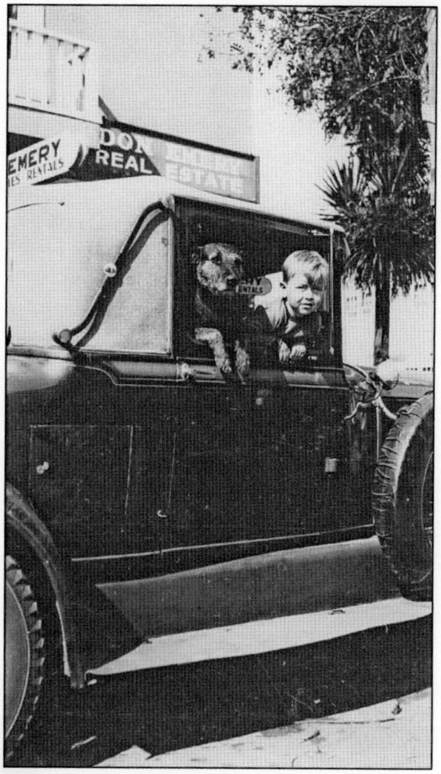

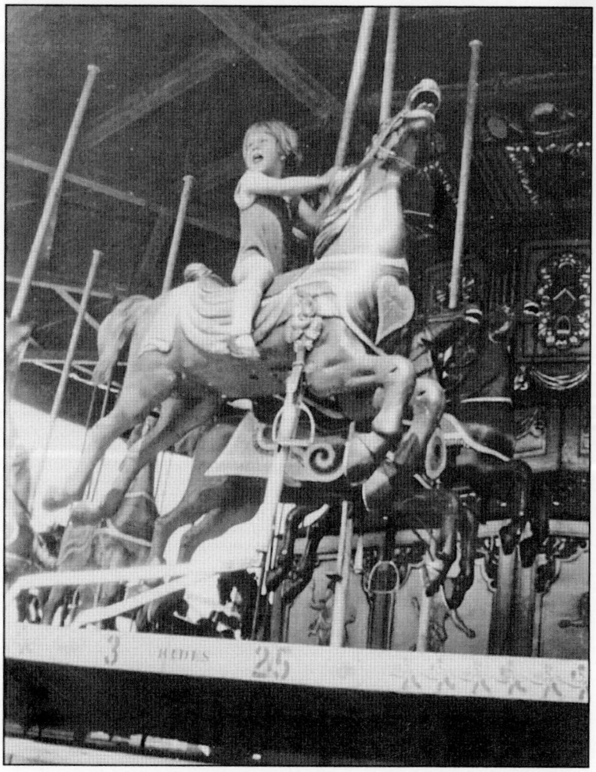

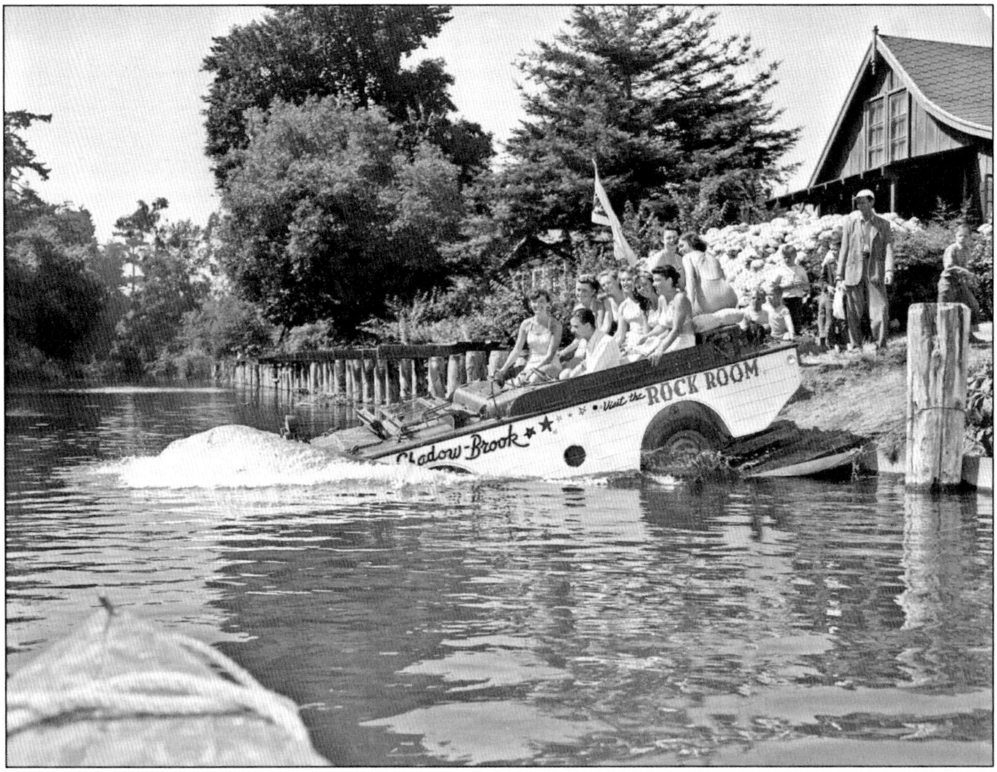

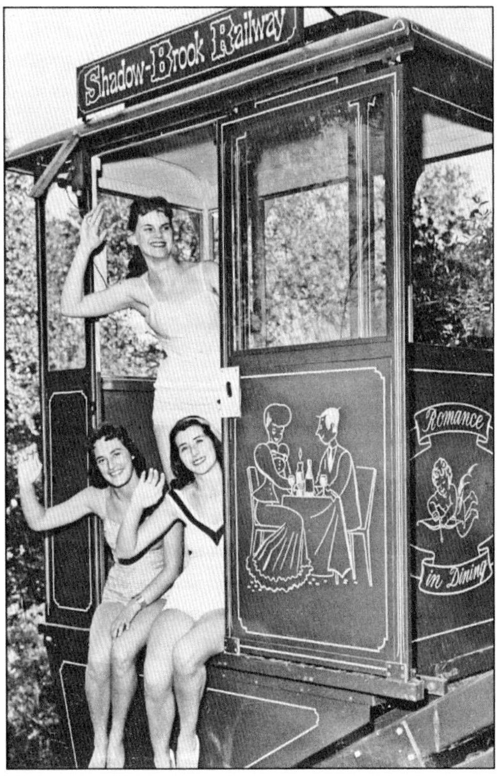

Raised in Capitola, Brad Macdonald knew when he bought the cabin along the creek below Wharf Road that it had potential as a restaurant. Macdonald, his wife, Bea, and business partner Ed Phillipet opened the landmark Shadowbrook Restaurant in 1947. Macdonald came up with an unusual scheme for getting customers to his front door. He bought an amphibious Duck and named it "the River Taxi." Guests, including famed film director Alfred Hitchcock, were shuttled across Soquel Creek. Later, Macdonald installed the funicular down the west bluff for easier access. Miss California pageant contestants, at left, crowded into the early tram for a photo opportunity in 1957. Artist Al Wiseman of Opal Cliffs created the tram illustration.

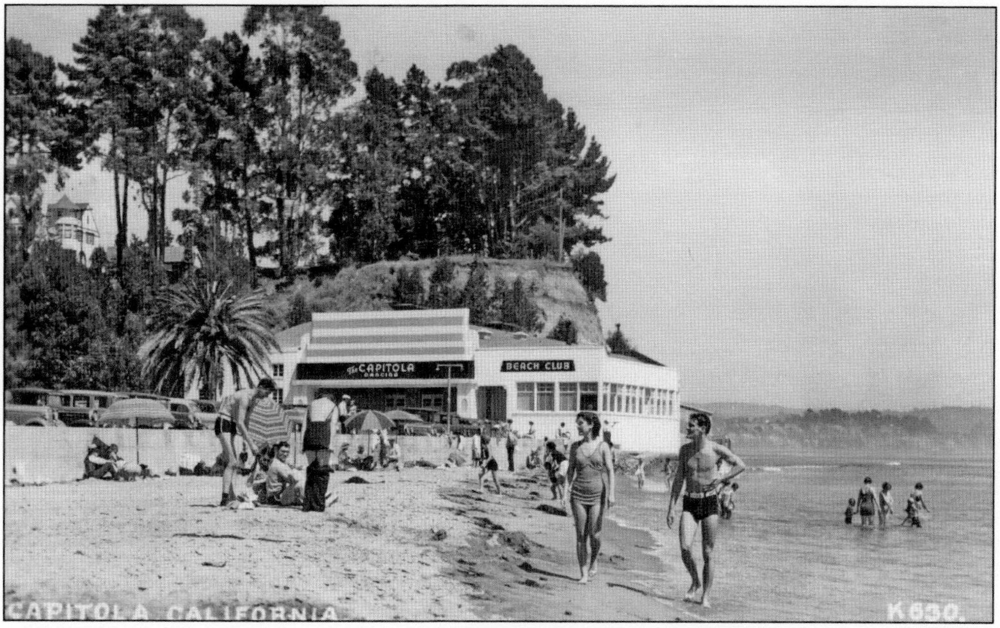

Lowell and Everett Vetterle, owners of Vetterle and Reinelt Hybridizing Gardens on Capitola Road, opened the Capitola Ballroom and Beach Club in 1935 on the former site of the Hotel Capitola. The building housed a dance pavilion, skating rink, and beer garden. In 1954, Brad Macdonald sold his Shadowbrook Restaurant and with his father, Jack, bought the building. They renovated it as a West Indies–style nightclub called the Saba (sayba). Great band performers were headlined—Dizzy Gillespie, Count Basie, and Lionel Hampton among them—but the enterprise struggled in a time when dancers preferred the jukebox. Lewis Sorensen was invited in 1956 to move in Sorensen's House of Wax, featuring life-sized figures. Unfortunately, a grease fire destroyed the entire structure the following year. (Below, courtesy of Covello and Covello Photography.)

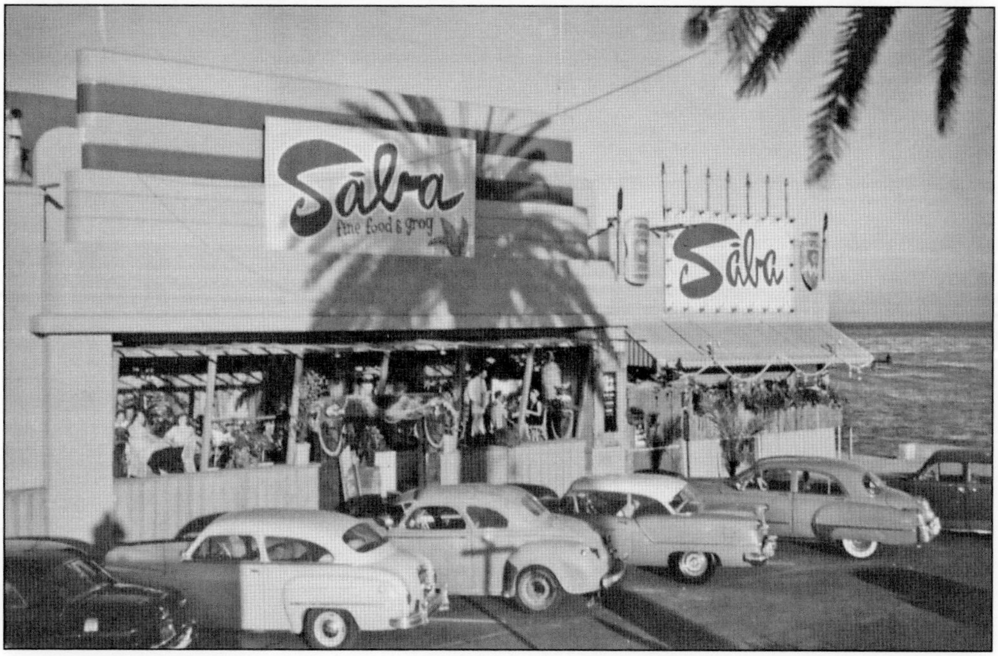

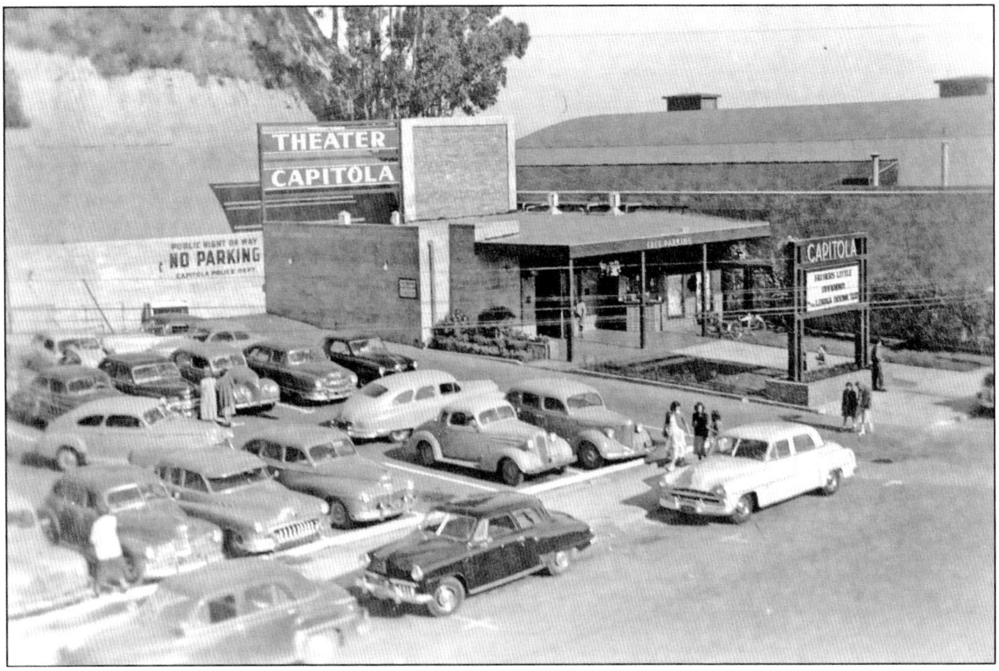

When Joseph Jacobs and Arthur Meyer built the Capitola Theater in 1948, they had no idea it would entertain several generations of children as a much-loved double-feature bargain theater with tasty popcorn and lenient rules. Jacobs's daughter, Audrey, was a young schoolteacher who came to help her parents out on opening night in 1948. She stayed nearly a half-century. The theater closed shortly before her death in 1997 and was torn down in 2010.

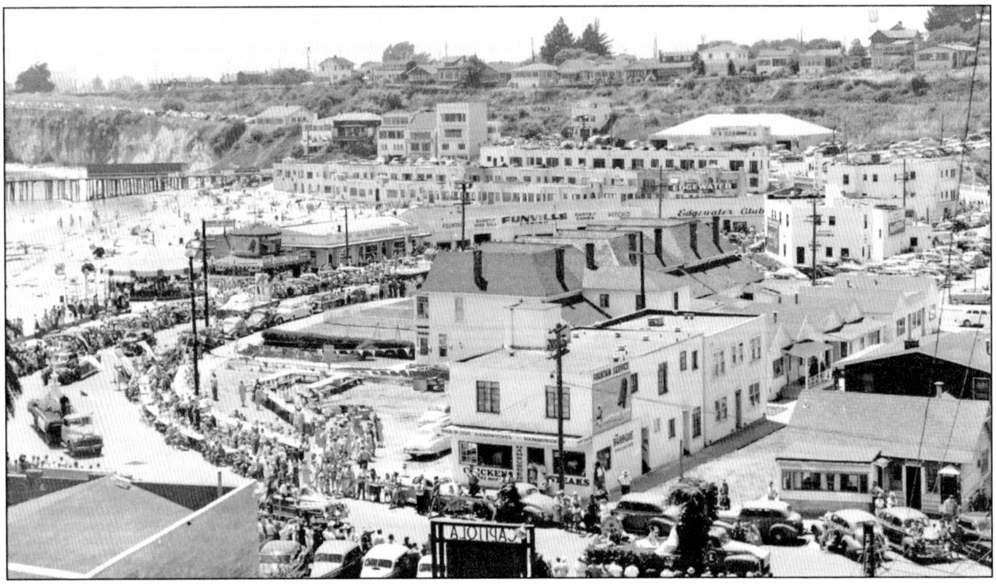

Capitola Improvement Club members buttonholed voters on behalf of a cityhood election drive in 1948. Their tenacity paid off when, triumphantly, Capitola became a city on January 11, 1949. The resort won city status by a wafer-thin victory. The final count was 297 in favor to 243 opposed. The site of the first city hall can be seen at bottom right in a Fourth of July parade photograph. (Courtesy of Covello and Covello Photography.)

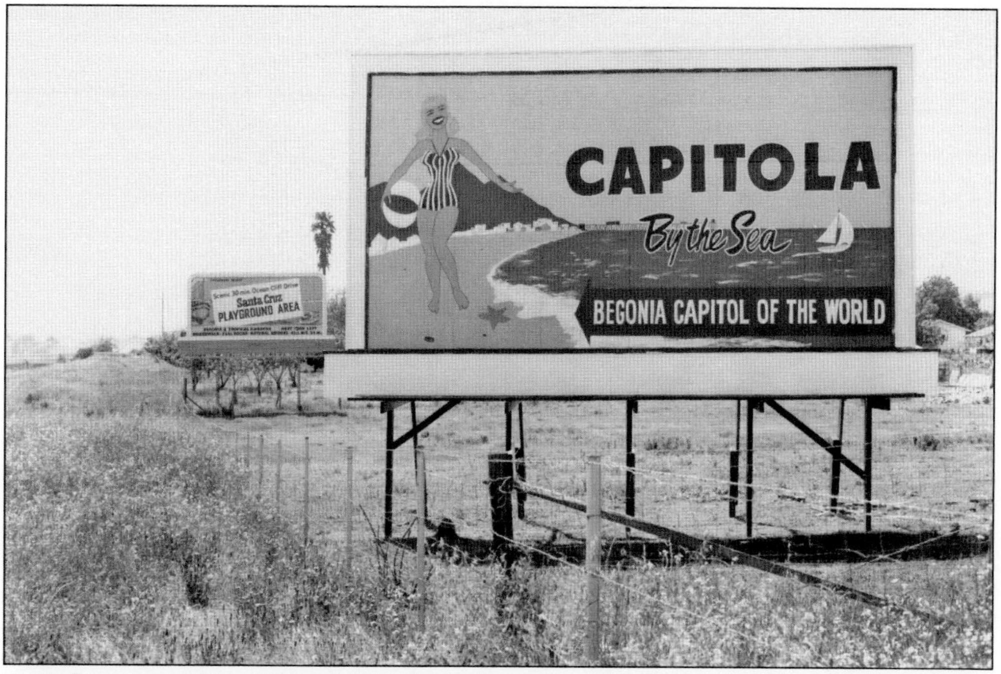

Capitola incorporated in 1949 with boundaries that embraced the fields of nearby nurseries spreading out to the west. When a symbol was needed for an annual celebration, the choice was easy. Award-winning begonia growers were within walking distance of the beach. Inspired by a Water Fantasy event staged from 1950 to 1954 by Peggy Slatter Matthews, the first official Capitola Begonia Festival was inaugurated in 1954. A patient crowd of several thousand spectators watched the 1957 festival, below. The five decorated floats waited in turn as a single motorboat towed each one down the creek to the lagoon and back again. The Labor Day weekend celebration continues today as a famed and high-spirited event. (Both, courtesy of Covello and Covello Photography.)

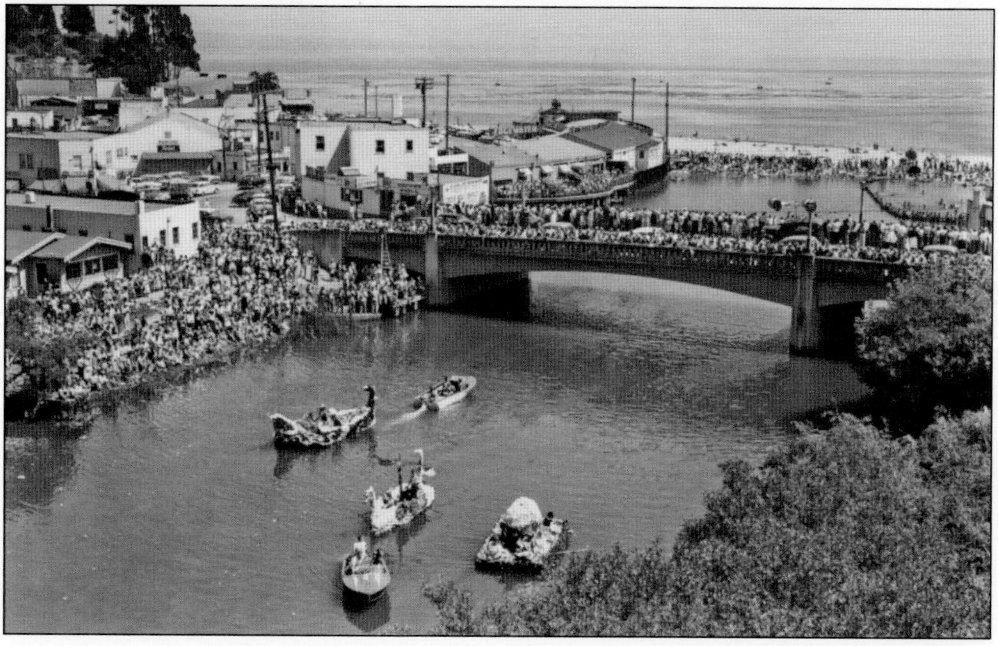